Europe vs USA and China.
How to reverse decline in the age of artificial intelligence.

LUIS MORENO
ANDRÉS PEDREÑO

EUROPE vs. USA AND CHINA

HOW TO REVERSE DECLINE

IN THE AGE OF ARTIFICIAL INTELLIGENCE

Europe vs USA and China.
How to reverse decline in the age of artificial intelligence
Authors: Luis Moreno Izquierdo and Andrés Pedreño Muñoz

Review of the first edition: Laura Cárdenas
Review of the English ed.: Rebecca Rippin and Marilú Hernández
Cover Design: Trini Mora

First edition (Spanish): May 2020
ISBN: 978-84-09-21211-8

First edition (English): June 2021
ISBN: 978-84-09-30986-3

For any matter related to this work
please contact the authors through the website:
www.prevenireldeclive.com

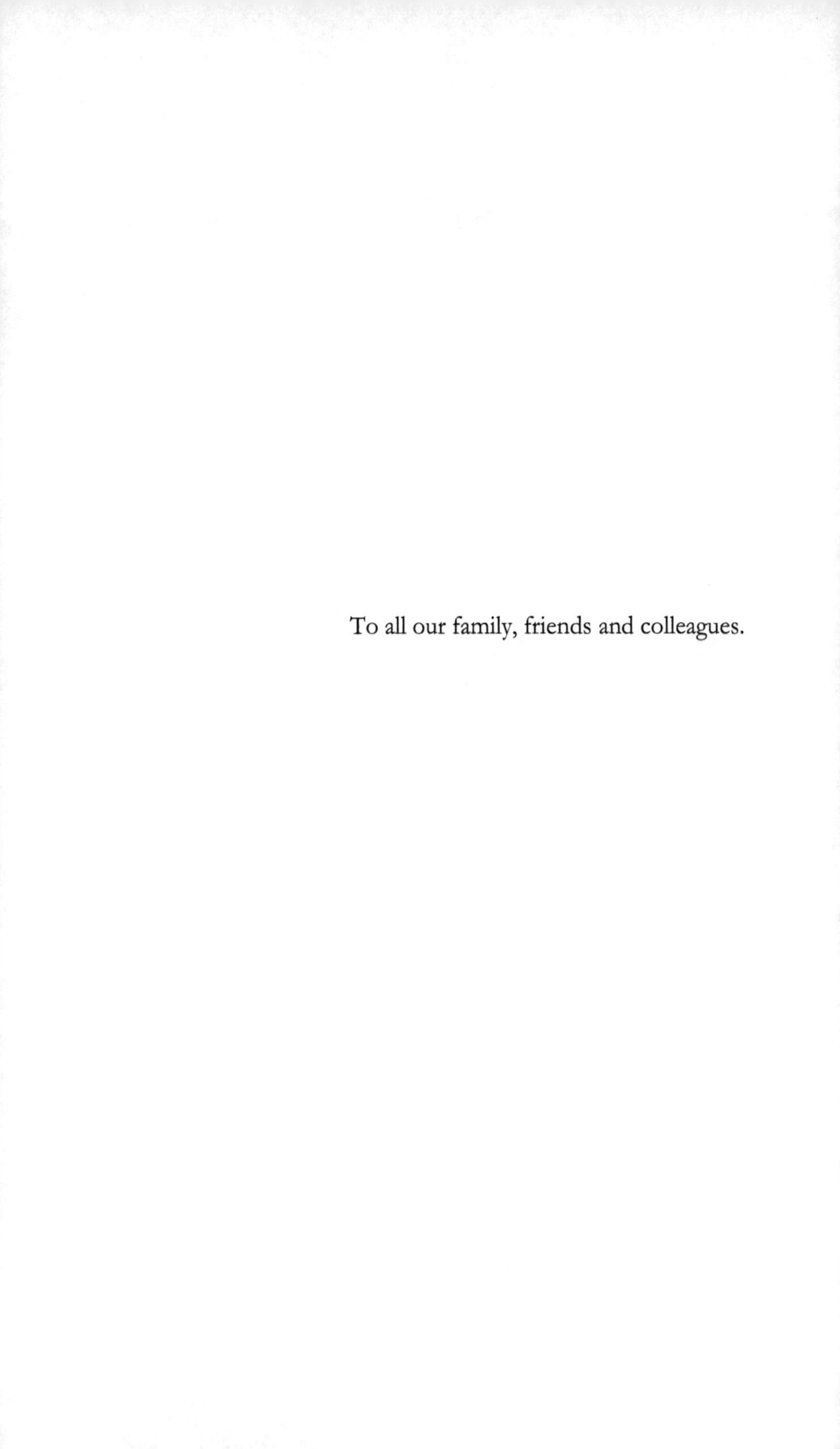

To all our family, friends and colleagues.

INDEX

2nd PART: POLICIES AND PROPOSALS FOR ACTION

SYNERGIES AND ENTREPRENEURIAL CULTURE

PREFACE, BY VINTON G. CERF

Artificial intelligence has been a topic of curiosity for over 60 years. Even as the earliest computers were developed with names like ENIAC, EDVAC, UNIVAC and WHIRLWIND, they were characterized as giant brains and speculation was rampant that these machines might someday exceed human capacities and somehow take over. In the 1960s, pioneers like John McCarthy, Marvin Minsky, Allen Newell and Herbert Simon were already energetically exploring ways to program computers to solve problems thought to be the sole province of human ingenuity and reasoning. Board games were a popular target with TIC-TAC-TOE falling quickly, chess somewhat later and GO very recently. Building on earlier work from the 1940s, Frank Rosenblatt at Cornell developed in 1958 a single-layer neural network he called a perceptron. This was intended to demonstrate automatic image classification using a training method that adjusted functional parameters to increase the likelihood of correct automatic classification of images. Minsky and Seymour Papert wrote a critical analysis of Perceptrons in a book by that title in 1969 that put a pall over this avenue of research. However, a few people persisted in this work, notably Paul Werbos, Judea Pearl, Yoshua Bengio, Geoffrey Hinton and Yann LeCun, among others. Their multi-layer neural network successes were partly a consequence of hardware catching up with concept, allowing networks hundreds of layers deep to be built and exercised.

These systems have been successfully applied to natural language translation, speech recognition and synthesis, medical image analysis, fusion plasma stabilization, self-driving cars, discovery of exoplanets and uncountable other applications. Such successes have, not surprisingly, generated a substantial degree of hyperbolic enthusiasm and national level determination to be first in the field of artificial intelligence. It is important not to confuse effort for progress. The US, China and the European Union, inter alia, are investing heavily in these technologies and it is likely that some important and beneficial results will materialize. At the same time, it is important to recognize the limitations of multi-layer neural networks. They can be very brittle, failing in unexpected ways when presented with unfamiliar inputs. A classic example is illustrated by what are called Generative Adversarial Networks that try to fool an image recognizing neural network into getting the wrong answer. When you see an image recognition system concluding that what you think is an image of a cat is actually a fire truck, you quickly realize that absolute dependence on these technologies might be premature.

The authors of this book draw attention to the European reaction to digital technologies which they characterize as regulatory out of concern for privacy, ethical abuse and perhaps also job losses in consequence of automation. Their worry is that in their zeal to protect Europeans (and others) from real or imagined harms, regulators have also hobbled the development of new applications enabled by AI and other digital technologies. Coupled with limited technology transfer from research into applications, these ingredients have baked a fallen soufflé which only radical response can remedy. More eggs need to be broken!

This is not an argument for reckless application of AI, machine learning and other digital technologies without consideration for the protection of citizens from harm. However, economic decline is itself a significant potential harm and can only be combated with vigorous exploration of new technologies. Nothing more powerful than computing has come along in the last century in terms of enabling innovation. Everywhere one turns, "computational-X" for many values of "X" looms on the horizon or is already deeply embedded in research, business and daily life. Viewed less as threats than as enabling technologies, it is possible to see the augmentation of human capacity that was so central to Douglas Engelbart's vision[1] of communities getting better at getting better.

Although the expression "move fast and break things" has been justifiably discredited, there is a kernel of truth in the "moving fast" part. Rapid and broad exploration of possibilities is called for in a globally competitive environment. Some paths may be dead ends and failure is a possibility. It is vital to discover productive paths and to share openly successes and failures, at least at the research level.

---

1. https://en.wikipedia.org/wiki/Douglas_Engelbart

Openness has been key to so much progress in the digital space. The open standards of the Internet and World Wide Web are testament to the value of sharing at fundamental technological levels. Open-source software has offered similar acceleration. It is wise, however, to look that gift horse carefully in the mouth. Open source does not mean free of flaws and vulnerabilities.

There is an element of risk taking that is closely associated with the digital successes seen in the US and China. European practices of late have tended to favor caution, regulation and low-risk approaches to new developments. And yet, the 19th Century industrial revolution has its roots in Europe. Perhaps now is the time to take note of that history and to infuse the EU business and academic/research sectors with new freedoms and support to explore possibilities. Rather than stifling the free flow of information across national and regional boundaries, perhaps now is the time to encourage that exchange and to accelerate the rate at which discovery and invention can happen. There is ample evidence that collaboration and sharing of knowledge has delivered capabilities indistinguishable from magic, seen through the eyes of a 19th or even 20th Century citizen. At the very least, the European gears of progress need to mesh and not clash, for the region to prosper.

Vinton G. Cerf

Vice President and Chief Internet Evangelist,
Google LLC

October, 2020

PREFACE TO THE SPANISH EDITION, BY J. CARLOS DÍEZ

Finding authors with an academic and strongly entrepreneurial background such as Andrés Pedreño and Luis Moreno is not easy.

It requires considerable effort to combine research and university classes with projects that hybridize economics and technology in the private sector; a cross-cutting vision to ensure that academic innovation ends up becoming an open training program for more than half a million students around the world; and a very special sensitivity to catalyze entrepreneurship in the classroom, or reinvent yourself on the brink of retirement to found your successful startup, something within reach of very few.

Perhaps because of this strangeness, the book you are holding is a real breath of fresh air; a new approach to the consequences of the digital delay in Europe, with a critical tone from those who suffer the absence of impulse to digital companies and the exhaustion imposed by university research; an essential vision of the weakness of the European Union in the face of the US and China, which are strengthening their positions (especially the latter) at the dawn of the artificial intelligence (AI)-driven industrial revolution.

Such a book was much needed.

The European Union (EU) is now a victim of its policies and doubts about leaving its comfort zone and transforming its traditional production system. However, economists for decades have paid little attention to regulatory issues, almost ignoring the impact of their measures on a country's growth or the opportunity costs they can bring to their businesses.

The coronavirus crisis has once again reflected this European backwardness, as well as the need for an in-depth analysis of its consequences and policies to boost economic development.

The COVID-19 pandemic has shown how many of our companies were not telework-ready, public school teachers barely had the means to give online sessions, and our right to privacy constantly created conflicts with potential technological solutions to contain the infection - a situation similar to that in the United States, and completely contrary to the experience of China, Taiwan, or South Korea.

Asia, already consolidated as a leader in the digital economy, has emerged successfully from this new global crisis, and by reading this book, you will understand why.

If there were something special about this work, it would be that its authors, Andrés and Luis, have dared to draw a roadmap beyond criticism as recommendations for closing the digital divide.

In a solid way, they explain why the honing of talent, the creation of digital ecosystems, a regulation that weighs its effects on the development of cutting-edge technologies, and an intelligent administration are topics that should become a "state business" for a European Union that is rapidly approaching its economic decline.

AI and the software economy as a whole are emerging as the general-purpose technology of our time, the epicenter of many other innovations that will forever transform any sector the reader has in mind.

Medicine, tourism, transport, and agriculture are subjected to a profound disruption that will surface in a short time, generating a revolution similar to that of electricity in the 20th century.

That is why the authors constantly insist that all European leaders, academics, businessmen, and professionals should urgently become fully aware of the disruption that embraces us, enable sufficient funds, establish an intelligent open data policy, specialize in new branches of knowledge, and facilitate, when not impelling, the transformation of the productive sectors.

Europe, if it does not promote strategies to take advantage of cutting-edge technologies, will be relegated to a secondary role in a market that will generate tens of billions of euros. However, the authors warn that it will first have to get out of the crossroads in which it finds itself, more politically concerned with watching over its "dissatisfied gods" than with containing the perfect storm that is the aging population, Brexit, public debt, and even the new economic scenario opened after the coronavirus.

Finally, they want to draw the attention of faculties, professors, and economics students with an exercise in reflection and debate on the new demands of a very renewed science in its functioning and its foundations.

Based on their own experience and previous studies, the authors propose a theoretical adaptation of some of the aspects exposed during the book, asking in a practical way and with concrete examples if the classic models can explain the effects and alterations caused by autonomous learning on fixation of prices, automation in employment, the collaborative economy on supply, or cryptocurrencies and Blockchain on monetary theory.

The change we face will generate fears that will have to be managed, and potential victims that must be protected and accompanied by social policies to minimize the negative externalities of technological transformation. If Europe does not start the path of change towards an eminently digital economy, it will inevitably be overwhelmed by "creative destruction". Cutting-edge technologies will be generated outside our borders. Our irrelevance and technological dependence will make the social market economy model that characterizes us unsustainable, a loss of well-being for millions of Europeans that the authors try to anticipate by proposing an intelligent adaptation and progressive and profound transformation towards the new era of artificial intelligence.

For all these reasons, after reading this book, it will be more apparent than ever that we are in that state that in classical Greece they called Kairos, the right time to do something crucial. As Heraclitus of Ephesus, Plato's teacher, taught us, "everything flows, nothing remains"; to which he added, "nothing is permanent except change."

José Carlos Díez

Professor of Economics at the University of Alcalá
and partner of the VC investment fund LUAFund.

April 2020

WHY READ THIS BOOK

«The greater the obstacle, the more glory in overcoming it. »
MOLIÈRE.

«I think everyone guessed it, although they didn't ask questions.
When you can't have reality, dreams are enough. »
RAY BRADBURY. *The Martian Chronicles.*

You are holding in your hands the fourth edition of "Europe vs. the US and China: Preventing Decline in the Age of Artificial Intelligence". At the time, the authors doubted whether our unorthodox and critical view of economic reality would be well received, but after two years of work combining a dose of humility and daring, we felt ready to tell, as Al Gore did, a series of *inconvenient truths*. And time has proven us right.

Massively positive feedback soon followed, which helped to correct some errors and discover new bibliography. Three months after its publication, this book was already at the top of the Amazon Spanish bestseller list in sections such as artificial intelligence, technology, and macroeconomics, and it remains in very high positions as this preface is being written (March 2021).

Our goal has been achieved: we raised interest and debate about a predicted decline of the European economy, while events proved our hypotheses to be true.

Why do we keep encouraging people to read more than 450 pages? Let us recall the arguments we made in the first edition:

- The overall GDP weight of the EU has decreased from 25.6% in 2008 to 18.6% in 2018. Europe is losing a fundamental race to maintain its global economic positioning, well-being, and freedom.

- We live in the Europe of digital laws, yet we barely have leading innovation companies and we are increasingly technologically dependent.

- Technological lag and lack of focus on digital skills endanger the future of labor, especially in southern Europe, with high rates of youth unemployment and specialization in old sectors.

- The role of economists[2] is not proactive enough in identifying the opportunity cost of delay and dependence on world-changing technologies.

- Some experts question for the first time since World War II whether the next generation of Europeans will improve the level of well-being of their parents and grandparents.[3]

- Our political leaders get lost in criticizing the American and Chinese economic models, without paying enough attention to Europe's competitive loss.[4]

Unfortunately for this new edition, the reasons have not changed. The coronavirus continues to highlight our limitations and disadvantages. We have come face-to-face with working remotely, educating and training online, selling over the internet or developing an e-government, and the shortcomings have been notable. We have fallen prey to debates and ambiguities on privacy, leading to a state of inaction when what was most needed was to secure jobs, welfare and health.

---

2. It is important that not only economists, but also engineers, lawyers, politicians, educators... get out, let's get out of our comfort zone and work together to provide robust and effective solutions.

3. Gill, I. S., & Raiser, M. (2012). *Golden growth: Restoring the lustre of the European economic model*. World Bank Publications.

4. Europe has precisely criticized both the Asian giant and the US for their lack of involvement in matters of social integration or in the fight against climate change; but in this self-satisfaction and criticism, Europeans - even with reason - have forgotten that without future technologies, without economic growth, and without quality jobs to retain talent, it will be impossible to sustain all our achievements and social commitments.

Europe still needs to regain hope, and to do so it will need to reinvent itself on digital talent and ecosystems where creativity and leadership achieve scalability and curb youth unemployment and the knowledge diaspora. We must give solid and well-founded hope that women and young people will embrace technology and play a leading role in achieving new milestones for humanity such as curing cancer, stopping climate change, eradicating poverty or reaching Mars.

The only possible way to do this is to invest ambitiously in the future, and to abandon contradictory discourse in which the advances made by AI in the medical field are applauded, while regulations for data exploitation are tightened; or millions are invested in campaigns to prevent traffic accidents, but autonomous driving is called into question; and even the technological giants are fiscally targeted while the EU has tax havens in its territory.

The old Europe cannot be a brake on the future of its young people. We must change the discourses and be braver: regulate to lead, not to be led. Every new technology carries with it risks and dangers, but just as humans mastered fire thousands of years ago and learned not to burn themselves, our generation must face the challenges of AI with determination, knowing that the next evolutionary leap of our species depends on it.

The authors of this book represent two very different generations: the one that has had to reinvent itself digitally after a life on the analogue stage, even after suffering the Spanish post-war period, and the one that has had to face a volatile labour market, very different from the one taught in universities, hit by an accumulation of economic crises.

But despite an age difference of 33 years, we share a vision of the future and a need for change. We both come from rural areas of Spain, far behind the big cities. After a lot of effort, we have both managed to live our time: to be university graduates, to integrate into the European project, to be digital, to be entrepreneurs... Europe has made us stronger, and has helped us to overcome our complexes. That is why we want it to have the leadership and the future it deserves.

Europe needs to unite all forces, no more brexits or governments that call into question the future of the EU. We must learn from

Europe's collective intelligence, from Finland's good practices in education or Estonia's efficiency in public administration. Encourage and value our start-ups and entrepreneurs. Use our own technologies to tackle the processes of digital transformation and digitization.

In this new edition of "Preventing Decline in the Age of AI" we continue to invite you to participate in a debate and a reflection that will hopefully take Europe out of its comfort zone and position it once again as a driving force in the world economy.

STRUCTURE AND CONTENT

This book has been structured in three main sections and twelve chapters which, although related, can be read independently, with differentiated recommendations and conclusions.

Although a logical order has been established starting with the basic concepts, followed by the diagnosis and problems of the lack of digital leadership in Europe, then policies and proposed solutions, and ending with a reformulation of theoretical postulates to provoke debate among teachers and students, the reader can feel free to start with the part that most interests him or her.

Specifically, this is the structure of the book:

1st Part. Diagnosis: Reasons for European digital decline, an announced chronicle of the coronavirus syndrome

Ch. 1. Why is Europe not a digital economy superpower?
Ch. 2. Traditional sectors and the "perfect storm" in southern Europe
Ch. 3. European research and development (R&D): insufficiency or inefficiency?

The data shown should set alarm bells ringing in an EU that is approaching a perfect storm caused by ageing, youth unemployment in southern countries, the weakness of the productive fabric and its technological ecosystems, and the fragility of its R&D; problems that have historical roots and whose lack of solutions is bound to cost too much in terms of welfare.

Ch. 4. Regulation as culture

We argue why European regulation is not efficient, raising a very critical debate on the so-called *Brussels Effect*. The European regulatory does not understand digital nature, generating relevant costs for companies and being highly inefficient. The proof is in the lack of

European digital companies and unicorns of relevance. We also put forward a proposal to finance press freedom, the Achilles heel of digital disruption, and why oversized privacy has prevented a rapid and effective highlight to the COVID-19 crisis.

2nd Part. Policies and proposals for action

Ch. 5. A strong commitment to AI in Europe

Will AI be the electricity of the future? In this chapter, we identify the potential of AI in economic growth and its enormous sector impacts, with some industries already facing radical transformations. Finally, we contrast the weakness of Europe's involvement in AI leadership compared to China and the United States.

Ch. 6. Prospects for job creation and destruction in the digital age
Ch. 7. The education and talent revolution in the context of disruptive technologies

Are automation and AI a threat to employment? Are our education systems generating the skills and knowledge needed for the jobs of the future? Given the results observed at European level, we propose giving absolute prominence to a new education policy focusing on aspects such as computational thinking in primary and secondary education, university employability and the digital education of society.

Ch. 8. Entrepreneurship and startup scalability issues
Ch. 9. Digital ecosystems- in search of the European model

Why is the scalability of European digital businesses so limited? What ingredients are needed to generate successful entrepreneurial ecosystems? How to develop and retain talent in less technology-driven economies? This section discusses the characteristics of European digital entrepreneurship and the guidelines for developing digital environments, after analyzing some international success cases. We also discuss the idiosyncrasies of what we call *digital small-holdings*, a new concept that aims to address how to take advantage of existing entrepreneurship in Europe.

Ch. 10. Public administrations in the digital age

To what extent can Blockchain revolutionize the efficiency and transparency of public administration? How can AI and the age of data revolutionize attention to citizens? Experience shows that public digitalization plans are impossible without the awareness of politicians, administrative staff and citizens themselves.

While in many "advanced" countries we are still queuing in long lines to resolve the most absurd bureaucratic formalities, in India properties are registered at the click of a button and in Estonia any citizen can do everything, except get married, from his or her computer screen.

3rd Part. Dissatisfied Gods and a New Economic Theory

Ch. 11. Europe at the crossroads. Bringing dissatisfied and irresponsible gods into hell.

What are the future prospects for Europe? How will it be affected by changes in the geopolitical context such as Brexit or the rise of populism, or the digital gap? Using some references from the book "Sapiens: A Brief History of Humankind" (Y. N. Harari, 2014) we reflect on whether today's Europe should continue trying to break the "unsatisfied gods" with regulatory crusades, or assume that the "fire" of technology can burn but, as primitive tribes did, "controlling it" is the only way to continue to evolve.

Ch. 12. Proposing new theoretical approaches to the digital economy

Do our economics manuals explain everything that is happening in the digital economy? To what extent should we pay attention to the variable time and prospects? What are the implications of price formation in digital sectors for resource allocation? Based on the concept of *black swans* (N.M. Taleb, 2008), in this chapter we suggest the need to propose new theoretical and conceptual tools that allow us a more precise economic analysis to interpret the new digital economy.

We invite critical comments

At the time of writing this book, numerous specialists linked to education, law, economics, and entrepreneurship have fundamentally helped us by proposing very valuable changes and notable suggestions that have improved the original versions. All are referenced in the acknowledgments section at the end of this book.

Even so, we, the authors, are fully aware that we not in possession of the truth.

Surely an ambitious and multidisciplinary treatment like the one we propose is full of many gaps and weak points. We hope that you understand that some sections and theoretical concepts have had to be synthesized given the breadth of topics addressed. Nevertheless, you will find at all times the references to the original works.

To make amends for this situation we propose that the book in your hands be interactive. Our intention is to provoke debate, share ideas and incorporate value and knowledge in a lasting way, for which constant changes and updates will be introduced based on the observations those critical, incisive, and generous readers get across to us.

This is what we have done so far, having introduced more than 200 suggestions from some experts and our readers. To contribute you can visit the website reverse-decline.com or contact us on social networks.

INTRODUCTION

BASIC CONCEPTS

«Confusion is the welcome mat at the door of creativity».
MICHAEL J. GELB

The purpose of this introductory section is to differentiate and clarify the meaning, at least as far as our use in this book is concerned, of terms used in the field of the digital economy yet among which there is plenty of confusion or a lack of de-limitation.

They are as follows:

1. Digital economy.

What we understand today as "digital economy" has little to do with its meaning just a few decades ago. If at the beginning of the millennium the digital economy was assimilated to an "internet economy", the emergence of disruptive technologies such as deep learning, Blockchain, the internet of things (IoT) or quantum computing have given us a completely different approach.

The digital economy is now seen with an unpredictable capacity to concatenate new developments. It is therefore more intelligent to talk about the singularities and differences with respect to the traditional economy than to rigidly specify a closed description.

Don Tapscott[5] at the end of the 90s included concepts such as "knowledge, disintermediation, innovation, immediacy, globalization, and discordance" in his interpretation of the emerging New Economy. These attributes, even in spite of the continuous revisions, are those that still best characterize the digital economy.

---

5. Tapscott, Don (1997). The digital economy: promise and peril in the age of networked intelligence. New York: McGraw-Hill.

2. Digital transformation and digitization.

Although they are sometimes used as synonyms, we must differentiate between "digital transformation" and "digitization".

The first of these terms will be used to refer to innovation processes that integrate new technologies in products, companies, or markets without altering their nature. For example: a public administration that invests in online communication or incorporates a chip to the national identity cards to speed up some procedures.

By "digitization", we mean the general process that leads a conventional economy or sector to be completely digital, taking advantage of technology to reinvent itself and not just to transform itself. A good example of digitization is the use of distributed accounting technology by public administrations to make any process telematic, from submitting documents to voting in elections.

Digitization changes the rules of the game, threatening even the survival of traditional practices in the medium and long term. A transformation process similar to or even greater than that brought about by industrialization and tertiarization in previous technological revolutions.

3. Innovation and disruption.

Understanding the difference between *innovation* and *disruption* is fundamental to understanding most of the arguments in this book. These concepts have been discussed in one way or another in the economic literature by such influential authors as Joseph Schumpeter, Jürgen Hauschildt, Peter Drucker and Clayton Christensen, with perhaps the relationship established by the latter being the most precise: "disruptive technologies" are innovations that give rise to new, cheaper and better products, causing economic powers to rise and fall[6].

However, this definition must be qualified in the current technological context, as we live in a era of so many changes that from a

---

6. Christensen, C., Craig, T., & Hart, S. (2001). The great disruption. Foreign Affairs, 80-95.

traditional perspective many innovations could be understood as disruption.

In this book, innovation refers to linear change processes, derived from the application of existing technologies or new discoveries, but which have limited growth potential. These limits may be set by dependence on third party technologies, by the impossibility of scaling up, or even by regulatory issues.

The concept of disruption is associated with large-scale, high-speed change. It would be a concatenated and exponential innovation, allowing a relevant and continuous alteration of products or processes. An idea that brings us closer to a radical Schumpeterian "creative destruction", transforming the competitive nature of products or services.

Let's take an illustrative example: a traditional bank could invest a large amount of its funds in constant innovation to improve its productivity (mobile apps, smart ATMs, big data, etc.). But fintech, cryptocurrencies and the big tech are reinventing the financial system, turning software companies into its new leaders. In a few years' time, the sector will look very little like what we know today, and only those that are part of this revolution will survive. This will also be true for health, agriculture, education and all other sectors. All will be "reinvented" from the top down, and a new economic reorganization will begin on the basis of international productive specialization.

This approach will lead us throughout this book to identify three groups of countries: those that adopt a passive technological position, those with a high capacity for innovation and digital transformation, and those that are committed to reinvention and disruption. The first two are followers (on a different scale) and the third will be the leaders.

The difference between innovation and disruption will lead us to question the usefulness of indicators such as investment in R&D, the number of patents or the publication of scientific articles. As we will see in the following chapters, policies focused on innovation and not on disruption are directly responsible for Europe's loss of economic leadership.

4. Kondratieff waves and new disruptive waves.

Since the early 20th century economists have formalized the evolution and replacement of technological paradigms under the so-called *Kondratieff waves* (1935)[7]. These waves were originally used to draw the course of economic cycles (expansion, stagnation and recession), and were popularized by Schumpeter (1939)[8] to demonstrate the effect of innovation on the development of countries[9].

Although this model could be adapted to any era and socio-economic transformation experienced by human beings since the agricultural revolution, the Kondratieff waves have been used for the analysis of the last two hundred years, coinciding with the technological acceleration brought about by the three great industrial revolutions.

According to Schumpeter's observations and subsequent revisions, each technological paradigm develops over 40 and 60 years, with the knowledge that gives rise to each new leap occurring several decades earlier. This reasoning has held up remarkably well with linear transformation technologies, but do traditional waves withstand the exponential concatenation of new technologies?

One of the solutions proposed by economic orthodoxy has been to shorten the technology waves (**figure 1**), with the AI revolution, the internet of things (IoT) or 5G taking a steeper, shorter and more intense form.

---

7. Kondratieff, N. D., & Stolper, W. F. (1935). The Long Waves in Economic Life. *The Review of Economics and Statistics*, 17(6), 105-115.

8. Schumpeter, J. A. (1934). *The Theory of Economic Development*. Cambridge, MA: Harvard University Press.

9. Although Schumpeter's contribution is decisive in explaining the use of these waves, the original name is retained in recognition of Nikolai D. Kondratiev, who was condemned to death by Stalin's orders for criticising massive state industrialisation and agricultural concentration.

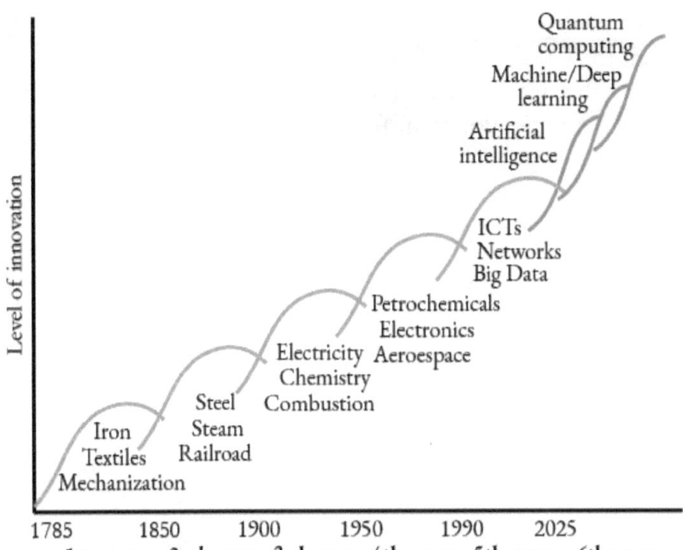

Source: own elaboration

However, this way of drawing the new waves misses the feedbacks that occur between these technologies. Artificial intelligence and Blockchain, for example, are two high-intensity waves occurring at the same time and with a strong relationship to each other. And the same is occurring with the Internet of Things, 5G connectivity and even quantum computing. On the other hand, as new waves converge, the size of previous waves will shrink in comparison to the degree of innovation provided. In Kondratieff waves model, this means that, by comparison, technological innovations that occurred more than half a century ago will no longer be visible.

We can only understand how the age of AI will affect our economy by leaving our usual theoretical comfort zone. If we ignore this, we will lose capacity to analyse and interpret relevant changes in the new technological paradigm. We must comprehend the stress that variables such as employment and wealth will be put under by the advance of new technologies. Because it is highly likely that no industry, not even our own way of life, will be recognisable in a few decades' time.

35

Ray Kurzweil, Google executive and AI expert, stated that "the explosive power of exponential growth, the 21st century will be equivalent to 20,000 years of progress at today's rate of progress"[10]. Translating this leap into traditional models, such as Kondratieff waves, will be tremendously difficult.

<hr>

10. www.kurzweilai.net/understanding-the-accelerating-rate-of-change

DISRUPTION IN THE ECONOMY: KEY FACTORS

«The way for a nation to project itself better into the future is to assume that only by innovating can it catch up with the most prosperous countries»
JOSEPH A. SCHUMPETER.

«If everyone else is already doing it, don't do it»
ROBERT KIYOSAKI. Rich Dad Poor Dad.

Before embarking on the reading of this book, we believe it is worthwhile to introduce some fundamental theoretical issues in relation to the digital economy in order to situate the reader. All of them will be analyzed in more detail in the following chapters.

1. Short-term gaps between countries.

The main objective of this book is to identify how the hegemony of China and the US in AI and other cutting-edge technologies affects the economic development of Europe, which is left in a weak and lagging position. The intensity of disruptive change generates a competitive gap both between companies and countries, causing geopolitical frictions that threaten the economic order shaped over decades.

The curious thing is that these tensions emerge in the form of protectionist and conservative policies that have been reviled throughout history and that threaten both growth forecasts and global stability. European regulations that penalise American digital giants, or the technological trade war between the Trump Administration and China are clear examples of this.

The new era of AI cries out for clear-cut global rules, and while the EU has tried to define itself as a digital regulatory leader, it will never be able to impose global regulation as it is technologically dependent on China and the US. Europe must stop going to war on its own and seek global pacts in which to shape internationally adopted rules of the game. Any other alternative will have too high an opportunity cost.

2. Prospective for decision making.

In an era of rapid, complex and interlinked change, economic agents' decision-making will depend more on anticipation than on trends. Leading firms devour and commission predictive reports from consultants, knowing that expectations formed from a previous period may introduce more bias than guidance.

The variable t (time) is changing for economic science, and 21st century economists will need to use less econometrics based on the models we understand and use more predictive algorithms even if we do not know what is going on inside them.

3. A new price formation and the animal spirits.

The concept of *animal spirits* (J.M. Keynes, 1936)[11] describes how the emotions and feelings that influence human behavior also influence their economic decisions. An idea that became relevant for modern economic theory thanks to Shiller and Arkeloff.[12]

Because it is clear that the understanding of consumer behavior has reached its maximum expression in the new technological paradigm, that of data and information. In this sense, companies that adopt AI algorithms to individualize and personalize their prices by segmenting behavioral patterns or user profiles are called upon to maximize loyalty and profits. The result is an already evident competitive distance, even causing monopolies that tend to be natural because of the difference in access to data.

---

11. *The General Theory of Employment, Interest and Money.*
12. Akerlof, G. A., & Shiller, R. J. (2010). *Animal spirits: How human psychology drives the economy, and why it matters for global capitalism.* Princeton University Press.

4. Disintermediation and the digital perspective of value.

Economies base much of their wealth on the added value generated by intermediation. Any sector aggregates professionals and activities in extensive chains of production, services and logistics until food arrives in our kitchens, vehicles reach the dealerships, or bank loans are granted.

The digital economy, and in particular the link between automation and disintermediation thanks to Blockchain - known as the "internet of value" - is set to validate all these processes in the near future, in order to unmask inefficient structures. In this way we could even measure the cost to business and society of analogue bureaucratization, excessive departmentalization, or group meetings dedicated to covering the agenda.

David Graeber defined Bullshit Jobs as "a form of paid employment that is so completely pointless, unnecessary, or pernicious that even the employee cannot justify its existence even though, as part of the conditions of employment, the employee feels obliged to pretend that this is not the case."[13] Blockchain can be the key to identifying them.

5. The efficiency of regulatory processes.

Special attention should be paid to public administration, which is generally conceived as a cumbersome apparatus whose inoperative nature, accepted and hated in equal parts, entails significant economic costs borne by all citizens and businesses.

The public sector economy needs to assess the opportunity cost of its unsuitability for new digital environments, both at the regulatory and administrative level. Because the digital economy needs a flexible, fast regulation, adapted to relocation, that does not take entrepreneurs and researchers, for whom talent and creativity are the most important assets, away from their daily tasks.

---

13. Graeber, D. (2018). *Bullshits Jobs: a theory.* Simon & Schuster.

6. The fundamental input: talent.

The emergence of the *knowledge economy*[14] established the idea that human capital is the most valuable input for the development of a region. References such as Silicon Valley were built thanks to the specialization of its universities in new technologies and the attraction of bright young people, and in recent decades we have witnessed a global empowerment of talent.

In the coming decades, the combination of technologies such as AI, IoT, Blockchain and quantum computing promise a phase of exponential growth that will take other disciplines such as biotechnology, medicine and physics to unprecedented levels. The cure of diseases, the fight against climate change, the protection of species or the understanding of the universe will depend on the impulse of the digital economy and its technologies.

It would be a mistake to be left out of the promising era of global knowledge acceleration, which requires a firm commitment to computational education, but also agile economies with the capacity to assimilate change, as well as to promote practices such as collaborative intelligence.

7. Cryptocurrencies and monetary policy.

Far from disappearing, cryptocurrencies are experiencing a rebound in Europe, with very interesting legal doubts included. While in Spain, the High Court ruled against their consideration as currency in ordinary use, France accepted them.[15]

To what extent could a digital economy and its aspects such as global online commerce refuses to pay with cryptocurrencies? And how will each country's monetary authority and its monetary policy have to reinvent itself in the face of decentralized money? Although these questions are difficult to answer, China has already gone beyond the rest of the world by supporting a regulated and national cryptocurrency.

---

14. Drucker, P.F. (1994). *Post-capitalist Society.* Routledge.
15.   lesechos.fr/finance-marches/banque-assurances/la-justice-francaise-assimile-le-bitcoin-a-de-la-monnaie-1182460

8. Efficiency and effectiveness of digital ecosystems

Digital ecosystems are fundamental pieces for the economy of a country that dares to declare itself innovative. But are they easy to create, and why do disruptive innovations emerge in some areas and not in others? European economic policy must make a deep reflection on why in the old continent there are no laboratories where entrepreneurship, professional networks, universities and venture capital funds interact.

The above eight points serve to show how our economy, its science and economists themselves are being disrupted by new concepts, hypotheses and working tools. Even if we try to stretch brilliant ideas such as "disruptive innovation", "creative destruction" or even the scope of Kondratieff's waves, we must be aware of the scale and complexity of the changes linked to the digital economy.

In the following chapters, we will address these and other issues in order to understand the seriousness of the economic and technological decline into which Europe may fall, the urgency of policies to prevent it, and the need to think positively in order to restore its deserved geostrategic prominence.

1ˢᵀ **PART:** DIAGNOSIS

*Reasons for digital decline. An announced
chronicle of the coronavirus syndrome*

CHAPTER 1: WHY IS EUROPE NOT A DIGITAL ECONOMY SUPERPOWER?

«Since we cannot change reality, let us change the eyes which see reality»
NIKOS KAZANTZAKIS

In the following chapters you will find the first of our inconvenient truths. Perhaps the most painful: those that demonstrate, based on an exhaustive analysis of the most recent European economic and technological history, how and why the old continent is losing strength and global influence, moving away from being a powerhouse of the economy of the future.

We don't want you to take what you are about to read as dogma. Some data could lead to second interpretations, and it would be very positive if this were done. In fact, we hope to feed and justify a necessary debate that we will address in detail later on: can a country be a benchmark in the technology sector without disruptive companies? Can centenarian companies be digital leaders? Is European welfare sustainable without an industrial transformation?

Although in our opinion the European starting situation in the face of the digital era is very worrying, we must maintain a positive tone. Amartya Sen[16] said that the future is not a single and continuous line but is as plural as the degrees of freedom that human beings have to decide. Preventing the technological and economic decline that Europe is approaching is possible, but it will require the right political, business and social decisions.

---

16. Nobel Prize in Economics for his study of well-being

1. EUROPE, THE US AND CHINA: AN ANNOUNCED TRANSITION?

Europe and the US have dominated the changes of every new technological paradigm since the first industrial revolution. Both, established especially in the last half-century as undisputed economic leaders (not forgetting Japan), saw from afar how emerging countries lacked sufficient potential complete with them.

Until now.

China has broken all growth schemes in a few decades, overcoming cultural distances and economic restrictions. Although in per capita levels it is still far from the Europeans and North Americans, the power struggle that will mark the 21st century is evident.

Nowadays, these 3 powers contribute 60% of the world's wealth, 55% of the value of all exports, and more than half of the global R&D investment. Three major economic and financial engines of the world whose influence far crosses its immense borders. But in this new geopolitical balance that is taking shape, there is one big loser, the EU, and one fundamental reason: its technological backwardness.

Europe and the US: industrial and technological evolution

During the eighteenth century in Europe experiment a unprecedented stage of industrial innovation unprecedented until then. Continuously and in a belt that runs through the Netherlands, England, southern Germany, northern Italy, and some regions of France, Spain, and Portugal, numerous technological advances were fed back and channeled exceptionally[17]. The UK became the great technological catalyst. It led the Industrial Revolution and the growth rates, becoming the first economic power of the contemporary era.

---

17. Grinin, L., & Korotayev, A. (2015). *Great Divergence and Great Convergence. A Global Perspective.* Springer International Publishing, Switzerland.

Decades later, the US would lead the sectors that gave rise to the second Industrial Revolution and thus positioned itself as the new economic benchmark. European countries maintained their innovation policies, but North America decidedly aimed at the then leading industries (electrical, chemical, petrochemical, etc.), later adopted by the rest of the Western world.

American hegemony was further consolidated in the next technological leap, that of telecommunications and computing. As a result, it was able to maintain its privileged position despite the loss of political influence after the Cold War and the Japanese awakening and despite the oil crisis (the 70s), the dot-coms crisis (the 90s), and the financial crisis at the beginning of the millennium.

During this time, especially in the last half century, Europe was restructured with the formation of the European Union and the Eurozone. However, the scant specialization in the cutting-edge sectors of each technological wave has increased their dependence day by day, mortgaging its future and its well-being.

China, from factory to world mastermind

During much of this era of revolutions and profound transformations in the West, China suffered the terrible effects of a policy of isolation that began several centuries earlier. The Japanese invasion, a civil war, and popular uprisings formed the rest of the ingredients of a cocktail of stagnation.

If at the end of the 14th century, in the pre-industrial era, the Asian giant was considered an even more advanced economy than Europe, by the middle of the 20th century it still had feudal structures alive, and its per capita wealth was lower than the average of Sub-Saharan Africa[18].

The human and resource potential of the vast Chinese territory suggested the awakening of the sleeping dragon, but its momentum has surprised everyone.

---

18. Maddison, A. (2001). The World Economy: A Millenial Perspective. Development Centre Studies. OECD.

In just half a century, it has gone from being an eminently agricultural country to matching US investment in digital companies[19], from being a forgotten economy to becoming the second-largest gross domestic product (GDP) on the planet. China exhibits economic growth that exceeds the takeoff of Europe in the 18th century and the "economic miracle" of Germany and Japan in the second half of the 20th century.

China thus joined other dynamic economies in the Asia-Pacific region such as South Korea, Hong Kong, Singapore and Taiwan (the *Asian tigers*) in driving their economic and technological transformation to reach record levels of wealth and well-being.

But the largest power in Asia does not rest to revel in the progress made. China knows that AI and current disruptive technologies are key to confirming the leadership transition from the West to the East. They need to abandon the role of the world's factory to become the brain of the world, and the Made in China 2025 (MIC 2025) plan of industrial modernization promoted from Beijing is the best reflection.

We'll talk about it later.

In this scenario, the US and China have started a Cold War 2.0 for technological hegemony with billions in investments, sanctions and tariffs.[20] Europe, sadly, barely presents a battle to lead the AI era: with no globally relevant digital companies, no government leadership and regulations focused on revitalising its traditional sectors, the technological and competitive gaps are opening faster and faster, showing a chasm of economic slowdown, unemployment and public debt.

---

19. When Google was founded in 1998, only 0.2% of the Chinese population was connected to the internet compared to 30% of the US. See: elmundo.es/papel/lideres/2020/02/17/5e4ae1cd21efa01d5b8b45a5.html

20. "The Trump Administration Blacklisted Chinese A.I. Startups. But That Might Not Slow Them Down". Published on Forbes in October 2019. fortune.com/2019/10/10/trump-china-entity-list-ai-blacklist/

2. WHY IS EUROPE RESISTING THE TECHNOLOGICAL REVOLUTION?

2.1. US initiative, Asian planning, European lethargy

The digital era has led to a transformation of the economic environment from two complementary perspectives:

- A vertical by creating industries that are the direct product of new technologies such as AI,

- A horizontal one, which consists in the adaptation by the sectors of these technologies in their value chain (production, logistics, marketing, sales, communication, etc.).

Although both are powered by the same technologies, they have a well-differentiated impact on the innovation or disruption capacity of regions. Aiming predominantly for specialization in one perspective or another has marked the economic growth and leadership capacity of the US, Asia, and Europe in recent decades.

Government push in the United States and Asia

The United States owes its leadership in the Internet age to the proactivity of a succession of governments focused on innovation since the mid-20th century.

In the middle of the Cold War, the US military industry became the world's leading buyer of microchips and computer advances, even paying above-market prices for experimental products. Many of the advances we use today (the internet, telecommunications satellites, drones, etc.) are the result of this type of relationship that continues today with agreements such as those reached between SpaceX and NASA[21] or with the Robotics Collaborative Technology Alliance (RCTA), which China and Israel replicate in their AI investment strategies.

---

21. futurism.com/nasa-spacex-partnership-saved-nasa-hundreds-millions

To this public impulse we must add a business culture that empowers ecosystems like Silicon Valley, the constant mobility of workers and universities truly committed to entrepreneurship.

On the other side of the Pacific, the role played by Asian administrations has also been essential for their economic modernization. Japan became the most paradigmatic case at the dawn of the third Industrial Revolution. With non-existent military investment after World War II, Japan based its industrial conversion on plans devised by the Ministry of International Trade and Industry, which included promoting technological import, investment in business R&D, domestic innovation production, zero-cost financing of new technology companies, providing tax incentives worth billions of dollars for the acquisition of machinery and computer products, or implementing educational plans to promote careers in science and engineering, among others.

In just 30 years, the planning orchestrated in Japan led to a production specialization focused on technology that allowed it to fight for global leadership with the US in the 1990s. The reinvention of a symbol like Toyota based on the idea of "continuous improvement" and robotics is a clear example of this transformation process. Japan even led industries as relevant as microchips at that time (**figure 1.1**).

Although today, Japan has lost strength as a technological disruptor, other countries in the Asia Pacific region have taken over, also thanks to a high-tech-based planning system. South Korea, Singapore, Taiwan, and China are examples of a model of innovation impulse that seems to adapt well to the Asian socio-economic idiosyncrasies.

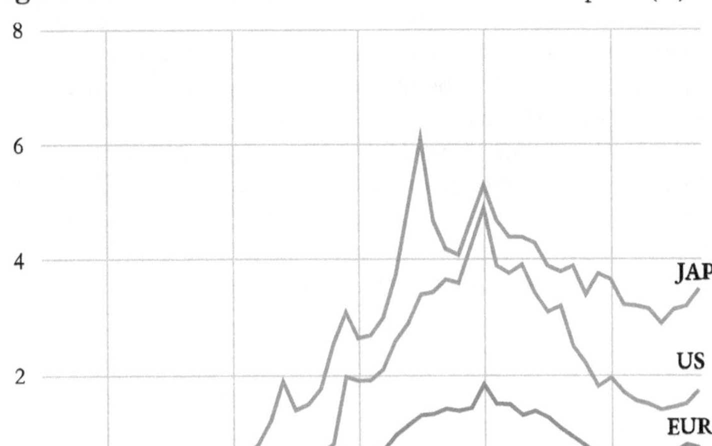

Source: UN Comtrade Database (SITC Rev. 2)

Cardwell's Law and traditional sectors in Europe

Europe's industrial transformation efforts have not been ambitious in leading technological advances. Neither national nor EU policies, such as the eEurope plans, have generated a flow of digital ecosystems and companies capable of competing on a global scale. In brief, and with exceptions such as Ireland, Estonia and Sweden, Europe has been generationally committed to technological adaptation, and not to the vertical transformation of its industries.

More than half a century ago, the historian Servan-Schreiber identified a European fear of technological progress,[22] characterized by hostility from its industrial tradition towards computing. He detected a belligerence over "invading companies" like IBM. Decades later, neither the push from emerging countries nor the opportunity cost of technological subordination has caused a necessary change in behavior.

---

22. Servan-Schreiber, J. J. (1967). Le défi américain (The American challenge). *Paris: Denoel.*

Europe seems to have installed a kind of institutionalized "Luddism",[23] a defense of traditional sectors often promoted by governments that limits the ability to explore new business models or markets. Google, Facebook, Uber, or Airbnb among others have seen their activities undermined because they are a threat to the press, banking, or the tourism sector in its many ramifications. The European attitude fits in with what is known as **"Cardwell's Law"**,[24] or the preference of countries to maintain the advantageous position and experience in their traditional sectors even if it is detrimental to development in the sectors of the future.

The opposite case occurs in countries that have had to redefine their economic structures in recent decades. China, Estonia, India, and Kenya have promoted much more radical transformations in the public administration or in their economic sectors than the most innovative European countries.

The lack of muscle in the European digital economy compared to traditional sectors could be the main reason for this defensive policy. While the European stock exchanges are led by banking, energy and traditional sector companies, in the US and China it is the recently created digital companies that have the greatest room for manoeuvre and capitalization. An unimaginable reality for the European technological fabric, which still today has its privatized telecoms, some with more than a century of history, as its main references.

---

23. The Luddite movement refers to the uprisings and protests in the 19th century against industrial modernization that began in England and spread to the rest of Europe. Juma, C. (2016). Recommended: Juma, C. (2016): *Innovation and its enemies: Why people resist new technologies*. Oxford University Press.
24. Cardwell, D.S.L. (1972). *Turning Points in Western Technology*, Neale Watson, New York.

3. EUROPEAN STAGNATION SINCE THE 1960s

3.1. Asian convergence and European divergence

In the second half of the 20th century and until the economic crisis of 2007, we witnessed an unquestionable process of improvement in global well-being - measured as human development (**figure 1.2**). This is the result of the process of opening and integration, improvements in education and health systems, and the increase in productivity thanks to technological leaps, among others.

In this stage of progress, China and emerging Asia have tripled the growth rates of the most developed economies over the last few decades Their industrial modernization and their inclusion in the global trade value chain have been key.[25]

Figure 1.2. Values of the human development index (1990-2017).

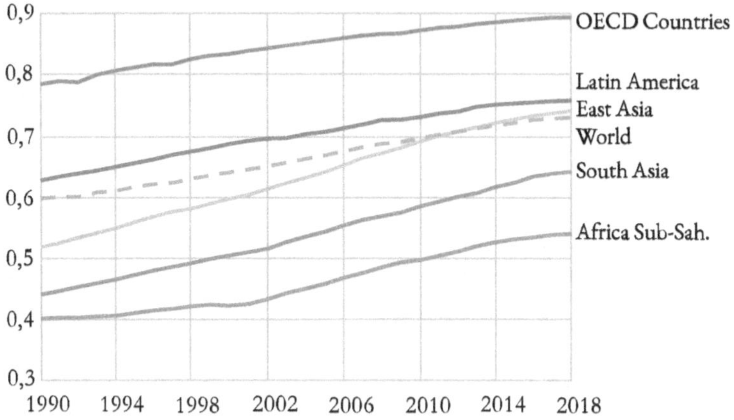

Source: Human Development Report Office, UNDP

---

25. Something that has enabled China to lift 700 million citizens of rural regions out of the poverty trap. Ver: Ang, Y. Y. (2016). *How China escaped the poverty trap*. Cornell University Press.

Meanwhile, Europe has seen its wealth levels move away from the American economy since the end of the 20th century (**figure 1.3**), even though it experienced a period of economic splendor with the construction of a single European market, a common currency and the coexistence of several "economic miracles" in the Mediterranean arc.

In 2008, the EU's share of global GDP was 25%, higher than that of the US (23%). China barely reached 7.5%, measured in current values. A decade later, in 2018, the EU's share of global GDP has fallen by more than seven points to 18.5%. The US share has increased to almost 24%, and China has doubled its contribution to global GDP to over 16%.

Figure 1.3: Comparison of economic growth between the EU, the US and China (GDP per capita, US $ at constant 2010 prices)

	1960-1990	1990-2000	2000-2018	1960-2018
USA	3.6%	3.8%	2.1%	3.1%
EU	3.7%	2.5%	1.5%	2.7%
Eurozone	4.1%	2.5%	1.3%	2.8%
China	6.6%	11.6%	9.7%	8.1%

Source: World Bank

Why this European structural weakness? How do we explain that the EU has grown less than the US and Asian economies despite being in a boom phase?[26]

Traditional and disruptive steady state

Growth and economic convergence theories try to answer questions such as the above. Without going into developing their

---

26. In De la Dehesa, G. (2004). Quo vadis Europa?: *por qué la Unión Europea sigue creciendo más lentamente que Estados Unidos*. Anaya-Spain, the reader will find interesting answers to the stage immediately prior to the economic crisis.

fundamentals,[27] we will say that each economy has a maximum potential income in the long term given its characteristics (inputs) and its savings capacity. It is known as the steady state point[28], and it marks the level at which countries stabilize their growth.

The greater a country's income distance from its stationary equilibrium point, the higher becomes the rate of growth, with so-called diminishing returns as we approach the optimum. Why is this happening? Simply because of the productive potential of each input. To explain it better, let's imagine that a leading country "A" and another developing country "B", both of equal size and population, have 100 million euros to invest in education.

While country "A", with a full schooling rate, could use the investment for scholarships or equipment, country "B" could double the enrolment ratio in agricultural areas to allow thousands of families to escape the poverty trap, with a noticeable impact on the well-being of its population.

However, this convergence relationship between countries with different levels of income does not always occur. In the period before the 2007 crisis, China and Senegal grew at very similar GDP rates (6.6%), and so did Estonia and Togo (4.8%), Israel and Mozambique (3.4%), and South Korea and Afghanistan (2.7%). The reason for this is that countries are constantly changing their steady states (improving their economic planning, incorporating new technologies, renewing their productive fabrics...). This could imply, as in the case of the US and Europe, that a leading economy will grow faster than its pursuers thanks to a future economic projection that is further from its current moment.

Between the years 1970 and 1990 Europe started with a lower per capita income, and its aggregate growth exceeded that of the United States. Countries such as Spain, Ireland, Austria, Finland, Portugal, and Germany converged with respect to the US economy

---

27. If the reader is interested, we recommend the updated work: Solow, R.M. (2018). *La teoría del crecimiento: una exposición.* (The theory os growth: an exhibition). Fund of Economic Culture.

28. Solow, R. (1956): "A Contribution to the Theory of Economic Growth", *Quarterly Journal of Economics*, 70 (1), 65-94

(figure 1.4). The impulse of sectors such as the automobile, chemical, energy, and tourism sectors, which in the US were already showing signs of stagnation, were the engine of the EU.

Figure 1.4: Per capita income (1970) and accumulated average annual growth until 1990

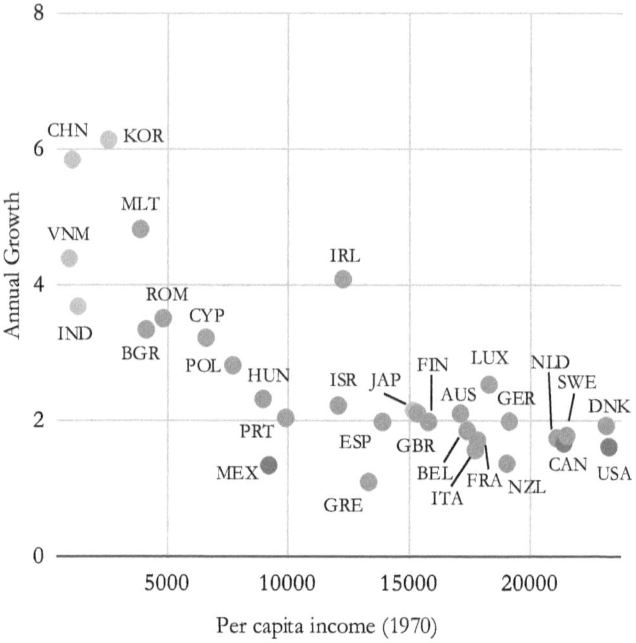

Source: own elaboration based on data from Penn World 9.1

Since the 1990s, however, and with the explosion of the "internet economy", the process has been reversed: the US has re-asserted its role as technological leader, renewing and creating sectors and increasing the wealth potential of its economy. Europe, on the other hand, failed to seize the opportunity of technological change. Without specialization in disruptive sectors, it increased its steady state to a lesser extent, leading to a process of divergence. The differences between the US and countries such as Spain, Italy, Greece, Portugal, Austria, Germany, France or Finland (**figure 1.5**) started to open up, especially after the economic crisis of 2008.

The Asian economies have maintained a very high rate of convergence, boosting their growth thanks to a very ambitious specialization in future sectors. China is going through a stage of economic modernization that took the US and Europe more than a century, prioritizing the improvement of the average income of its inhabitants and closing the technological gap with the West.[29]

Figure 1.5: GDP per capita (1990) and average annual growth accumulated until 2017

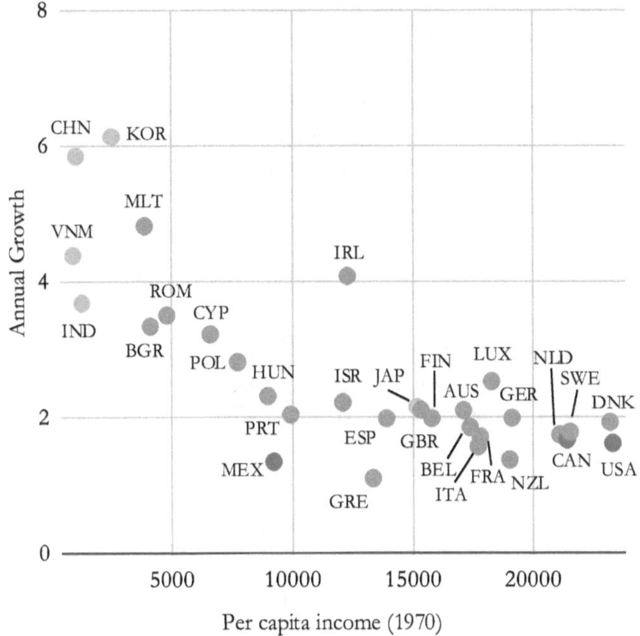

Source: own elaboration from data from Penn World 9.1

Considering these three cases, economists should begin to differentiate between traditional European growth and the disruptive growth, supported by cutting-edge technology, that is driving the

---

29. Asian convergence shows that there is a large amount of its assets away from its optimum, but at the same time it uses some of the wealth to specialise in forward-looking sectors that continue to raise its steady state.

59

Asian convergence and the divergence with the US. Despite the current differences in income with respect to Europe, it is quite possible that the steady state of countries such as South Korea, Singapore, China, or Israel is already higher.

This means that decades in advance they have been projected as leading economies. Now they only have to travel the marked path.

3.2. False economic miracles

The work of the Nobel Prize winner in economics Robert E. Lucas [30] can help to better understand these growth differences from the study of economic miracles. For the author, *miracles* only occur when income growth is accompanied by a productive transformation, something that has not happened in Europe but has in Asia. From the end of the '80s and until the beginning of the 21st century, the peripheral economies of Europe promoted a renewal of their productive fabrics that allowed a period of splendor. Spain reached a growth rate of 5%, Greece of 5.6%, Italy of 3.7%, and Portugal of 4.8%.

However, this growth was anchored to low value-added industries, without an effective introduction of new technological sectors. They modernized their economic structures but maintained their almost exclusive specialization in sectors such as construction, tourism and basic manufacturing.

Except in the case of Ireland, which reached 11% growth, the booming Europe marked a tremendously unstable and short-lived growth path, which collapsed with the financial crisis. Naively or deliberately, European political leaders confused conjunctural effects with structural ones. They let the tailwind of the single market, the privatizations of strategic sectors, and the lack of competitiveness of the emerging countries to give wings to the European economy, while they scored the goal of having fostered economic miracles that turned out to be false.

South Korea, Taiwan, Singapore, and China did work on the complete industrial transformation, and their miracles continue to

---

30. Lucas Jr, R.E. (1993). Making a miracle. Econometrica: Journal of the Econometric Society, 251-272.

bear fruit. First, they became competitive in the less innovative sectors (textiles, toys, footwear, etc.), then in high value-added manufacturing (technological assembly, microchips, domestic consumer technologies, etc.). Nowadays they excel in the most disruptive technologies such as AI, targeting global leadership.

4. A FRAGMENTED DIGITAL MARKET AND THE WEIGHT OF TELECOMMUNICATIONS

4.1. European plans and their inability to close the tech gap

The technological gap between the US and Europe in the 1970s was already too evident to sit idly by, so the European Commission promoted its first commitments for a common policy. Successive eEurope plans (1999, 2002, 2005), the Lisbon Strategy, and programs such as Europe +30 or ESPRIT, aimed to promote economies of scale and incentivize a very weak domestic demand.

Have these strategies achieved the proposed objectives?

Very partially. All have encountered barriers in European fragmentation, in limited budgetary capacity, and in the lack of interest in drawing lines of joint action. Each member state has maintained a well-differentiated economic and technological transformation policy that outlines a Europe of different speeds with distant objectives and specializations **(figure 1.6)**.

First of all, northern countries such as Finland, Sweden, and Ireland have better understood the need to drive the digital change. We could not leave Estonia out of this group, nor of course, the United Kingdom, which, although it no longer belongs to the EU, is indisputably the technological benchmark of the old continent, especially in fintech.

A step below the digital momentum would find countries like Germany or France, with traditional industries but working at a forced pace to maintain their global significance, something that is not easy because of the pressure of Asian competition. This effort is already visible in sectors such as automotive, with Renault leading the sustainable vehicle market in Europe, and brands such as Audi, Mercedes, and even Porsche showing off their traditional technological power by adapting their high range vehicles to the autonomous and electric trend.

Figure 1.6: Regional Innovation Scoreboard[31]

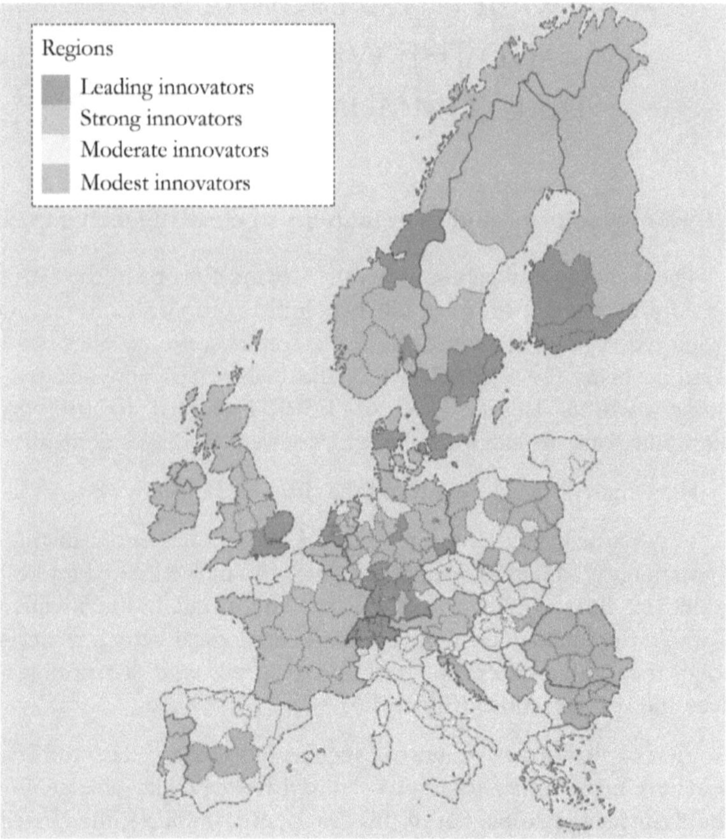

Source: Eurostats

The last place is for southern Europe, whose specialization in mature sectors and under-invested in R&D slows down the possibilities of a digital transformation. Its situation of public debt and high youth unemployment calls for a profound change in its productive model.

---

31. The index is derived from variables such as public and private R&D investment, population with higher education, employment in high-innovation sectors and patents, among others.

4.2. The liberalization of the telecommunications market

These differences, which cause a paradoxical "fragmented common policy", prevent the EU from being able to compete with the two global technological powers,[32] which present unique markets for hundreds of millions of people. One of the examples of European fragmentation at the technological level can be seen with the liberalization of the telecommunications sector in the 1990s, a process that, although it had notable successes, was too conditioned to safeguard the interests of each country independently and their privatized companies.

The telecommunications markets (1): connecting people

In the 1980s, the existence of eight digital communication systems in a twelve-member European Community forced all countries to work together.[33] So many systems represented an extra cost for governments and excessive rates for users traveling in the European area. It was incoherent to boast of union between countries when their citizens could not even communicate with each other.

The European Commission (EC) had to lead a process that was as revolutionary as it was necessary. The reports '*Growth, competitiveness, employment*' (1993),[34] and '*Europe and the global information society*' (1993),[35] were key to promoting connectivity throughout the Community. The results were swift, with central and northern European countries rapidly outpacing the US in networked population **(Figure 1.7)**.

---

32. See: Jacques Delors (1985): *Completing the Internal Market: White Paper from the Commission to the European Council* (Milan, 28-29 June 1985) COM(85) 310, June 1985 (EC), and Ungerer y Costello (1988): *Telecommunications in Europe*, Published 04/19/1990, registered as CB-PP-88-009-EN-C. (EC).

33. At that time, there were only three systems in the US and two in Japan.

34. Growth, competitiveness, employment: The challenges and ways forward into the 21st century: White paper. Published 09/03/1994.

35. Report on Europe and the Global Information Society: Recommendations of the High-level Group on the Information Society to the Corfu European Council. Bulletin of the European Union, Supplement No. 2/94.

Figure 1.7. Population with active internet connection

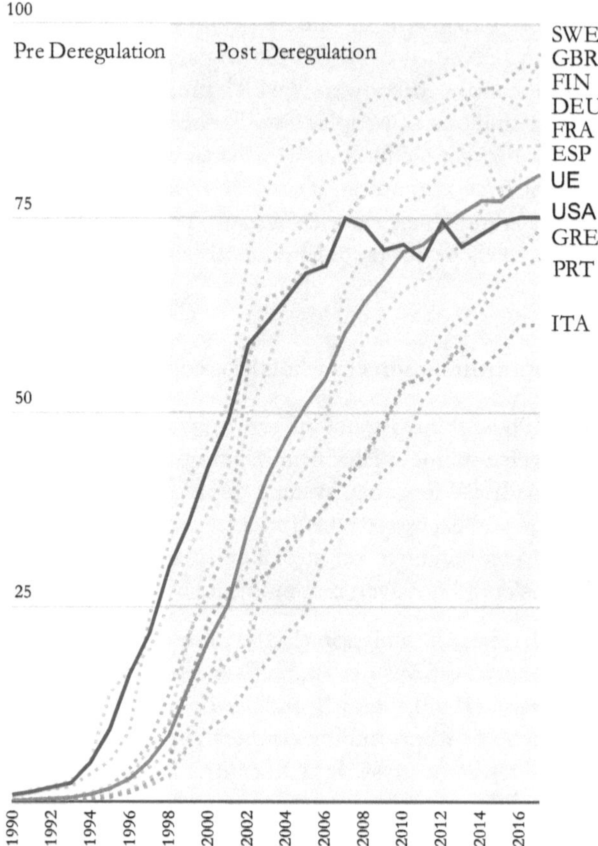

Source: International Telecommunication Union

It is true that the European *sorpasso* occurred once the US had practically reached its connectivity ceiling, given its geographic and demographic characteristics. [36] Its size and lower population density negatively affect its Internet connection service. Even today it is difficult for an American city to have more than three telecom operators.

---

36. Wu, T. (2010). *The master switch: The rise and fall of information empires*. Vintage.

However, this does not detract an inch from the European achievements, with successful policies such as the implementation of the GSM network, roaming between countries without changing the mobile card (though at that time paying exorbitant and abusive prices), and the guarantee of several competitors in the market.

Even at this time, top-tier European technology companies such as Ericsson, Siemens, and Nokia were consolidated.

The telecommunications market (2): the European failure in the internet economy

The extraordinary effort to connect the European population had little reflection in its industrial sector. The EU was losing prominence both in the new communication protocols (3G, 4G, and especially 5G) and in the manufacture of devices. The giant Nokia collapsed before Apple, Google, Xiaomi, and Huawei, reducing to a minimum the European participation in mobile technology.[37]

And after Nokia, the desert.

The failure of the internet economy in Europe is largely explained by an erroneous bet on connectivity per se. The Lisbon Agenda made sure that all Europeans could connect with each other, reaching a complex common framework[38], but left out of its objectives concrete measures to promote the creation of digital companies and ecosystems in which to scale. In this context in which communication was the only important thing, the telecommunications sector turned out to be the great beneficiary. However, while the US process served to end AT&T's monopoly,[39] the European liberalization

---

37. Simon, J.P. (2016), "How Europe missed the mobile wave", *info*, Vol. 18(4).

38. They were looking for achievements such as "bringing the digital age and online communication to every citizen, home, and school and to every company and administration" (eEurope 2000), "increasing the number of Internet connections in Europe" (eEurope 2002), or the "accessibility of services in favor of all European citizens" (eEurope 2005).

39. Mueller, M. (1997). *Universal service: Competition, interconnection, and monopoly in the making of the American telephone system*. American Enterprise Institute.

process protected the privatized telecoms, which maintained leadership in their respective markets at times through blatant anti-competitive practices. For example, in Spain, Greece, Portugal, Hungary, and Italy, the *flagship* companies appropriated the public networks, applying royalties to the new competitors. A few decades later, these countries have some of the most expensive fares in the world **(figure 1.8)**.

Figure 1.8. Price of telecom services (USD, PPP)[40]

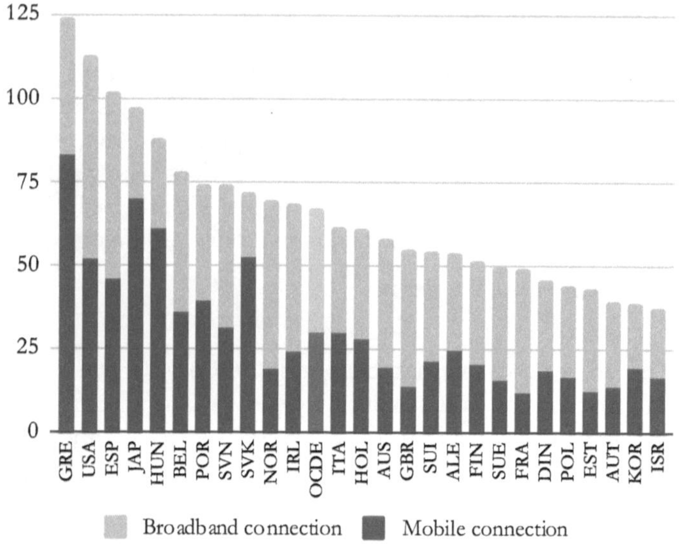

Source: OECD

The results of this entire process, characterized by fragmentation, have been devastating for Europe. While in the American and Asian markets, a wave of young companies that emerged in the last 25 years (Google, Amazon, Tencent, Huawei, etc.) took the pulse of disruption and the leadership of world economic growth, the old continent maintains as technology references the centuries-old privatized companies such as Telefónica, France Telecom/Orange, and Deutsche Telekom.

---

40. Estimate made from broadband connections of 200GB and 25 Mbps, and mobile contracts of 300 calls and 1GB of data in 2017.

Companies that, despite painstaking and willful attempts, have proven in most cases to be very far from understanding the new digital possibilities. Their structures and business models led these corporations to resounding failures with dotcoms businesses twenty years ago (we'll talk about that further on), and later to a disdain for the web 2.0 that is the seed of their delay in some of the new disruptive technologies.

5. THE DOTCOM CRISIS AND THE WEAKNESS OF WEB 2.0

5.1. No news on web 2.0 in Europe

During the 1990s and the first decade of the 2000s, strategic plans emerged in almost all advanced economies to exploit the advantages of the internet. In the US it was the Clinton-Gore Administration's "information highways"[41]; in the EU, the eEurope plans; and similar documents are found in Japan, South Korea, Canada, Australia, France, the United Kingdom, and Sweden.

However, not all dedicated the same effort to delve into ICTs. The US marked early differences with respect to the hard core of the EU, whose commitment and investment was late and less solvent in digital assets **(figure 1.9)**. Only the UK and Sweden come close to US ratios. These first differences became an insurmountable gap at the time when the first generation internet was transformed into a collaborative system with exponential growth. This "internet 2.0" was supported by social networks, wikis, video platforms, communication between companies, etc., and required a fully participatory society, administration, and business fabric; a digital culture that is not built overnight.

In this leap, American ecosystems ended up establishing themselves as the protagonists of the third Industrial Revolution. In 2006, amid investments in web 2.0, private funds invested in American startups more than 700 million dollars. European companies barely reached 100 million dollars. By that year, companies based in California owned 40% of all collaborative websites created in the world.

---

41. The National Information Infrastructure: An Agenda for Action, September 1993.

Figure 1.9: Investment in ICTs (% non-residential gross fixed capital formation)[42]

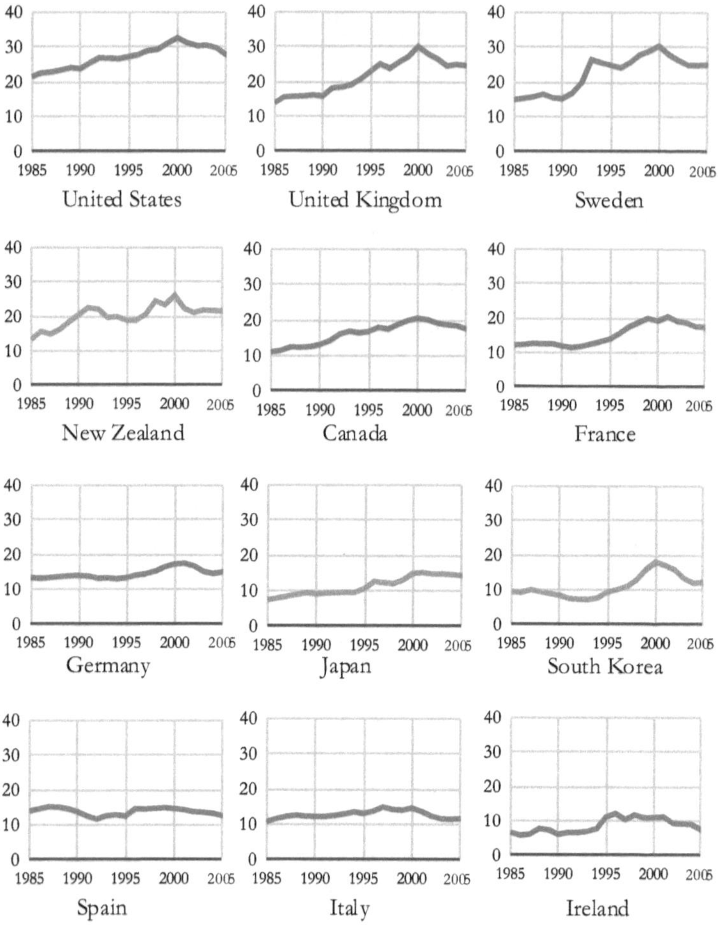

Source: OECD

42. Non-residential gross fixed capital formation refers to the investment and acquisition of tangible or intangible durable goods carried out by companies, non-profit organizations, and administrations.

5.2. The dot-com bubble, or how the old economy fouls the digital economy

The development of the dot-com crisis deserves a careful study, as it synthesizes the behavior of the US and Europe in digital matters; a crisis that in a wrong and opportunistic way has been used as a warning of the "limits" of the knowledge economy, but that was the result of speculation by investors and ignorance of the sector in the 90s.

In 2000, and after a constant revaluation of companies in the technology sector, the Nasdaq exceeded 4,500 points. It thus multiplied its value by 400% in just 5 years, with thousands of shareholders who were carried away by the promises of innovation.

However, the fall was faster than the rise. The lack of profits and an evident oversizing of the sector caused a 75% loss in the price of the selective in a year and a half **(figure 1.10)**, a collapse of billions of dollars that went to companies like 3com, Yahoo!, Digital Insight, Infoseek, Lastminute, Cisco, Intel, and Radvision. It took fourteen years to return to the Nasdaq values before the crisis began. Europe also suffered the effects of the bubble, with the German Neuer Markt doomed to close after losing 98% of its valuation between 2000 and 2003 (more than 200,000 million euros).

Figure 1.10. Nasdaq Index Quote (1990-2002)

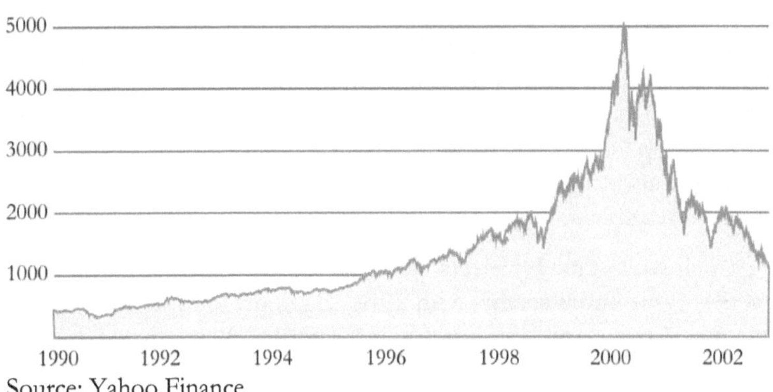

Source: Yahoo Finance

The internet of traditional sectors

The dotcom bubble doesn't have "too much" mystery. It happened as a result of a misunderstanding of the mechanisms of an Internet economy that was just waking up. Traditional giants guarded the first era of ICT, applying an extension of the analog economy over new companies. Teleoperators, banks, electric companies, and relevant entertainment and communication groups searched the internet for a means to expand their businesses, even with speculative profits in the short term. It was an internet of "portals" with one-way communication - almost a full-color teletext that gave information to users but ignored their real needs and the very potential of this new technology. The support of big renowned business groups for new internet enterprises encouraged and gave confidence to investors, who responded decisively to the IPOs of modern technologies without understanding the market.

In this current of new opportunities, Telefónica founded in Spain the internet portal "Terra" (1999) and reinforced it with million-dollar acquisitions (ZAZ, Infovía, Infosel, etc.). A year later, it was the fourth company by capitalization on the Spanish stock market and the principal reference on European websites. However, shortly after the debacle came: Terra's market value fell by more than 90%, with losses exceeding 5.5 billion euros in 2001, and the website Lycos, acquired for 12.5 billion euros in 2000 by Terra, was sold in 2004 for only 100 million euros.

The British online service provider Freeserve also went through a similar process. In 1999 it became the first internet company to go public. It reached a record market value of 10 billion pounds, exceeding the capitalization of the Bank of Scotland. In 2000, and after a 70% drop in the price of its shares, it was acquired by France-Telecom (Orange) for an amount close to 2.0 billion euros, one fifth of its maximum value.

Meanwhile, small projects like Napster, with hardly any funding, were shaking entire sectors with the idea that the internet was a channel for sharing and not just for information. Beyond the debates about its legality, the trends of users on the Net were being clearly defined, though almost traditional companies ignored it to stand firm on ideas that did not work in the digital world.

Substantial differences after the dot-com crisis

After the burst of the dot-com bubble, the disinterest of large companies ended the first internet revolution in Europe. Not only were their investments in the technology sector abandoned for fear of a repeat crash like Terra-Lycos,[43] but in many cases, this skepticism led them to delay their digitization processes for many years.

At the same time, in Silicon Valley, there was the opposite effect, with a 2.0 revolution driven by startups born in garages, but with infinite possibilities to scale in an environment conducive to second chances. Dozens of startups took off driven by new business models and millions of connected users. In just a few years, some small companies were already a benchmark for a new internet, absorbing entrepreneurial talent from around the world and creating a self-sufficient ecosystem, alien to the old economy and its traditional sectors. There were no business plans or long-term growth projections; agility and the ability to pivot ruled.

The evolution of a company like Google, started by two young students, going public before having a clear business model, and with a brand value of more than 30 billion dollars in less than five years since its founding, would have been unthinkable in Europe; nor would others such as Amazon, Apple, or Microsoft have achieved a capitalization in the old continent several times higher than their oil companies, manufacturers, or the most representative automobile firms. Success stories were repeated one after another in the US, with China always attentive, copying and improving ideas 100% adapted to its territory, limitations and censorship.

Europe, without realizing it, was already irrelevant. The internet economy of the old continent had been devoured by unresponsive juggernauts, and the few startups that stood out were only willing to be acquired for a few million euros at best, not to stand up to the digital giants.

---

43. Historians of the economy will enjoy reading how the speeches of the presidents of the telemarketers changed every five years. Telefónica is a paradigmatic example from 1997 to 2002.

6. FROM WEB 2.0 TO THE FIGHT FOR LEADERSHIP IN AI

The European Commission in the 2009 report "Web 2.0: where does Europe stand?"[44] recognized the weak business situation of the EU in the ICT sector and the urgency to propose common policies that will promote the digital economy.

To reach these conclusions, patents were used related to 2.0 technologies (social network, blog, wiki, RSS feed, etc.), an interesting approach that we want to update by comparing two periods, 2000-2010 and 2010-2020, and adding to the exercise the cases of China, Japan and South Korea **(Figure 1.11).**

Figure 1.11. Technology patent registration 2.0

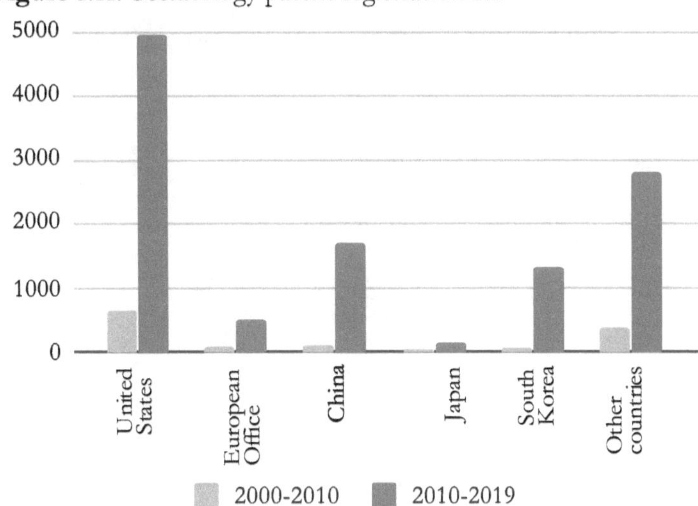

Source: World Intellectual Property Organization

---

44. Lindmark, S. (2009). Web 2.0: where does Europe stand? *Joint Research Centre, Institute for Prospective Technological Studies, European Commission,* http://ftp.jrc.es/EURdoc/JRC53035.pdf.

With this exercise we can see how the EU has lost weight in the internet economy despite the warnings of the report. In the first period observed (2000-2010), the US has 655 patents compared to 71 in the EU, a ratio of 9 to 1. In the second period (2010-2020), the figures are 4,900 patents compared to 500, almost 10 to 1. Even more eye catching is the comparison between China and South Korea, which have multiplied by more than ten their activity between periods (they go from 91 to 1,700 and from 67 to 1,350 patents, respectively).

Although the 2.0 revolution started two decades ago, its development is still making a difference. It is the basis for the success of companies that depend on the reputation of their users, such as Airbnb, Uber or Upwork. But it is also key to developments in AI such as improving machine language, predicting behavior, or optimizing pricing strategies. It is no coincidence, therefore, that Google, Microsoft and IBM stand out in the registration of patents for these technologies **(figure 1.12)**.

Figure 1.12: Registration of patents related to web 2.0 by different companies

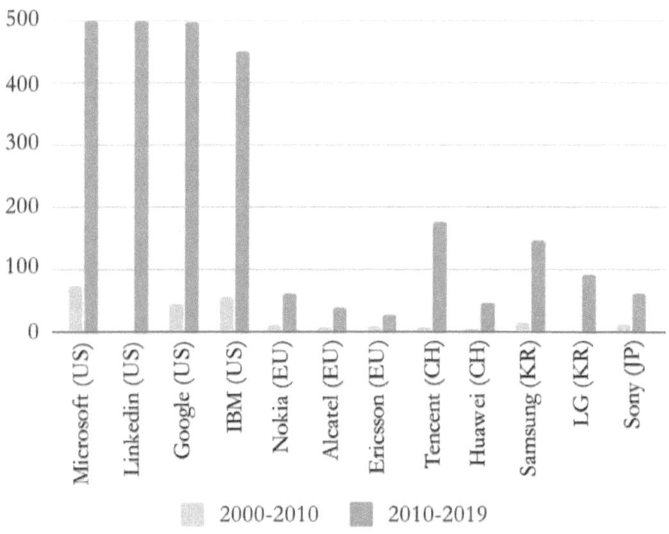

Source: World Intellectual Property Organization

Based on these data from countries and companies, we can advise, once again, how Europe is staying on the sidelines of digitization. European R&D stands out in sectors such as the automobile, with companies like Renault or Bosch leading patents in their industry. However, the lack of companies and digital ecosystems are weighing down the capacity for disruption in the European economy.

An overall assessment

A decade after the report "Web 2.0: where does Europe stand?" and the implementation of the eEurope plans to promote "information society for all", it has become clear that the goals and proposals set by the EC were insufficient in business matters.

As we show in the previous section, the EU has become the great benchmark for internet accessibility and connectivity throughout the planet, with huge benefits for telecommunications companies and regulations aimed at guaranteeing the security and privacy of users in their connections, yet with hardly any leading companies in any branch of internet 2.0.

Indeed, only the UK's Telegram and Denmark's Momondo would fit in a top 25 global 2.0 digital companies by funding volume updated to 2020 (**figure 1.13**). A ranking totally dominated by American and Asian firms.

These numbers are the best reflection of the failure of the European digital policy, whose excessive guarantee conditions the competitiveness of companies and, with it, their ability to generate wealth and employment, as we will see in the second chapter of this book. No region can afford to stand as a leader in innovation or disruption without a private ecosystem capable of sustaining its arguments.

Figure 1.13: Internet 2.0 companies by volume of financing[45]

	App/Website	Country (Region)	Visits (1000/month)	Funding (million $)
1	Facebook	US (California)	19,984,072	2,335
2	Telegram Mess	United Kingdom	12,.500	1,700
3	Pinterest	US (California)	744,568	1,466
4	Twitter	US (California)	3,929,307	1,460
5	Groupon	US (Illinois)	43,462	1,387
6	Weibo	China (Beijing)	222,456	1,286
7	Douyu TV	China (Hubei)	99-146	1,127
8	Weimob	China (Shanghai)	769	589
9	FriendFinder	US (Florida)	31	551
10	Reddit	US (California)	1,600,000	550
11	Renren	China (Liaoning)	7	478
12	Yimidida	China (Shanghai)	269	403
13	Cornerstone	US (California)	312	344
14	PT Link Net	Indonesia	11	275
15	Hike	India	215	261
16	Quora	US (California)	590,000	226
17	Farmers Buss.	US (California)	47	193
18	Linkedin	US (California)	915,000	154
19	Mail.Ru	Russia	262	165
20	Momondo	Dinamarca	440	152

---

45. Order established by volume of funding, not acquisition. YouTube is not on the list as Google acquired it when it had only raised $11 million in funding rounds.

OTHER EUROPEAN STARTUPS				
-	Vinted	Lithuania	357	119
-	Depop	United Kingdom	5,050	105
-	Culture Trip	United Kingdom	16,400	102
-	JobandTalent	Spain	426	101
-	Research Gate	Germany	141,200	87
-	Cinesite	United Kingdom	60	70

Source: own elaboration from crunchbase.com and Alexa

CHAPTER 2: TRADITIONAL SECTORS AND THE PERFECT STORM IN SOUTHERN EUROPE

«When there is a storm, the birds hide, but the eagles fly higher».

MAHATMA GANDHI

«It is better to sail with a moody good captain than a laughing bad one.».

HERMAN MELVILLE. Author of Moby Dick

The effects of Europe's technological catch-up are noticeable in most of its sectors, although they have not yet reached their peak. Analog demand is still sufficient to sustain companies that are not yet digital enough, and more than a decade after the last financial crisis, Europe is still lacking an adequate economic transformation strategy.

The old sectors that led us into an economic abyss are still the most representative, especially in southern Europe, and in the absence of investment, market and political decisions, it seems wiser for entrepreneurs not to embrace radical changes.

However, even if the European economic structure remains in place, there is a nest of termites eating away at the foundations of future development that will become evident with the rise of AI.

1. THE ARGENTINEAN SYNDROME OF EUROPE

To understand the situation the EU is currently going through, we will use the process that Argentina experienced a century ago as a comparison.

Believe it or not, at the end of the 19th century, between 1895 and 1896, Argentina became the richest country in the world.[46]. It was not a technological or industrial powerhouse; nevertheless, the demand for agricultural goods from around the planet allowed sustained growth for decades. In fact, in the mid-20th century, it was still considered one of the seven most developed economies, and its situation was so comfortable that it was allowed to help hungry postwar Spain very generously.

However, in just over half a century, they switched positions: Spain became the 8th economic power, and Argentina sank to 60th place.

What were the causes of the Argentinean collapse and the rise of other economies such as Spain or Italy? The industrialization processes experienced in southern Europe from the fifties and sixties and the maintenance of a traditional economic structure in Latin America are the answer.

Under the protection of the single European market, Spain, Greece, Italy, and Portugal were positioning themselves as leaders in labor-intensive industries, while capitalizing and modernizing their agriculture. Argentina lost any differential competitive advantage and was relegated to a marginal position in the global context, even in the primary sectors.

Today it seems that it is Europe that is undergoing a process similar to that of Latin America in the 20th century. The anachronism is resolved if we change the terms "industrialization" and "modernization" for "digitization". The sectors leading European growth in

---

46. Source: Maddison Project Database.

the early 21st century have become excessively volatile, especially in Mediterranean economies where they show symptoms of extreme depletion. Compared with more innovative countries such as Israel, Ireland, South Korea, and New Zealand, southern Europe is languishing **(figure 2.1)**.

Figure 2.1. Evolution of GDP per capita PPP (2000-18) (NI: 2000=100)

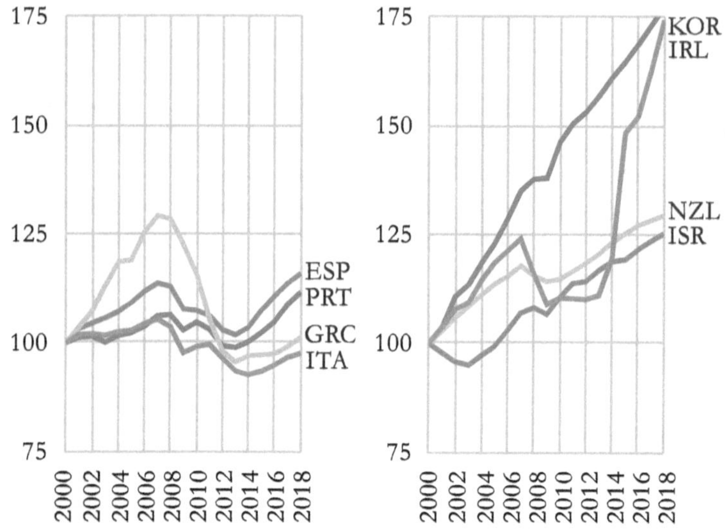

Source: World Bank

We should not forget the drama experienced a few years ago when the financial and brick sectors dragged southern Europe into a state of near despair. Public administrations had to bail out banks, freeze public salaries, and cut social services. Business closures were numbered by the hundreds each week, jobs were destroyed, public debt increased, and the purchasing power of families plummeted. Meanwhile, the most disruptive countries and sectors emerged stronger from the crisis. Only the famous "Whatever it takes" by Mario Draghi in July 2012 confirming the purchase of debt by the European Central Bank kept away the ghosts of a breakdown of the single currency that could have further depleted the fragile economies of Italy, Greece, Spain, and Portugal.

86

Patches, indebtedness, and policies to protect traditional sectors are no longer working. The conventional press is going bankrupt, Amazon closes all corner stores one by one, and Uber and collaborative driving undermine the customary transportation business. Nevertheless, digital companies that can generate jobs and wealth in Europe in the age of AI are practically non-existent.

2. DETERIORATION OF THE COMPETITIVENESS OF TRADITIONAL SECTORS

The competitiveness reports of the most important organizations detect a continued deterioration of the European economies to the detriment of the emerging economies of Asia-Pacific, with spectacular growth of China in any document analyzed **(figure 2.2)**.

Figure 2.2. World competitiveness index (years 2007 and 2017)

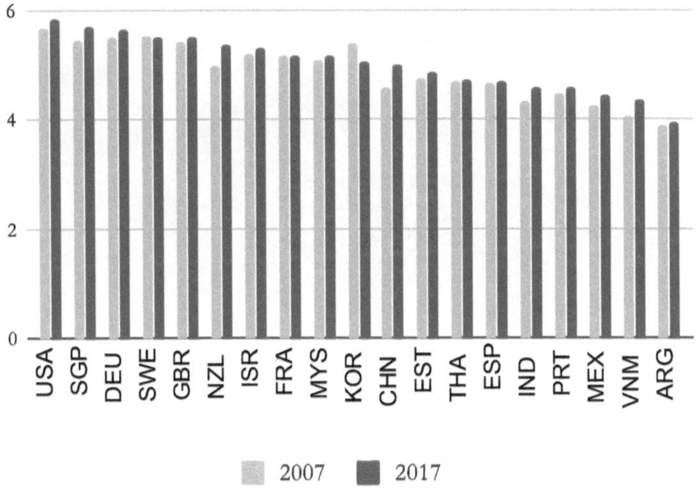

Source: World Economic Forum

Although we are not particularly forums for these indices as they show too much volatility and methodological bias, they demonstrate a particularly alarming change dynamics for Europe. The EU, aware of its deficiencies, is brandishing taxes on technology companies, applying restrictions to the development of AI, or putting a stop to Uber and Airbnb, as we will see in subsequent chapters. All this to progressively protect its most representative sectors from the threat of the countries that innovate the most and their disruptive companies, even if this leads us directly to the precipice. That should remind us of the aforementioned Cardwell Law.[47]

To give a simple example, the awakening of Asian electric cars could cause a loss in German exports of over € 20 billion,[48] which would have direct consequences on their growth rate, employment, or debt capacity. Also, the Spanish tourism sector is losing its capacity to adjust the balance of payments as digital companies such as Booking, The Fork or Airbnb are taking revenues away from local SMEs. And this situation will be repeated in the rest of the industries in which Europe maintains a technological dependence or disadvantage.

____

47. Chapter 1.2.
48. wsj.com/articles/rise-of-electric-cars-threatens-to-drain-german-growth-11565861401

3. A CLAMP BETWEEN THE U.S. AND EMERGING ASIAN ECONOMIES

Economists have been studying the "international division of labor", the productive specialization of countries, and the distribution of global trade for decades[49]. Of all the factors that could explain its causes, wages and innovation are arguably the most prominent, although in this book we include a new one: disruption. Let us explain these three elements.

Wages are undoubtedly the greatest advantage of the so-called emerging or developing countries. Sectors in these economies often specialize in labor-intensive activities and mature technologies, as China has done for years, making it the factory of the world. European and American companies have historically taken advantage of wages to locate production plants. Large and medium-sized enterprises, from textiles to consumer technology products,[50] set up their factories in Asia, reducing costs and jobs in mature sectors in economies of origin.

Innovation is the element that enables advanced countries to compete with the low costs and lower wages of emerging regions: the creation of patents, training of human capital, improvements in performance and productivity, investment in marketing, advances in logistics, etc. Sweden, Germany, France, and Spain have managed to remain leaders in sectors such as the automotive, rail, textile, and

---

49. Comparative advantages are a fundamental ingredient in explaining trade in goods and services. In short, countries specialize in those products in which they are more competitive in a relative (not absolute) way compared to the rest of the possibilities. Those goods or services that cease to be produced due to dedicating efforts to those with the greatest comparative advantage must be acquired in the foreign market. Since David Ricardo and subsequent theoretical updates (to highlight the Heckscher-Ohlin model), economists have tried to clarify the factors that explain specialization in specific sectors that they try to make profitable while abandoning others that must later be imported.

50. I'm sure a lot of readers have heard of "Designed by Apple in California. Assembled in China".

chemistry, thanks to a constant transformation of its most representative industries. However, more and more emerging countries are climbing to this innovation "zone", also counting on salary advantages. The competition in this strip is increasingly fierce.

Finally, disruption must be understood as the advantage of the countries that lead the world economy. AI, IoT, Blockchain, 5G networks, or quantum computing renew, differentiate, and give competitiveness to all sectors until they are unrecognizable. Amazon has become the world's greatest warehouse, Google the first advertising agency, Netflix the fastest growing entertainment company, Spotify the most listened to radio - and all at a lower cost and bigger expandability than with analog practices.

Europe, stuck in a position of innovation, receives pressure from below by emerging countries that are beginning to monopolize increasingly advanced sectors; and from above, China, the United States, and others such as Israel or South Korea, which are putting the entire European production and services sector in danger through automation and global competition based on the most advanced technology.

The weak commitment on disruption is locking the old continent into a commercial clamp whose effects are expected to be devastating.

4. JOB DESTRUCTION AND WAGE GAP

Loss of competitiveness is leading Europe to face a really tough labour market scenario. As Asia, and even Latin America or Africa make their way into increasingly advanced industries, the survival of traditional sectors in European economies will be seriously at risk, limiting the possibility of job creation.

After the outbreak of the financial crisis and until the coronavirus pandemic, Europe had experienced a continuous reduction in unemployment, although its structural values continue remain between 2% and 5% higher than the US average **(figure 2.3)**.

Figure 2.3. Unemployment rate (% active population)

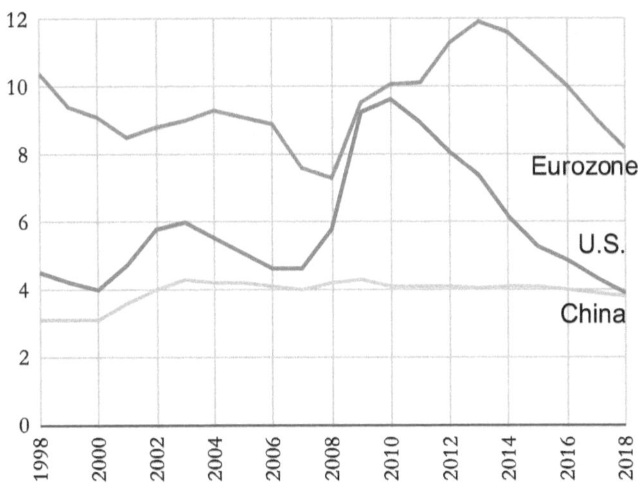

Source: World Bank, Knoema and Eurostats

Within the European economies, southern labor markets (especially in Spain, Italy, and Greece) have shown greater fragility, with very high numbers of job losses during economic crises and a very slow recovery. However, other countries such as France, Sweden,

Finland, and Ireland have more than 5% of their workforce unemployed, while that of the United States and China as a whole remain below 4%.

Despite the fact that these structural differences are a reality with decades of history, many European politicians and union leaders remain fearful of introducing AI or digital transformation into their agendas. However, it is precisely the most high-tech economies (Israel, Ireland, South Korea, Finland, the United States, etc.) that have lower youth unemployment rates and greater resilience to the crisis **(figure 2.4).**

Figure 2.4. Youth unemployment in Europe, the U.S., and China

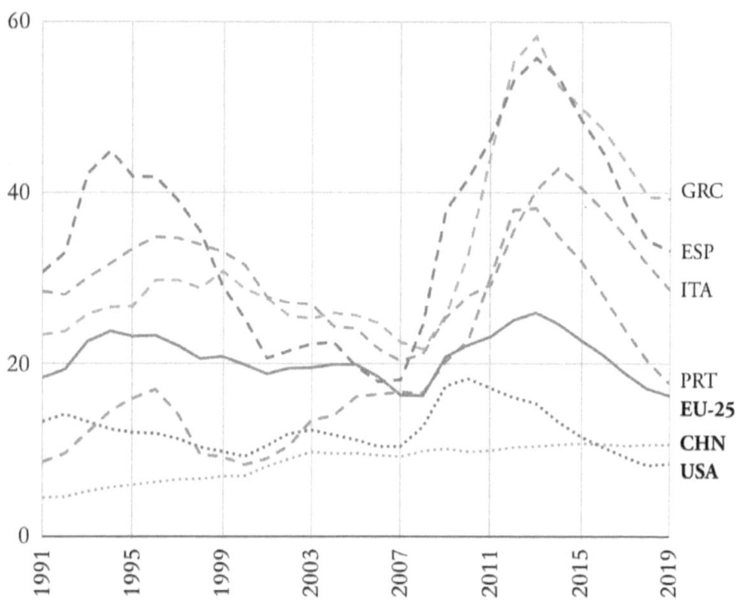

Source: International Labor Organization

5. THE PERFECT STORM: AGING AND PUBLIC DEBT

In this global context of digital transformation, Europe also has a handicap in its population structure. Its aging **(figure 2.5)** leads to cost increases in public services at the same time that productive capacity is lost.

Figure 2.5. Population over 65 years (% total population)

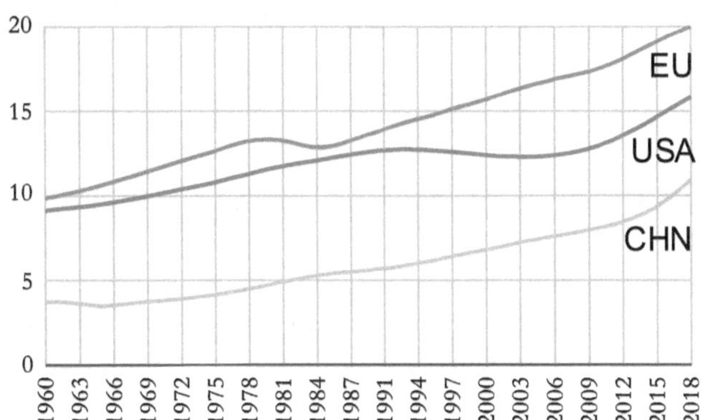

Source: elaboration based on data from the World Bank

The brain drain experienced by the less innovative economies exacerbates this problem. The numbers of the misnamed "external mobility"[51] after the financial crisis were very worrying, with Greece losing 58,000 professionals with higher education between 2007 and 2012, Spain 87,000, and Italy 133,000 **(figure 2.6)**,[52] a situation that could be repeated with the coronavirus crisis.

---

51. elplural.com/politica/espana/mientras-el-pp-se-lo-toma-a-broma-el-gobierno-aleman-alerta-a-espana-de-la-fuga-de-cerebros_40349102

52. These figures do not reflect the real situation. Many did not formalize their residence abroad and others did so intermittently.

Figure 2.6. Migration balance between EU countries by level of training (2007-2012)

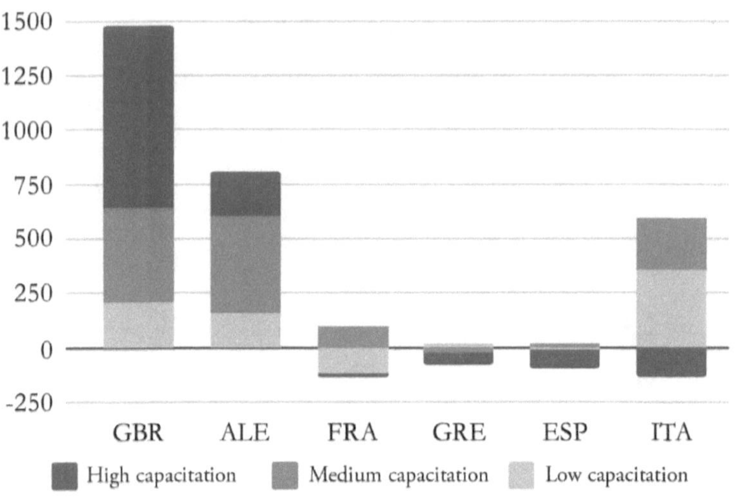

Source Report: "EU Mobile Workers: A challenge to public finances?"

Considering this dynamic, sustaining the European welfare state -with public spending 15% higher than in the US and China-[53] and the rights acquired by citizens (pensions, subsidies, universal health care, etc.) seems complex.

The response to this challenge has been financial "suicide": creating debt. In Italy, Portugal and Greece, their public debt exceeded 100% of GDP years ago, and France and Spain are close to that level. This means that even if these economies set aside all the money they produce for a year, they would not be able to service their debts.

The EU, faced with the need to inject capital due to the coronavirus crisis, could mistakenly follow in the footsteps of Japan, whose central bank holds 70% of the national debt (which exceeds 200% of GDP). A major challenge that could provoke discomfort in the northern countries and bring back the debate on the two-speed euro.

---

53. This and other macroeconomic data for the US, China, and a selection of countries can be seen in the Annex table at the end of this first part.

6. THE COST OF NOT TRANSFERRING THE ENTIRE ECONOMIC SYSTEM INTO SOFTWARE

A decade ago, Marc Andreessen bluntly warned us that "software would eat the world".[54] Many understood it as an opportunity. No fewer saw it as a threat. And many others even denied it.

The rise of new disruptive technologies, the exponentiality of their implementation, and the impressive technological advances that await us around the corner, such as quantum computing, mean that no one has any doubts anymore: "everything that can be software will be software", says our friend Benjamí Villoslada[55].

The question is to guess at what speed each sector will transform, venturing the margin of time that a company has to embrace digitization or lose competitiveness at a forced march.

AI and drones will revolutionize our agriculture with smart crops and high precision farms. Robotics, automation, and 3D printing will have a brutal impact on the manufacturing industry, reducing the cost of chain production and eliminating any possibility of error. Autonomous driving will reinvent the transport sector and our cities will become smart 'sensorized' entities to 'talk' with our cars.

Subsectors such as healthcare or medicine will be unrecognizable with personalized care and treatment and disease prevention. Public administrations will sooner rather than later include transparency, traceability and authentication platforms through technologies such as Blockchain. And this could be just the beginning.[56]

---

54. Why Software Is Eating The World, published by Marc Andreessen on August 20, 2011 in The Wall Street Journal. wsj.com/articles /SB10001424053111903480904576512250915629460

55. Benjamí Villoslada is a digital reference in Spain and co-founder of the Menéame website, which was seriously threatened with the approval of the Google tax that protected digital media from news aggregators.

56. If nanotechnology managed to reach a real industrial phase for many of

The digital economy is not a mere à la carte option that a government can dose, delay or limit as it pleases. It is a real question of survival, the only ship capable of navigating the waters in this perfect storm that Europe seems to be heading for.

By way of conclusion

European administrations continue to grant too much credit to the old economy, something that directly and indirectly cuts the wings of the digital sectors. It seems our leaders are not aware of the high economic and social costs of resistance to change.

The plan to be drawn up in Europe is a continuous strategy for the future, a joint commitment to a single digital market, the creation and reception of talent, the promotion of digital companies that create high-wage jobs, and mass inclusion of disruptive technologies in our most traditional sectors. A complex and long-term goal, yet mandatory to prevent the economic and social disaster that may befall the old continent.

---

its potential advances in molecular engineering, the industrial and economic impact would be of such magnitude that it would be beyond imagination.

CHAPTER 3: EUROPEAN R&D: INSUFFICIENCY OR INEFFICIENCY?

«The mind is not a vessel to be filled but a fire to be kindled».
PLUTARCO

«Every day we know more and understand less».
ALBERT EINSTEIN

The objective of increasing investment in innovation proposed by Europe is a major approach. Indeed, there is a general consensus on the low contribution to R&D in the old continent, especially in the southern countries.

But the problem goes far beyond gross figures. Before raising the issue of insufficiency, we should question its efficiency. If we entrust our R&D with the challenge of being a driver of disruption and development, we must link most of our investment to correcting the technological gap and the decline of the European economy in the global context.

1. THE EUROPEAN SITUTATION IN TERMS OF R&D

For more than a decade, the EU set the objective of investment in R&D with over 3% of GDP, a figure that would have allowed it to establish itself as a leading power in innovation. At present, the European investment effort is barely 2%, far behind the US, Israel, or South Korea, and below China **(figure 3.1)**.

Old Europe is going out of date. The innovation locomotives such as Germany or France are finding it increasingly difficult to propel the rest of the wagons, and Brexit has meant the exit from the EU as the continent's leading digital technological power.

Figure 3.1: Investment in R&D to GDP

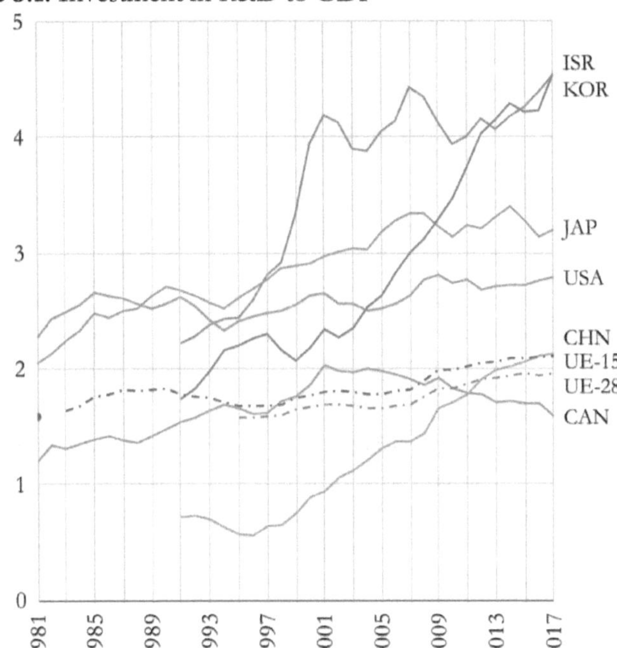

Source: OECD

Indeed, only Denmark, Germany, Finland, Austria and Belgium have exceeded the 3% mark set by the European Commission, while thirteen countries, especially in the south and east of the continent, invest less than 2% of their GDP in R&D. This includes Romania and Latvia, with a depressing 1% national investment in innovation[57] **(figure 3.2)**.

Figure 3.2: European investment in R&D relative to GDP (2017)

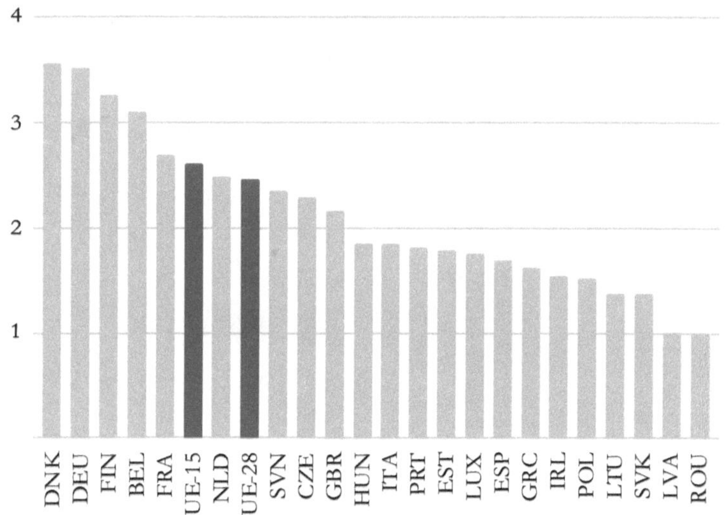

Source: OECD

But in addition to these disparities within the EU, it is necessary to highlight two elements of concern that should motivate a change in European innovation policy:

1. The gap with the U.S: Although some European countries spend more on innovation than the U.S., the fact is that North American investment is higher than that of twenty-four of the twenty-eight EU members (including the United Kingdom). However, what is really relevant is that when the US economy is

---

57. See statistical tables as an Annex at the end of this section.

102

disaggregated, no European country can compete with the leading states of the US economy

For example, California's investment (5% of GDP) is 1.5 times that of Sweden, 1.7 times that of Germany, triple the British investment, and four times that of Portugal or Spain.

Figure 3.3: Investment in R&D relative to (2016)[58]

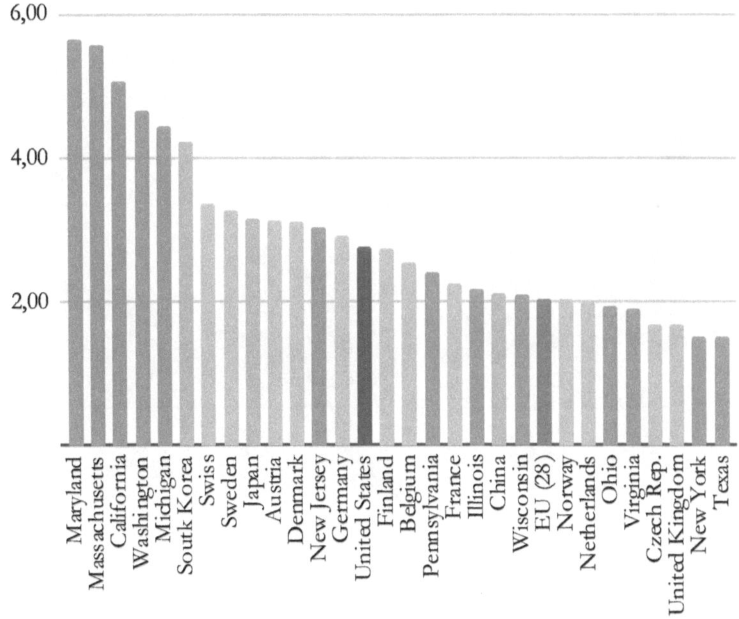

Source: Eurostats and National Science Foundation

2. The weakness of investment in private R&D: The second reason for concern is the public dependence of European investment.

---

58. In the comparison, the 15 states of the United States with a population of more than 7 million have been used, which corresponds to the statistical limit established in the NUTS1 population level of Eurostats. For example, California has a population of 40 million people, almost half of all of Germany; and Maryland and Massachusetts have larger populations than Ireland, Norway, or Denmark.

In the US only 26% of investment in R&D is made by government administrations, in China it is 22%, in South Korea 20%, and in Israel, California or Washington, it barely reaches 13%.

In Greece, public investment in national R&D reaches 51%, in Portugal 49%, and in Spain 45% **(figure 3.4)**. Not even the European leaders (Sweden, Germany and France) are able to compare the private investment effort of the digital powers.

Figure 3.4. Public and private investment in R&D (2017)

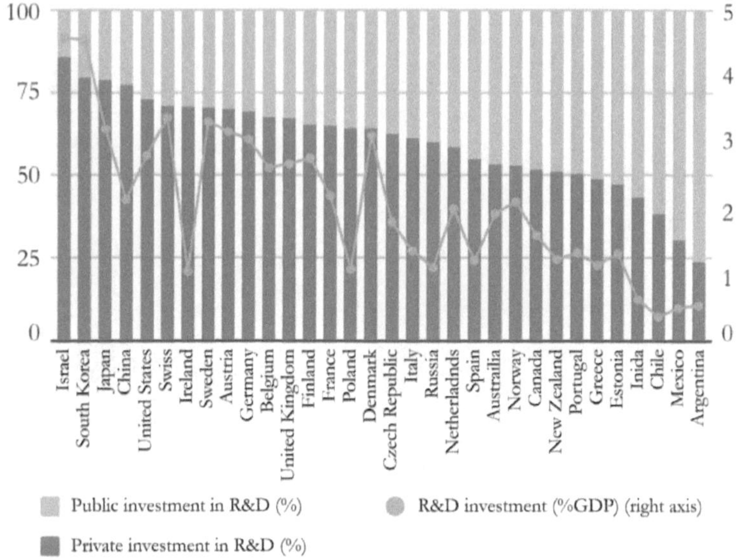

Source: UNESCO

2. INNOVATION AND PRODUCTIVITY IN EUROPE AND THE US

Unlike China and the US, the European public sector is not exercising its role as a driver of private R&D investment, nor is it compensating for the lack of disruption with commitment and leadership in the sectors of the future.

In order for the agents involved to take action, it is necessary to understand the factors behind this problem. We identify the most relevant, which will be explained in later chapters in greater depth:

1. **Oversizing of academic research:** R&D in European public universities is excessively focused on academic research, especially oriented towards publications in prestigious journals, but with a limited transfer of scientists and PhDs to the private sector and no incentives for the creation of technological and start-up companies.

2. **A R&D focused on traditional sectors:** while the European R&D maintains its focus on traditional sectors, in China and the US leading companies are emerging in disruptive technologies such as 5G, AI, IoT and Blockchain.

3. **Weak patent conversion:** one of the corollaries of the previous items is the deficit in trade and industrial research. California, Massachusetts, and Washington each multiply the number of patents by four per 100,000 inhabitants of Sweden, the most prominent country in the entire EU, which is also surpassed by 12 other US states **(figure 3.5)**.

4. **The EU must rethink its innovation objectives:** in a world where open innovation is gaining more and more weight and small startups are reinventing sectors, the EU should focus on bringing the technological specialization of its regions to the technological forefront and on renewing a productive fabric that is losing competitiveness, and not on reaching 3% investment.

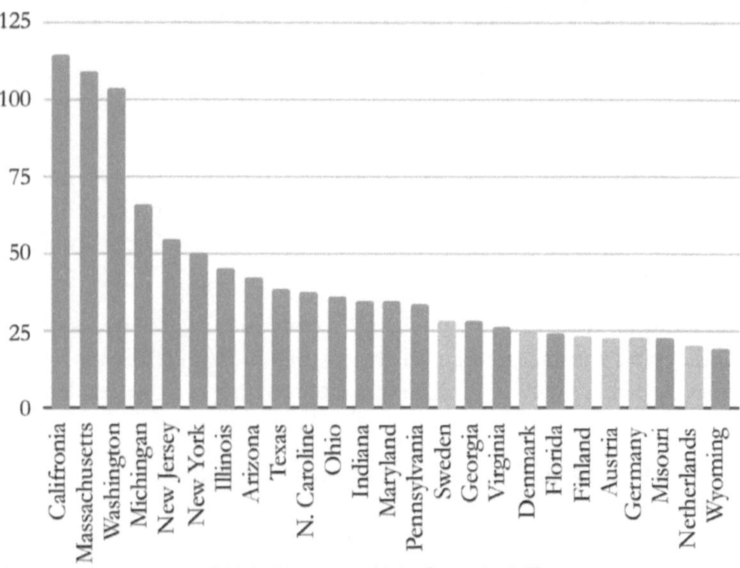

Source: Eurostats and U.S. Patent and Trademark Office

5. **Lack of efficiency in the management of R&D and the allocation of resources:** EU member states should be obsessed with measuring and monitoring the impact of public R&D spending. Billions of euros are allocated to projects with practically no impact on society or employment. With inflated expenses for travel and meetings and no subsequent follow-up.

   The efficiency of the innovation funding system must be called into question, with tedious bureaucratic procedures that prevent prestigious research teams from bidding for public funding, and with companies that make a business out of their knowledge in applying for calls for proposals, regardless of their nature.

In summary, the European public sector investment effort in innovation should always have the competitiveness of the economy as the first option, and through this, obtain gains in employment and well-being.[59] The private sector must be understood and empowered as the driving force behind new advances that will ultimately improve the well-being of all citizens and act accordingly.

We must therefore move away from looking at the entrepreneurs as a public enemy (something common in certain political circles) or at the public sector as a drag on companies (a current that predominates in other spheres) to become obsessed with the search for efficiency and disruption in our innovation system.

59. Andrés Domingo, J. y Doménech Vilariño, R. (2020): *La era de la disrupción digital.* (The era of digital disruption). Deusto.

3. BREAKING THE SOLOW PARADOX: R&D AND PRODUCTIVITY

The European stagnation is also observed in productivity levels, influenced by industrial specialization, and with a notable divergence between all EU countries and the US from the 1990s **(figure 3.6)**.

Figure 3.6. Productivity (GDP per employmee) (US$ 2010 PPPs)

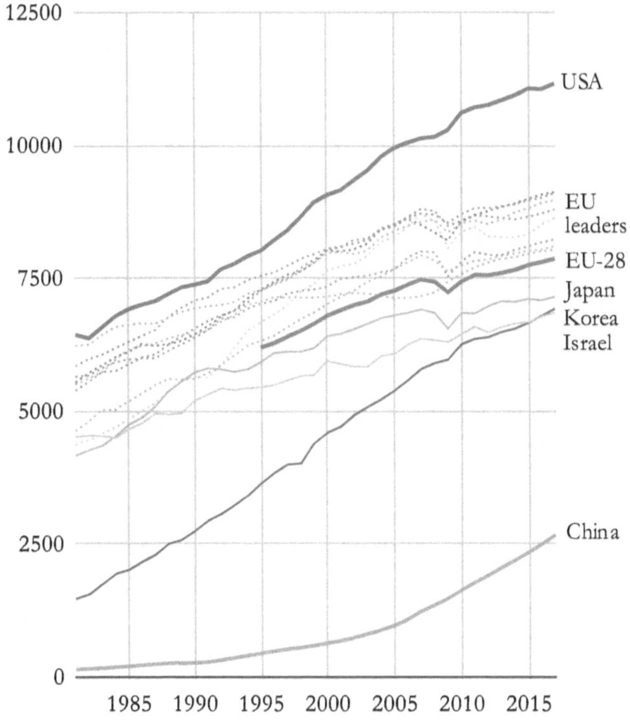

Source: OECD

In the last two decades, the US has increased its average productivity per worker (2.9%) almost one point more than the EU as a whole. Only Finland (3.3%) and the United Kingdom (2.6%) have shown close values, while Spain (0.6%), Italy (0.4%), and even Germany (1.7%) have left far behind. The ICT sector has contributed most to the gap been between the U.S. and the EU (**figure 3.7**), confirming that although the U.S. technological advantage has taken a few years to assert itself -as the well-known Solow Paradox warned[60]- it is already having a significant effect on productivity.

Figure 3.7. Increase (%) of productivity per worker since 1950 and contribution of each sector in the period 1995-2007

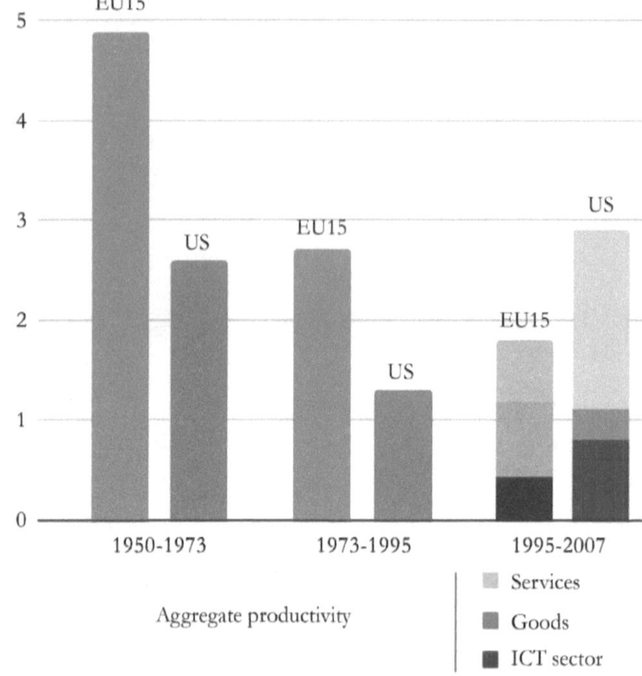

Source: Timmer, Inklaar, O'Mahony y Van Ark (2011)[61]

---

60. Paradox enunciated by the Nobel Prize winner in Economics R. Solow: You can see the computer age everywhere but in the productivity statistics. "We'd better watch out", *New York Times Book Review*, July 12, 1987, pp. 36.

Erik Brynjolfsson showed that this paradox was not true, and that the effect of innovation, although it took time to appear in the statistics, was differential for companies. See: Brynjolfsson, E. (1993). The productivity paradox of information technology. *Communications of the ACM*, *36*(12), 66-77.

61. Timmer, M. P., Inklaar, R., O'Mahony, M., & Van Ark, B. (2011).

These indicators should be analyzed with great caution and concern from Europe in the age of AI. If the internet economy is causing such evident productive and competitive differences, what effects will the new disruptive technologies, with a transformation capacity far superior to the ICT that emerged in the 90s, not have?

With an insufficient investment in R&D and inefficient in its spending (little oriented to disruptive technologies and excessively dependent on the public sector), it will be difficult to achieve productivity advances comparable to those of the US and China.

Europe should start to correct its course and direct its strategy towards new sectors, starting with replacing the traditional R+D+i[62] with a new R+D+d: research, development, and disruption.

Productivity and economic growth in Europe: A comparative industry perspective. *International Productivity Monitor*, (21), 3.

62. R+D+i: research, development and innovation.

4. THE BATTLE OF THE OUTDATED R&D: SOME REFLECTIONS

José Manuel Leceta, former director of the highest state body promoting digitization in Spain, red.es, and of the European Institute of Innovation and Technology, published in the newspaper Cinco Días [63] a truly enlightening article on the situation of the European Mediterranean and its commitment to technological transformation.

The title of the article "Viajar sin moverse" (*Travel without moving*), alluding to the iconic album of Jamiroquai, could not be more revealing. Leceta, both in his article and in the subsequent book *La innovacion fractal*[64] criticizes the fact that in the last 25 years there has hardly been a commitment to digitization in Spain. He also highlights how innovation indicators fail to capture the reality of the problem, and even points out the excesses of R&D spending that are wasted redundantly.

Encouraged by his publications, we will now make a series of reflections on investment in innovation that will serve to synthesize some of the ideas of this chapter:

First reflection: R&D without technological innovation has reduced impacts.

Investment in R&D is traditionally considered the best indicator of innovation. Even in this book, we have used it to reflect the different trends in China, the US, and the EU. However, R&D is too broad a concept, which includes any type of action and expenditure intended to obtain knowledge regardless of its branch of research or performance.

---

63. cincodias.elpais.com/cincodias/2019/08/29/economia/1567095224_443-399.html

64. Leceta García, J.M. (2020): *Innovación Fractal. Navegando la complejidad.* (Fractal Innovation. Navigating the complexity)

Experts such as Professor Charles Edquist of the University of Lund[65], raise doubts about the payoff that R&D indicators deserve, especially about their effect on society and its well-being. In his own words, "in the utopian defense from politics and science to bet on growing investment in R&D, we run the risk of losing ourselves in non-technological innovation in an increasingly technological world."

As we have pointed out, the European innovation discourse has been constructed precisely with a certain distance from private businesses. Public administrations and a notable absence of leading digital companies prevent the EU economies from taking the pulse in terms of 'speed' and 'intensity' of technological change, reflected in the number of industrial patents, scientists in companies, and digital startups.

Second reflection: The statistics do not hide reality – quality vs. quantity.

The Lisbon Agenda and the eEurope plan to create an information society in Europe established at the beginning of the 21st century the objective of 3% of GDP investment in R&D by 2010 in the EU as a whole, about a point more than that in 2000. Two decades later, the figures are still anchored at 2%, which seems to have become our ceiling. Europe continues with the gap of one point and without specifying its digital bet.

Has the European strategy been so disastrous? To be honest, it is not that this 2% data is very positive... but we should not be obsessed with quantity but with the quality of the investment.

Ireland, one of the few references in the digital economy in Europe, invests in R&D less than Spain, Portugal, or Greece. However, in a few decades Ireland went from having the worst average income in the EU to the highest thanks to a strategic plan of attraction and creation of technology companies. And Estonia, also with scarce investment, points to the same path since it is the country that creates the most digital companies in the entire EU.

---

65. Charles Edquist: High R&D Intensity Without High Tech Products: A Swedish Paradox?

In contrast, Sweden has a higher **R&D** investment effort than the U.S., and no one would hesitate to point out which of the two economies lead in cutting-edge technologies.

R&D plans must be an absolute priority for any country and sector; however, they must be accompanied by clear strategic lines, with effective control of expenses, without excessive bureaucratic procedures, and above all, with companies leading the process. Otherwise, the investment will have more impact on the taxpayer's pocket than on improving welfare.

Third reflection: What if we are not so bad? On the self-deception of overly biased and optimistic index.

Any reader could go to the latest report "Innovation Scoreboard 2019" of the European Commission and find that 'for the first time in the index of "Innovative performance",[66] Europe surpasses the USA',[67] the first global technological power. Confused, we could even look for other innovation rankings, such as Bloomberg's,[68] and contemplate how Switzerland, Germany, Finland, and Sweden surpass, year after year, both the US and the Asian leading economies.

How is it possible? Why is a country that counts on Google, Amazon, or SpaceX, that spends hundreds of billions to promote new technology companies, or that presents aggressive national plans for the development of the technologies of the future, not a leader in innovation?

The answer is in the Key Performance Indicator (KPIs); or rather, in an incorrect definition of KPIs to measure the innovation of countries. Variables such as the number of doctors, the population with higher education, the number of scientific publications, exports of medium and high-tech products, R&D in the public and educational sectors,[69] etc. are indicators that, though they have some social

---

66. europa.eu/rapid/press-release_QANDA-19-2998_en.htm

67. ec.europa.eu/regional_policy/es/newsroom/news/2019/06/17-06-20 19-2019-innovation-scoreboards-the-innovation-performance-of-the-eu-and-its-regions-is-increasing

68. bloomberg.com/news/articles/2019-01-22/germany-nearly-catches-korea-as-innovation-champ-u-s-rebounds?sref=mezxKzsV

69. See methodology here: ec.europa.eu/docsroom/documents/35946

relevance, do not accurately show the economic performance or multiplier of the investment made.

Disruptive innovation must be measured through its impact in areas such as employment, the attraction of talent, income, the inclusion of scientists in the private sector, or the generation of technology companies. The ideal would be to be able to measure it in terms of productivity, competitiveness, and economic growth, not as a mere percentage objective that an administration achieves

Fourth reflection: the battle against fragmentation, inefficiency, and superfluous expenses.

The great handicap of European innovation is not so much the public dependence on investment, but duplication, lack of agility, and expenditure destined for bureaucratized entities that are alien to the development processes themselves.

From our own experience we know that for certain grants the procedures are so complex or require so much time and resources that they discourage researchers and companies. Why doesn't anybody act on the opportunity cost of this complete nonsense?

Imagine for a minute a team of European scientists studying how to reduce CO_2 levels to fight climate change. If they require public funding for their research, they have two options: to outsource to a consulting firm instead of a new researcher or to put aside their valuable studies to spend too much time on tedious bureaucratic tasks.

This situation, wasting hours of work and resources of the research staff, generates a million-dollar business set up at the expense of companies and the public sector (i.e. the taxpayer), with work teams oriented exclusively to the application and management of public aid and whose only raison of existence is inefficiency.

The EU must optimize its processes to ensure that every euro devoted to research funding is put to good use. It must facilitate continued competition in public processes, while tightening real-time control and monitoring of the work and results achieved with open innovation platforms and work in the cloud.

The selection criteria for public funding should be based on the expected social impact, such as job creation, welfare or the fight against the social problems of the 21st century, and not on whether a hundred pages of unwieldy documentation are delivered in a timely manner.

Fifth reflection: business leadership and ambition to reserve the situation.

Current European, national, and regional research policies run the risk of becoming a kind of canonry for agents linked to universities, centers, states, regions, or companies that wish to invest in R&D, a situation in which innovation is confused or equated with a subsidy.

Europe seems to anchor itself to its academic comfort zone. Large sums of money are earmarked to achieve meritorious goals such as combating climate change or even creating smart spaces, yet there is no common strategy for integrating universities, businesses, and venture capital. It is forgotten that it is the private sector that must lead R&D in order for it to translate into wealth and employment.

Countries such as Israel, Korea, or even China, in addition to being major leaders in public investment in research, have very ambitious digital policies such as the Startup Nation,[70] investment in hubs, support for university-business relations, and funds earmarked for disruptive technologies, allowing the hiring of doctors and scientists in private companies.

Last reflection: start the house with the roof - a well-being-innovation paradox.

In a commendable way, the EU has since its creation concentrate on to promoting the well-being of all its citizens, developing regulations and actions that promote social cohesion, ecological sustainability, and universal access to quality education and health[71]. Nothing to object to… if it weren't for the fact that European living standards are at risk of collapsing in the absence of clear leadership in disruptive sectors like AI. These sectors, in addition to generating

---

70. startupnationcentral.org/
71. europa.eu/european-union/about-eu/eu-in-brief_es

more wealth and employment than traditional ones, are necessary to face the challenges of our time, from clean energy to diagnosing diseases.

We must also add a budgetary issue: without the creation of our own disruptive technology, guaranteeing European citizens access to the latest medical techniques or to live in a healthy environment will lead to a significant increase in public debt to the limit.

Think about it: what leader would refuse to import technological advances that can save thousands of lives? A situation that we have already experienced with the acquisition of vaccines to eradicate the coronavirus, with considerable distribution problems and controversy due to the delay in their administration throughout Europe.

With a society in the process of aging, high unemployment, and a slow rate of economic growth, we speak of a bankruptcy of the welfare system. The outdated R&D has a devastating corollary: there is no viability for our well-being without specialization in the sectors of the future.

CHAPTER 4: REGULATION AS CULTURE

« One thing is not fair because it's law, but it must be law because is fair».

MONTESQUIEU

«Where there is little justice it is a danger to be right».

FRANCISCO DE QUEVEDO

Law, as a legal order, has fulfilled its mission for thousands of years to serve as a framework for action for human beings and their communities, learning from societies and establishing their foundations around them.

However, what happens when society advances so fast that the law does not have time to assimilate the changes that occur? If we think about the debates on privacy, on the regulation of robots in the workplace, or autonomous driving, we will realize that the traditional formula of establishing rules is not efficient in the face of the cascade of new situations that require attention.

Discussions in committees and the achievement of agreements tend to drag on for years, with technology leaving resolutions out of date. It is also often the case that the conclusions involve exhaustive systems of facts and phenomena which nature is not sufficiently known.

Aware of our limited legal knowledge, our intention in this chapter is solely to provoke debate among experts based on arguments that European entrepreneurs continually put on the table. An anachronistic regulation is detrimental to the competitive development of companies, hindering the take-off of the technology sector and causing a loss of wealth and employment.

The European Commission, true to its traditions, has entered a dangerous state of "paralysis by analysis", with a particularly coercive digital regulatory framework. Most worrying, however, is that there is no clear political, business, or academic counterweight that invites us to reflect on the opportunity cost of Europe in regulating the economy of the future.

1. REGULATION AND ECONOMICS

Until the successes of U.S. deregulation in the 1970s and 1980s, and up to the first decade of the 21st century, economic science had paid little attention to the ordering of markets.

In 1987 one of the authors of this book was lucky enough to meet Joseph Stiglitz at Princeton, and his interest in this aspect at that time was almost null. The 2008 crisis, nevertheless, caused Stiglitz himself and many other colleagues to react vehemently[72] to the lack of regulation of the financial market, which had allowed Lehman Brothers to unleash a global collapse. That again activated economists' focus on the effects of regulatory deficiencies and excesses on growth and well-being.

A few years later the Nobel Prize awarded to Jean Tirole (year 2014) 'for his analysis of market power and regulation'[73] came to recognize this growing interest. His contributions, most of them together with the sadly defunct Jean-Jacques Laffont (1947-2004), are of undisputed importance, with excellent work that clarifies the impact of monopolistic companies on different areas of action.

Since then Tirole has warned and underlined how complex it is to regulate the technology sector and the desirability of prudent administrations. It is preferable to wait and learn rather than make mistakes that may be of clear harm to businesses and consumers.[74]

Digital regulation

European regulators have ignored these recommendations. If, according to Tirole, the simple ignorance of a subject as "traditional"

---

72. theguardian.com/commentisfree/2008/sep/16/economics.wallstreet

73. nobelprize.org/uploads/2018/06/popular-economicsciences2014.pdf

74. Tirole has spoken out about digital monopolies, their fragmentation, quality of service, and barriers to entry, among many other issues. qz.com/1310266/nobel-winning-economist-jean-tirole-on-how-to-regulate-tech-monopolies/

as company costs can cause problems for administrations to establish efficient regulation, imagine what happens in the case of the digital economy.

Regulatory authorities face the complexities of an economic model such as digital, which surprises and misleads economists themselves. These new realities change the conventional operation of markets and the very concept of value, price, or user. Let's see some reasons:

- The expansion of a digital company no longer requires investments in the location, beyond representative offices that barely generate income or even declare losses, which is a tax challenge of global dimension.

- The merger of the digital market, contrary to what classical economic theory tell us, translates into better products and prices for end-users thanks to the exploitation of millions of data.

- Neither should a merger be a barrier to competition. Google displaced Altavista and Yahoo! when it was just a research project. Nokia was surprised by Apple, and this, in turn, by Xiaomi and Huawei. Facebook acquired Instagram to avoid being overwhelmed by the generational change and now trembles at the rise of TikTok.

- The digital economy calls into question the traditional concept of intellectual property. Advances in the post-internet era have been made possible by the release of the code and collaborative work. You can even see conventional industries that add to this trend.[75]

- Finally, although Google, Facebook, Uber, and Amazon may jeopardize the survival of traditional companies (press, banking, taxis, etc.), they are also the surest way to promote and make new businesses or professionals visible.

Therefore, given the possibility that because of ignorance or lack of adaptation, the law limits digital growth or harms the consumer

---

75. Tesla has opened patents to facilitate the creation of chargers and batteries. See: tesla.com/es_ES/blog/all-our-patent-are-belong-you

or competition, Tirole himself has been in favor of seeking new solutions, such as self-regulation controlled by public managers.

Europe, however, preferred to over-regulate without valuing well the cost of opportunity and the impact of decisions taken, as evidenced by the gigantic legal and punitive structure created to preserve privacy in the EU. Because a solid and strong technology like Blockchain, a well-trained human capital, and powerful software developments would be infinitely more effective in protecting the security of citizens' data than the entire European legal tangle.

Before moving forward, let us summarize the most relevant aspects that, from our perspective, must be taken into consideration to establish an efficient digital regulation in Europe, that will be expounded below:

1. Knowing the nature and impact of the digital economy: talking about technological development and efficient regulation requires understanding the socio-economic scenario in which we operate. The speed set by mature sectors is not the same as that of the need to boost startups and digital ecosystems.

Administrations must take into account the economic cost of preventing the proper development and use of digital services. They must know to what extent digital regulation is impacting via costs of the delay in the development of the digital economy in Europe and its consequences.

2. Preventing the duality of treatment in the analog and digital world: the digital world has complexity and characteristics that associate it with specific regulations. Logically, once we understand the nature and real impact of digital phenomena, we should design an efficient legal system adapted to the characteristics that occur in this digital world.

3. Preventing regulation from resulting in loss of competitiveness: when companies compete globally, regulation is key to explaining productive specialization in the global value chain. Digital policy decisions taken in the EU represent a lack of leadership in its sector.

Preventive regulation[76] around privacy multiplies the costs of any European start-up on legal and technical advice compared to their Chinese or American counterparts.[77] Yet many complain that consultancies do not give them a full guarantee of avoiding harsh penalties, a very tricky question for those companies that work with AI.

4. Promoting exponential innovation and open-source software: in 1983 Tirole, in collaboration with Drew Fudenberg, Richard Gilbert, and Joseph Stiglitz, analyzed the effects of patents, technical advances, and strategic investments. All of them have traditionally shown themselves as triggers for competitive advantages for the most innovative companies, though their role loses weight in the knowledge economy.

The speed of changes we are experiencing is of such magnitude that many companies are moving away from conventional analytical schemes and discarding the limitations posed by patents or long-term investments. We have a clear example of the impact of free software.

5. Reducing regulatory complexity: many of Europe's regulatory requirements have a burden of subjectivity and uncertainty,[78] with 27 national data protection authorities, plus regional ones within each country, and without a guarantee of uniformity in the interpretation and rigor of the application of regulations. That potentially represents a fragmentation of competition and the market.

---

76. Benefit law.

77. The United States has fled European-style hyperregulation, with the principle that anything that is not forbidden is permitted. The US digital company informs the user of the data processing it does, and the user decides whether or not to accept it.

78. Some data protection agencies are putting out 200-page AI "introductory" documents. The application of the regulations open a strong arbitrary and subjective burden.

This regulatory complexity, uncertainty, and subjectivity can lead to a problem of business inhibition. Entrepreneurs in Europe complain of chaos and regulatory inefficiency: any startup that signs a partnership with a large company will receive from the legal department of the latter a protocol of no less than 40 pages to guarantee compliance with data protection regulations, without resulting in any real guarantee of citizens' privacy, something unacceptable for and economy - the digital one – which requires efficiency and speed in the processes to be competitive.

2. THE EUROPEAN REGULATORY LEADERSHIP TRAP

During the last decades, driven by an ideal of regulatory leadership, the EU has sought to establish itself as the champion of guarantees for internet users, dreaming of a supposed "Brussels Effect" that will spread to the rest of the world;[79] an initiative that is far from being achieved, and yet is currently stifling the European digital economy.

The European regulatory scene is marked by inconsistencies and paradoxes, with sanctions that border on the absurd and lower limits of freedom of competition and information, with entrepreneurs more aware of the bureaucracy than of innovating, and with European users who prefer those American and Asian products that mark the highest levels of disruption.[80]

Jean-Baptiste Say warned, back in 1803, that the lack of competence of an individual could ruin a family, but that the incompetence of our rulers can ruin a country.[81] Current European data protection policies have become a trap for the future of the European economics. They condemn their digital sector to a scenario that limits capacity for innovation and growth, engulfs the development of AI sectors, and accentuates technological dependence on the U.S. and China.

---

79. Bradford, A. (2020). *The Brussels effect: How the European Union rules the world*. Oxford University Press, USA.

80. "EU backs AI regulation while China and US favour technology"; Financial Times. 25/04/2019.

81. *Je sais qu'il importe que les hommes élevés en pouvoir soient plus éclairés que les autres ; je sais que les fautes des particuliers ne peuvent jamais ruiner qu'un petit nombre de familles, tandis que celles des princes et des ministres répandent la désolation surtout un pays.* J-B Say, Traité d'economie politique, p. 47.

2.1. Does the copyright directive jeopardize freedom of expression?

Many experts have described the new European copyright directive (2019/790)[82] as a grievance for companies, content creators, and bloggers.[83] Even Wikipedia founder Jimmy Wales deeply regrets his approval (**figure 4.1**).

Figure 4.1. Tweet by Jimmy Wales on March 26, 2010

Source: Twitter[84]

Due to pure ignorance in some areas, we will avoid debating the basis of the law. However, we denounce the inconsistency of a regulation - specifically its articles 15 and 17 - which is a brake on the development of the digital economy and society in Europe.

Article 15: The so-called Right of Authorship[85]

Article 15 of the directive stipulates that EU member countries must recognize the copyright of press publishers for the publication of content, opening the door to negotiate its use on other websites.

Although the possibility of a fee for the hyperlinks was even considered,[86] finally the regulation allows the use of "single words" or "short excerpts" in search engines without Google and others search engines paying publishers for the use of references to their content.

---

82. eur-lex.europa.eu/legal-content/ES/TXT/?uri=CELEX:32019L0790

83 Some see the ghost of the 2011 U.S. Anti-Piracy Act (SOPA), repealed in 2012 by popular pressure.

84. twitter.com/jimmy_wales/status/1110517366365044736

85. *Protection of press publications in relation to online uses.*

86. As surreal as the arrival of the printing press, a tax was decreed for joining and sewing the numbered pages of books.

But how much is a "short excerpt" and who will make the decision as to whether or not it is compliant? And if search engines cannot collect information from the site they are pointing to, how will users be able to compare and choose the best option?

Google, in a smart campaign, shared what its search engine would look like if the Article 15 were approved with all its consequences **(figure 4.2)**: no images to display and no lines of text. Only links.

Figure 4.2. Google search engine according to the application of the old article 11 of the Copyright Directive

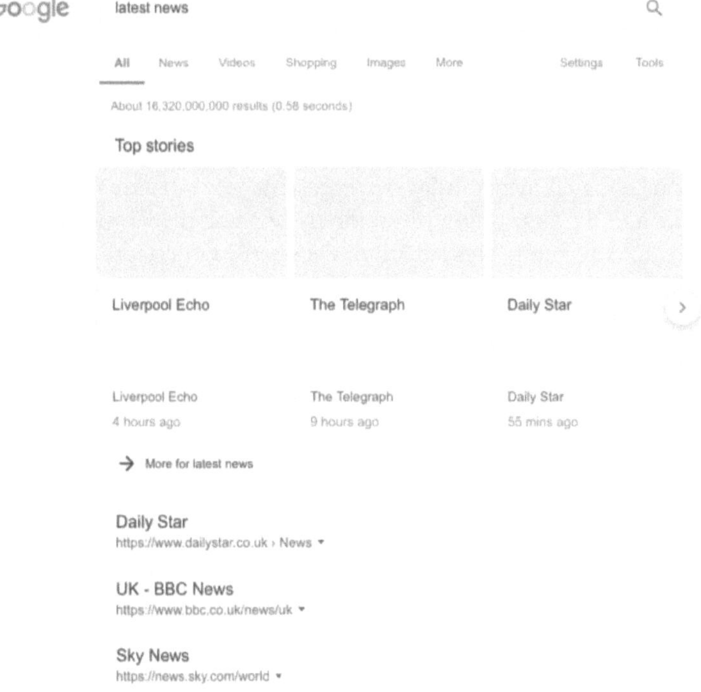

Source: Search Engine Land[87]

---

87.   searchengineland.com/eu-copyright-directive-nearing-final-form-as-google -tests-stripped-down-news-serps-310494

This new rule could lead to a Europe-wide expansion of the so-called AEDE royalty, driven by the Association of Spanish Newspaper Editors in 2014, which have had significant consequences:

- Spain was the first country in the world where Google News stopped providing its services.

- It caused a state of alarm from other aggregators like *Menéame* being unable to meet the million-dollar sanctions claimed by AEDE[88].

- Digital journalism lost quality. Aggregators allow us to channel articles according to our interest regardless of the medium, and avoiding the unfortunate generalized clickbait ("You will never believe…", "The last solution you'll ever need…", "Ten reasons why …"). Without these aggregators, small headlines lose visibility and ability to compete with large media.

The royalty imposed in Spain also prevented the independent decision of digital media. All were represented by a national managing entity and the opposition of hundreds of small media was not even taken into account. This situation was openly criticized by the Spanish National Commission on Markets and Competition, which suggested that "there are simple ways for digital media to avoid indexing in search engines."[89].

If the way we act in Spain spreads and consolidates across all countries on a reciprocal basis, we would be creating a "sub-internet" with restrictions that undermine its potential and corrupt its essence and measures aimed at weakening major technology and forcing a negotiation that favors traditional media. A clear violation of the fundamental of web users right to information.

---

88. "Nuevo intento de imponer el canon AEDE: piden a Menéame 2,5 millones de euros al año". (New attempt to impose the canon AEDE ask Menéame 2.5 million euros a year). El Confidencial, 07/02/2017. elconfidencial.com/ tecnologia/2017-02-07/canon-aede-meneame-internet-facebook-agregadores_1327333/

89. blog.cnmc.es/2014/05/28/propiedad-intelectual-editores-y-la-tasa-google

Article 17: the most sacred digital intellectual property[90]

Article 17 focuses on platforms such as YouTube or Facebook, which will have to do "everything in their power" to locate potential violations in the exploitation of copyright in millions of daily publications of its users - a titanic task, almost impossible to fulfill.

Until now, rights owners had tools such as Content ID to claim shares in their works. With the entry into force of Article 17, the platforms must check the prior publication of the texts, images, or videos if there is third-party content. This requires an investment only available to the big tech companies.

The norm has some exceptions. Small platforms are left out of the control that others like Youtube are supposed to have, although their scalability is hindered. Content used as criticism or to create memes is also outside the scope of the regulation. But it is hard to believe that the algorithms will be able to differentiate between those documents that do respect the spirit of the rule and those that do not. At the slightest suspicion, any ambiguous file will be deleted to prevent any form of sanction.

It is curious, on the other hand, that applauded and respected proposals such as Creative Commons, which consider flexible and also restrictive formulas on the use of intellectual property, remain outside European regulations.

Due to ignorance of the digital economy, or to protect the old forms of copyright in a completely new technological paradigm, Article 17 will cause a notable loss of content creation capacity in the European territory. In other words, a kind of censorship built to avoid sanctions.

The European approach may lead the Internet to a dual system, where on the one hand an open but rigid whole coexists, and on the other hand a creative but closed deep web, where all types of content are shared without being able to be channeled to the outside.

---

90. Use of protected content by service providers to share content online

2.2. Data protection policy: cookies, sanctions, and hackers

The current European General Data Protection Regulation[91] (GDPR), applicable since May 2018, was designed to, firstly, ensure the free flow of data in the EU and, secondly, guarantee the functioning of the Internal Market within a framework that secures the fundamental rights of European citizens.

Nonetheless, the two objectives have not had the same priority.

According to the legal expert Ricard Martínez, "The primary objective of the GDPR - securing the flow of data - has too often been lost sight of. And instead of balancing the two objectives, the issue has been approached from the privacy rights perspective alone by both legislators and regulators".

With this, although the rule itself poses logical reasoning, its application is doing more harm to the technology sector and its benchmarks than for the defense of citizens.

Problems for small companies

Since the mandatory application of the GDPR, all companies operating in Europe, as well as their products, websites, and applications, must take into account privacy and data protection as an inexcusable principle (privacy by design and privacy by default).

If the current regulation is not complied with, the sanctions could reach up to 4% of the income generated by a company, which implies that firms are jointly responsible in case of leakage of private information. Something that we have already seen in the largest airline in Europe, IAG, that was ordered to pay 205 million euros (1.5% of its income) after the theft by a hacker of the information of 500,000 passengers; a sanction imposed even though IAG immediately repaired the security breach, was immediately cooperative, and that it tried to restore and reward the trust of its users.

This situation forces companies to invest in security systems and technical personnel to the point of absurdity or even have an insurance company.

---

91. eur-lex.europa.eu/legal-content/… /?uri=celex%3A32016R067 9

However, in essence, any precaution or advice will be insufficient for any company. If the US National Security Agency (NSA) couldn't prevent Edward Snowden from bypassing all of its controls, how can any company in the world guarantee that an employee, a virus, or a hacker does not steal confidential information from its database?

The change in regulations penalizes SMEs, which must make an impossible effort to guarantee the right to privacy. Smaller companies lack in-house legal teams, and their small staff is not enough to prevent the possibility of sanction.[92] If they also plan to engage in AI-related issues, they must carry out a set of costly actions and specific requirements before dealing with a single piece of data, such as risk, security, and software assessment, or establishing procedures and conditions for suppliers and employees.

We are aware that entrepreneurs are willing to take a chance on their idea, even risking their assets. However, the norm, as it is conceived, is profound nonsense. The worst thing is that it highlights the predominance of a European dogmatic and civil servant culture. A bureaucratic establishment that disparages the knowledge and nature of digital technology and reveals with its actions a lack of understanding of the world of digital entrepreneurship and startups.

The spirit of tax collection and freedom of expression

The suspicion that we are facing a regulation that, in essence, has a marked anti-digital and tax collection nature was evident from the first moment after its application. Google and Facebook (specifically WhatsApp and Instagram services) received their first complaints upon applying the new regulation less than an hour after it came into force.

Half a year later, in January 2019, Google was again sanctioned with 50 million euros for collecting data 'massively and intrusively' on Google Maps and YouTube; information that, according to the

---

92. The human team must make an effort to adapt their websites and applications to a multitude of operating systems (iOS, Android, Windows, etc.) and browsers (Edge, Chrome, Safari, Firefox, etc.).

company, served not only to target ads, but also to improve free services that we all use such as detecting traffic jams or getting recommendations for the best route.

Faced with this uncertain panorama since the implementation of the current GDPR, more than 1000 US portals have blocked or limited access to their content to connections from Europe **(figure 4.3)**, among them the Los Angeles Times. Other media such as USA Today, The Washington Post, Business Insider, and The New York Times have changed their subscription models in EU countries to compensate for the reduction in advertising revenue. And this could be just the beginning. It is estimated that more than half of the websites to which European citizens have access violate some point of the GDPR. Faced with the risk of sanctions, it could mean a massive closure of portals, especially blogs.

2.3. Regulating AI: a call to caution

Since 2016, leading high-innovation countries such as the US and the United Kingdom have been trying to standardize AI development with different initiatives, although none legally binding to date. The difficulty of controlling the prediction process of algorithms, which can even learn on their own, makes it impossible today to set realistic goals and limits for technicians and researchers.

It is therefore more appropriate to act ex-post, with the results on the table, learning and severely punishing those who violate the general norms and principles. In the regulation of AI, we face scenarios never seen before, and caution should be the dominant trend in administrations, as Tirole warns.

Experiments like Tay, a chatbot created by Microsoft and whose awareness was developed from user feedback on Twitter, have shown that this is the best way to act. In less than a year, the algorithm could already communicate autonomously through the social network. But, surprise! Its messages were full of racist, anti-Semitic, and sexist hatred. It even advocated the construction of Donald Trump's wall between Mexico and the US[93].

---

93. "Tay, Microsoft's AI chatbot, gets a crash course in racism from Twitter", publicado por The Guardian el 24 de Marzo de 2016.

Source: Google y stltoday.com

Following these results, Microsoft withdrew its experiment. However, during that time, it was possible to work with a database and a volume of unthinkable interactions if it had been carried out in a closed environment or by imposing restrictions on quality or sanctions for comments made autonomously by the machine.

Even with errors in these early stages, only experimentation helps us narrow down problems and, in this case, look for formulas with the same technology that prevent future algorithms from radicalizing and even stave off hatred on social media. However, this should not prevent Microsoft from incurring in any criminal liability according to general principles of law, it should be sanctioned.

Nuria Oliver[94], one of the most authoritative and recognized

---

94. Nuria Oliver (Alicante, 1970) is a telecommunications engineer and a doctor from the MIT Media Lab, Academician of the Royal Academy of Spanish Engineering, National Engineering Awardee in 2016, and Fellow of the

voices in AI research, considers that the regulation of this technology should follow a series of ethical lines that aim at justice and non-discrimination, do not magnify the difference between people, and allow to recognize who is responsible when decisions are made based on algorithms. She also talks about an AI that is "transparent, to understand how algorithms work, and behaves in accordance with accepted ethical principles that we accept as a Society."[95]

All these principles have been reflected in the ethical guide[96] developed by the European Commission, and they are an important step in understanding where AI development should be directed over the coming decades.

We, the authors of this book, of course also support that moral line. Regulation must exist and be clear, although it must not give up digital development. And to do so it is necessary to get into the digital environment and experiment, work thoroughly with technical processes, and create knowledgeable standards. Economists must participate in multidisciplinary work with lawyers, technology specialists, and other disciplines to weigh whether the cost to be paid for the future growth and well-being of society is too high.

A good example of what we are referring to was presented by Geoffrey Hinton, a professor at the University of Toronto and a researcher at Google, at the alleged requirement that the results of the algorithms be transparent and explainable **(figure 4.4)**. If this is the case, we could miss great advances in science due to the connections between the data that occur in the algorithms are excessively complex, with results that work statistically, but are very difficult to explain and develop by humans.

Institute of Electrical and Electronics Engineers.
95.   muyinteresante.es/tecnologia/inteligencia-artificial/video/nuria-oliver-ya-hoy-vivimos-rodeados-de-inteligencia-artificial
96.   ec.europa.eu/digital-single-market/en/news/ethics-guidelines-trustworthy-ai

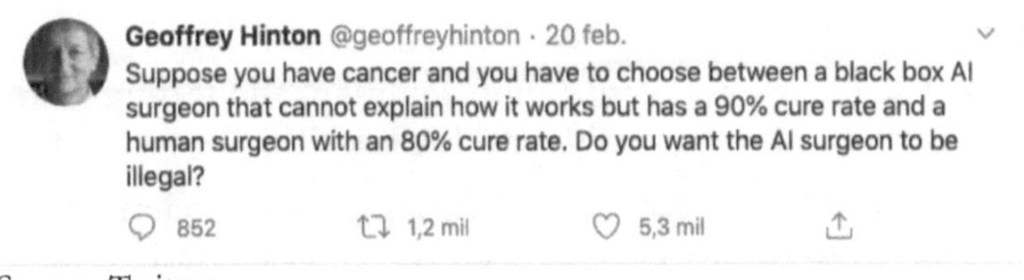

Figure 4.4. Tweet by Geoffrey Hinton on Febraury 20, 2020.

Source: Twitter

Europe needs a serious debate on AI regulation

Despite the political and academic tendency to justify Europe's ambitions for regulatory leadership, we believe that the old continent must put this aspiration to one side if it does not want to see its technological gap with the USA and China continue to widen.

This call for reflection would certainly arouse a consensus between Tirole's perception of prudent regulation and the concerns of Sargent and Sims[97]. Algorithms continue to surprise us every day with their ability to learn, and companies need massive access to data in order to continue to achieve competitive goals. In short, in the current phase of digital development, it is more important to generate trust - which also includes ethical rules - than to subordinate economic agents to a rigidity that may be inefficient.

The "European Digital Strategy" and the "European Commission's White Paper on Artificial Intelligence"[98] are fueling this debate: they recognize the weaknesses of a Europe lagging behind in the use of data and the need to generate common regulatory frameworks and workspaces among member countries, and nevertheless the recommendations made could further harm the competitiveness

---

97. T. Sargent and C. Sims, Nobel Laureates in 2011, developed tools to analyze the impact of changes in economic policies, as well as to isolate the impact of each of these changes. Their contributions were elaborated on macroeconomic models, but their recommendations extend to any area where policy has a relevant economic impact.

98. ec.europa.eu/info/sites/info/files/commission-white-paper-artificial-intelligence-feb2020.pdf

of companies in the EU[99]. Specifically, the following suggestions of the White Paper should be highlighted:

1. The request for certification, auditing, and testing of applications that are considered "high risk" by the authorities.

Knowing the bureaucratic inefficiency in most administrations, companies that carry out their activity in sectors such as medicine, defense, or education could face a funnel in the form of innovation offices and civil service that, in all probability, will have less knowledge in the field than the developers themselves.

We recognize the need to take care of these sectors because they are so critical; however, the debate must be opened in the face of the exponentiality of the advance of AI. What loss of competitiveness and well-being could mean less flexibility in the launch of algorithms compared to China and the US? How many SMEs can afford to meet the requirements and lose months of work evaluating their projects? And in the absence of homegrown innovation, how many foreign companies would be willing to go through the bureaucratic processes required in Europe or to allow third parties to dissect algorithms that can cost millions of euros?

2. A differentiation between European AI and that of the rest of the world is proposed with a quality seal for the applications, especially in high-risk sectors. A way to identify that an algorithm meets the European requirements for human verification, necessary robustness, and data protection.

This raises some questions in relation to international competition. Will US and Chinese companies be willing to limit their algorithm training to meet European demands? Will an algorithm that, for example, helps early detection of diseases stop being applied if it has been trained without a quality seal?

---

99. Prior to the publication of the White Paper, there were several rumors about even harsher recommendations, which, fortunately for the European digital sector, did not come to fruition: euractiv.com/section/digital/news/leak-commission-considers-facial-recognition-ban-in-ai-white-paper/

3. The White Paper devotes a specific section to facial recognition, which calls into question the identification of persons in environments with several individuals.

It is true that it is not specified under what circumstances it will be possible to carry out algorithm training or the application of technological solutions, although the precedents put us on alert. A good example occurred when the Swedish Data Protection Agency (DPA) based on the European GDPR sanctioned with 20,000 euros - it could have reached up to one million euros - a town hall that used facial recognition technology as an experimental measure to verify the attendance of 22 students, for which it had the express approval of all of them.[100] The Agency argued the existence of a "clear imbalance between the interested party and the controller".[101]

In other words, the educators were little less than accused of being madmen who had abused the privacy of defenseless students, unable to assess their ability to exercise their data privacy. But this way of understanding the use of AI and facial recognition limits other applications that are in the best interest. For example, the analysis of the attention, motivation, and understanding of students in class through facial recognition will be frankly impossible with this regulation.

Such advanced technology is indeed dangerous when it is exploited without restrictions, trampling freedoms and guarantees of citizen rights. In fact, in China and even the US, facial recognition has been the subject of strong controversy[102]. However,

---

100. thenextweb.com/eu/2019/08/27/facial-recognition-in-schools-leads-to-swedens-first-gdpr-fine/

101. lhr-law.de/magazine/swedish-school-violates-gdpr-by-using-facial-recognition-software-fine-in-the-amount-of-20-000-e-2?lang=en

102. The issue of facial recognition is one of the most controversial elements of AI. Today in the city of San Francisco, there is debate about whether cars can feed on the facial recognition of citizens walking down the street. Although many media outlets have treated the news as a ban on data collection, it is not at all a closed debate: there are numerous exceptions, and it seems that there is more need to justify the collection of information and transparency than the cessation of experimentation.

progress continues, and in China, facial recognition is already allowed as a means of payment[103] while Europe is putting bumps in the road for their research.

In summary, the European Commission seems to point once again to an excessively guaranteeing way of understanding AI, with strong restrictions on the use of data, and an over-dimensioning of privacy. We consider that this is a severe error, since the validity of the general principles of law, in most cases, are sufficient to preserve them in both the analog and digital world. No more guaranteeing regulations are needed which, we insist, are characterized by their inefficiency.

It is a time for debate, for a forceful assessment of the costs and opportunities of the rules that are approved in the European institutions and in the rest of the national congresses with their backs turned to entrepreneurs and citizens.

See: forbes.com/sites/lanceeliot/2019/06/06/bans-on-facial-recognition-will-impact-self-driving-cars-reciprocally-so/#dc1aa56650e3

103. Only in a country like Spain in 2018 were more than a million fraudulent card operations registered for an amount of 88 million euros. See: 'Annual report on the supervision of the infrastructures of the financial markets 2018' prepared by the Bank of Spain: ocu.org/dinero/tarjetas/noticias/fraudes-tarjetas-online

3. OVERSIZED PRIVACY IN THE DIGITAL AGE

Our description of a European digital economy facing stricter requirements and formalities than in the rest of the global economic powers does not suggest a call for the abolition of all regulation. A framework for action is needed to exploit sensitive information with guarantees for users, but at the same time to prevent superfluous costs and a loss of competitiveness that would have an impact on welfare and job creation.

The European regulatory tradition is almost Platonic in its orderly nature, seeking to ensure that everything is perfectly codified, and this is translated into a privacy understood as an "inviolable fundamental right" (Article 8 of the Charter of Fundamental Rights of the European Union of 2000),[104] as is the "right to life" or "human dignity" itself. Although the term "privacy" was not included in dictionaries even well into the 20th century and that today there is still an academic debate about its conceptual boundaries.[105]

The European Commission has surely not properly calibrated the opportunity cost of regulatory leadership, and GDPR is limiting our companies, compared to the other powers, to access new data, also preventing the use of the recorded information beyond the pioneering purpose for which it was specified, despite the fact that the combination of data enriches analysis and predictions.

In the U.S., citizens themselves own their information, which they can give away or even exchange for money. Not even the California Consumer Privacy Act (CCPA), one of the most restrictive, comes close to this European vision. The CCPA does not require a legal basis for all processing of personal data, nor does it affect aggregate databases, although it does threaten severe penalties for

---

104. eur-lex.europa.eu/legal-content/ES/TXT/?uri=CELEX%3A12012P%2-FTXT

105. Economides, N., y Lianos, I. (2019). *Restrictions on Privacy and Exploitation in the Digital Economy: A Competition Law Perspective.*

those who compromise sensitive user information.

China, on the other hand, lacks privacy and data protection regulations, and everything falls under the umbrella of other laws on property, intellectual property, civil liability or competition[106]. This is a situation that, fortunately and thanks to parliamentary and judicial controls, would not be possible in Europe or the USA, but which raises security and competitive concerns. [107]

Europe has radicalized and idealized its discourse around the individual and ownership of his or her data. A sacred privacy that we have never before demanded with such dialectical and legal vehemence, obliging countries to safeguard it at all costs and above all other rights.

Every new technology entails risks, but inefficiency over-regulation will not avoid them, and probably will not minimize them either. Hasty, preventive regulation has the cost of phagocytizing development.

Applying double standards

The authorities' concern for the privacy of European citizens does not manifest itself equally in all sectors, with a special comparative aggravation that harms the development of the technology sector. We will not say that the digital economy, in view of the existence of new types of crime and forms of fraud linked to information, does not require adapted regulations. In fact, just a few years ago the dissemination of private photographs or videos was not prosecuted as it is today, which demonstrates the necessary maturity of our legal system.

A clear example is the case of Olvido Hormigos in Spain. Let's remember: a politician records an intimate video, sends it to a third person with whom she has a relationship, who shares it with friends without consent. A few days later, the video was on hundreds of

---

106. Ibid.

107. Yuval Noah Harari, in his work Homo Deus: A Brief History of Tomorrow, refers to the differences in the genetic and biotechnology market, although it could be extrapolated to any sector dependent on data.

websites, and even television channels, especially tabloid shows, reproduced fragments of the recording.

As surprising as it may seem to us today, in 2013 the Justice Court of First Instance n. 1 of Orgaz (Toledo) closed the proceedings against the accused. According to the attorney there was "a legal loophole in the previous regulation of the right to privacy. The norm established that if a content was disseminated and there was an illicit capture of that image there was a crime, but this was not the case if the video had been voluntarily delivered to the recipient".[108]

This sentence, the interpretation of the norm, and the case itself describe the minimum zeal and little legal value of our privacy before the push of the digital economy. Just as we did not seem to be concerned about the right to privacy when telephone directories publicly displayed our surname, address and telephone number.

A rigorous application of the current GDPR, whereby the administrator of the information is responsible for safeguarding the data with the possibility of sanctions, as happened to the aforementioned AIG airline, would mean that the creator of the white pages (even the government itself) would be responsible for telephone spam as a result of the data published. To some extent this possibility has been limited by prohibiting reverse lookup in some countries, although it is obvious that telephone directories, considered an exception to the rule, are doomed to disappear.

The suspicion of data management in digital media does not apply to the sending of postal mails either. Again, it is a contrast that a webmaster has to almost protect with his life and honor the data of his users, while in the analog world millions of letters with medical or banking information are delivered with the only protection of a paper envelope, dropped in mailboxes that can be opened with a screwdriver. Again, as in the case of telephone directories, neither the postal workers nor the president of the neighborhood committee have ever been held responsible for criminals who have stolen letters or packages from a mailbox.

Along the same lines, even today some educational centers or

---

108. antena3.com/programas/espejo-publico/noticias/ley-video-sexual-ol vido-hormigos-iveco-video_201905305cefba0f0cf21b72629f4a84.html

public administrations hang on murals and panels the evaluations of students and candidates, accompanied by their names, surnames and even some numbers of their ID card. The new GDPR does not prevent this information from being kept in public panels and, although measures must be guaranteed to prevent the knowledge of non-interested parties, other colleagues, or even the parents of students, would be able to see the marks of all the others, even to take photos and share them privately. This exception - information open to third parties - is completely unthinkable on the web.

Finally, the privacy of many celebrities who appear on the covers of magazines and celebrity programs with stolen photos or videos accompanied by minors whose faces are covered with a blurred spot does not seem to be guaranteed either. People's intimate lives are commercialized in reality shows like Big Brother, or people are allowed to have their jobs or personal relationships ruined just because they are famous sportspeople or musicians, or they have to live in bunkers because their privacy ends when they walk through the door of their house.

In short, it is extraordinarily curious that privacy occupies such a diffuse and disparate place depending on whether it is an analog or a digital environment. That regulations are capable of protecting our privacy from the evil Internet, but look the other way in the face of the tabloid press, postal insecurity or advertising on corkboards.

We fully understand that the digital field requires specific regulations that are adapted to its attributes and peculiarities. What should not be justifiable is that with the same or greater harm the crime to analog privacy is conspicuous by its absence, while digital privacy is raised to the category of "fundamental right".

The right to be forgotten

The so-called "right to be forgotten" had not been the subject of debate before the existence of Google and Facebook. Newscasts and newspapers have historically published reports that recall events from years and even decades ago, with interviews or images that can hurt the sensibilities of victims or their families, open closed wounds, or negatively affect the reintegration of those who have already set-tled their accounts with justice. Paradoxically, the same information is a terrible problem if it is made public on the internet.

Since 2014, in Europe search engines must eliminate from their results the links that lead to information of the people who request so. And in 2016, the Spanish Agency for Data Protection already gave its first notice that it dealt with a capital issue with a specific objective in sight: Google. The company was sanctioned with 150,000 euros for not de-indexing from its search engine information related to fines, debts with the Treasury, or sanctions published in official gazettes. The Spanish National Court later dismissed the claim, but the line to follow by prosecutors was clear.

Accepting the spirit of a norm that grants citizens the freedom to appear or not in the media, we must reveal that a literal interpretation of it could have devastating effects. It could be used to make search engines and websites erase from the Internet the name of genocidal or military men who were the protagonists of the bloodiest periods in the history of mankind, if their direct relatives consider that their honor is being denigrated. For example, Adolf Hitler might continue to appear in all history books in a library but in Wikipedia we would read A**** H **** - or not even that.

To date, fortunately, the cases in which the removal of the name of war criminals has been requested have not been successful.[109] The courts have endorsed that the right to be forgotten is not applicable when it conflicts with other legitimate interests, such as the right to freedom of expression. However this does not prevent historians' collectives from looking with concern at how the right to be forgotten could mean a setback of decades in their research tools and techniques.[110]

---

109. We experienced a close case at the University of Alicante when the name of the secretary of the trial in which the poet Miguel Hernández was sentenced to death in 1940 was eliminated from an investigation by Professor Juan Antonio Ríos Carratalá. The request for the right to be forgotten about a relative of said secretary was enough for precautionary measures to be taken, although they were lifted after a short time Access: jstor.org/stable/24431934?seq=1

110. "El derecho al olvido puede borrar (también) la Historia". (The right to be forgotten can (also) erase History). El Diario, published on October 12,

Cookie policy

The most obvious example of the double legislative standard that separates the analog economy from the digital one is the cookie policy. Websites that can be accessed from Europe should alert with cumbersome texts that can occupy the entire screen that the footprint and information left by users can be used for different purposes such as advertising, performing analysis, or sharing statistics with third parties **(figure 4.5)**, something so obvious that it has caused many portals to take the warning as a joke **(figure 4.6)**.[111]

Figure 4.5. Cookies acceptance message.

PRISA y sus socios almacenan información no sensible en tu dispositivo, como cookies o identificadores únicos de tu dispositivo, y acceden a esta información para realizar tratamientos de datos, como medir y analizar las preferencias de nuestros usuarios, mostrar publicidad o contenidos personalizados a través del análisis de tu navegación, para lo cual es necesario compartir datos y perfiles no vinculados directamente a tu identidad con anunciantes, operadores publicitarios y otros intermediarios. Para aceptar y dar tu consentimiento a todas las finalidades y funcionalidades indicadas, puedes continuar navegando. En caso contrario, puedes configurar o rechazar dichas finalidades clicando en el apartado de Configuración. Para obtener más información sobre el uso de cookies y tus derechos, o para cambiar en cualquier momento tus preferencias, accede a nuestra Política de Cookies. Ver nuestros socios

Source: Elpais.com

However, data exploitation is also common in the analog world. Banks, phone operators, supermarkets and energy companies know more about our behavior and consumption patterns than even Google or Facebook. These long-established sectors have always used the information we generate as users and have even sold it to third parties or used it for multiple purposes without any warning raised for decades.

Why is there not the same debate regarding the exploitation of data beyond the digital environment? Why can't a user object to a bank using the balance sheet, or an energy company using our average consumption to offer us services?

2019. eldiario.es/hojaderouter/internet/derecho-olvido-Google-historia-milagros_del_corral_0_302369795.html

111. Something that some websites are using to sneak announcements and alerts; it could even be used by malicious websites to confuse users to enable the download of virus-containing software or facilitate the control of critical information on systems.

Figure 4.6. 'Alternative' messages for accepting cookies.

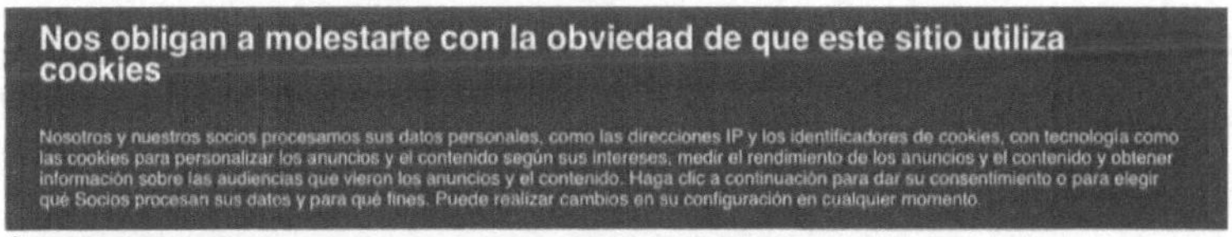

Source: meneame.net

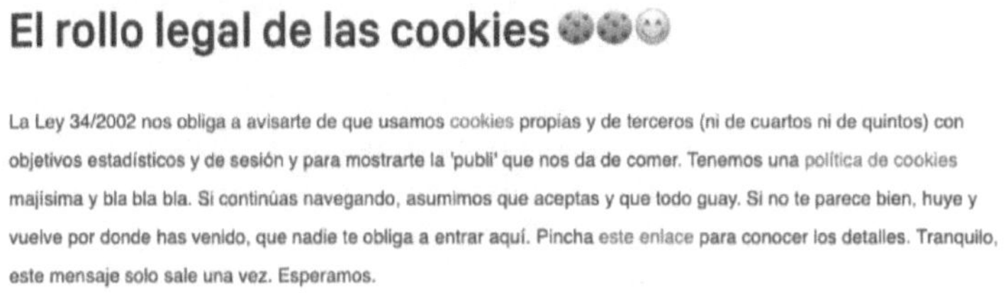

Source: Yorokobu.es

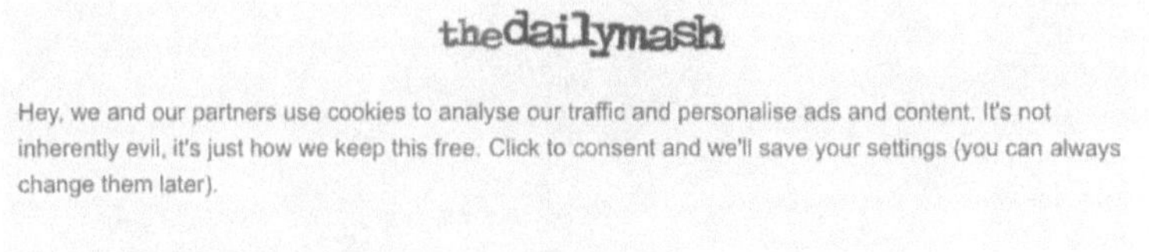

Source: thedailymash.co.uk

More technology, more education

It would be absurd to doubt the need for laws and regulations that protect us from companies that intentionally violate our rights or steal our information. Let the penalties be imposed as high as the government wishes! Millions if necessary! But let's not allow double standards depending on whether the activity takes place in the digital or analog world.

In the oversized privacy, interesting legal paradoxes could arise in the event of a strict reading of the regulations. For example, can a citizen with visual impairment be recorded by a closed-circuit camera if the notice is not in Braille? Can it be used as evidence of a crime? Isn't it an impairment of the right to privacy of thousands of people recorded without their knowledge?[112]

---

112. Example used by the Spanish law expert Ricard Martinez.

If Europe wants to set an example to the rest of the world in the responsible use of the digital medium, it should focus on education, not on punishment: educating citizens on what cookies are, why they are important for internet businesses and what real implications they have for their privacy, teaching how to protect personal accounts, the risks of having public profiles on Instagram or Facebook, and emphasizing the criteria to follow when trusting an online sales business.

Europe could also be a role model if it increases the use of technologies such as AI, facial recognition, or Blockchain to fight spam and guarantee the safety of users on social networks. These measures are much more efficient than regulations that any hacker can bypass. Everything else must be left in the hands of a justice that persecutes and severely punishes those who take advantage of users but does not penalize digital entrepreneurs with constant changes in regulations.

4. THE TEMPTATION OF REGULATION: THE CASE OF SPAIN

The regulation that Europe applies within the framework of the digital economy is no coincidence. It is largely due to the existence of an overly traditional productive fabric, which works on forced marches to adapt to changes and delaying a leap that should be immediate, while other regions create major disruptions.

In the EU, there are diverse positions within this common framework. From our perspective, Spain could be considered as the champion of 'digital regulation'. From a legal point of view, it has a large number of experts who have delved into privacy like no other country.

Surely, it has a lot to do with the fact that Spain has extraordinarily brilliant lawyers, listed worldwide, who create public opinion and set political and social trends. Its professional weight is also very important in Spain: according to the Census of the General Council of the Lawyers, there is one lawyer for every 284 inhabitants; twice as many lawyers work in Madrid alone as in all of France.[113]

The excellence of this professional group, especially of those who lead the large legal corporations, the state's general counsel and the judiciary in our country, arouses our deepest admiration, and their opinion and criteria are felt in most of the world's major companies, occupying prominent positions in Facebook, Apple or Google, especially in data protection matters.

Today they constitute the most important lobby in Spain.

In our frequent discussions with law experts on the subject, many -not all- are remarkably enthusiastic about the leadership of Europe and Spain in digital regulation. "Even the EU is serving as a model for Japan!", it is argued by proclaiming the said Brussels Effect. Also,

---

113.   periodistadigital.com/ciencia/educacion/20131204/madrid-hay-doble-abogados-francia-noticia-689400013653

some of our colleagues rightly say that the regulatory initiative is generating "new jobs" (lawyers, consultants, technicians adapting changes to regulations, etc.).

Wisely lawyers have paid more attention to the economy and digital society in the last decade than economists themselves. The Internet has been a very attractive field since its origin in the field of law, and recently technologies such as Blockchain, 3D printing, robotics, and AI have become a very recurring topic of study and opinion. But in this debate, the danger to the private sector of such pioneering regulation being ineffective has been downplayed.

The main problem is that there is a lack of communication between jurists and specialists in other areas of knowledge (economists, philosophers, computer scientists, etc.), as shown in the latest publication of the Spanish Data Protection Agency (AEPD). In this guide for adapting products and services using AI,[114] no relevant researcher who could have had a critical voice has been considered.

Legislators, far from contrasting positions from different fields, act with self-sufficiency and dogmatism, ignoring the voice of many of the agents involved. Even lawyers such as Manuel Desantes, former vice president of the European Patent Office in Munich, warns that ""if the continental system does not wake up, Europe will be the Jurassic Park of Law".[115] In other words: either the law, and especially legislators, understand the nature of digital and adjust it to its general principles, or we will die of legal "success", burdened with rules but without companies or jobs.

If the referred document of the AEPD or any other regulation such as the Organic Law on Data Protection (OLDP) had taken into account the opportunity cost that excessive collateral positions represent, they would surely be very different. Nevertheless, we economists must share the blame for this, as we have not been able to make our voice heard when it was most needed.

---

114. fundacionareces.es/fundacionareces/es/cargarAplicacionMediateca.do?identificador=6040

115. fundacionareces.es/fundacionareces/es/comunicacion/noticias/manuel-desantes-estamos-en-los-albores-de-la-quinta-revolucion-industrial.html

4.1. This comes from a long way: the Spanish regulation of Internet domains '.es'

One of the first issues subject to digital regulation in Spain was the internet domains "dot es", which like any other national (.de, .uk, .it, etc. called country code top-level domain, or ccTLD) are technically standardized from the Internet Corporation for Assigned Names and Numbers (ICANN) - formerly by the Internet Assigned Numbers Authority (IANA).

Despite being the same protocol, each country establishes its enrollment and accreditation procedures for registrars, and that is where the differences arise. In the 1990s and early 2000s, all countries accelerated the acquisition of these types of top-level domains that could be done online and in a matter of minutes.

Only Spain and Bolivia maintained from the beginning a cumbersome analogical regulation for their contracting, which even required them to prove paper documents according to the domain.

The intention of these measures? To "preserve intellectual property and trademark rights" and give confidence to a public that did not know very well what the internet was then, putting the bandage before the wound.

The results were dire. It was unthinkable that Spain, a modern country and a prominent member of the EU, had such a business card in the digital frame. Absolute ignorance from the administration was evident when this nonsense was put to an end in 2005: in just one month with the system liberated, more domains were registered than during the previous three and a half years.

4.2. Drone regulation in Spain

A decade later, drones suffered from inappropriate regulations. Through Law 18/2014 of October 15 (articles 50 and 51), drone users were obliged to pass a series of evaluations and examinations for their use at the professional level. Paco Nadal, a journalist for the Spanish newspaper El País, described them as "a confusing theoretical exam full of subjects that will not help you at all to pilot a drone better, another practical exam that serves little purpose other than to get from you a few hundred euros, and obtaining a medical certificate designed for pilots of light aircraft even though in reality you are going to handle a plastic gadget that weighs 750 grams."[116]

We wonder if it had not been more coherent to clearly decree de facto the ban on drones in Spain and not get involved in such complex administrative issues. We do not discuss the need to preserve the privacy and respect for the privacy of people, in addition to not flying in protected air spaces (airports, military bases, etc.). However, it is imperative to find a balance that allows experimentation with devices that are having invaluable uses in controlling poaching in Africa, sending medicines after natural disasters, searching for missing persons, pest control, pollution analysis, the fight against drug trafficking, traffic management, and fire detection.

Even so, the Spanish drone technology once the regulations were relaxed proved its worth, breaking international patterns.[117] Wouldn't it have been smarter to facilitate their use and experimentation from the beginning?

4.3. Renewal of the digital canon

Another controversial example of digital regulation in Spain is the "private copy compensation system" approved in 2017. The history of this royalty begins back in 2006 when it was established that, as it is impossible to know who copies or downloads digital content illegally (movies, music, books, etc.), all users must indiscriminately compensate authors, artists, producers, and publishers.

By executive order, the "private copy fee" or "digital fee" was established in Spain. When someone bought any device that could store or record digital files (such as a CD recorder or a smartphone), they paid an extra rate of up to 6 euros for the possibility of its use for criminal purposes.[118]

---

116. elpais.com/elpais/2017/03/09/paco_nadal/1489060374317707.html
117. Spanish drone inspired by hybrid vehicles breaks all flight times records. https://xataka.com/drones/hybrix-2-1-dron-espanol-hibrido-muy-especial-capaz-volar-durante-2-horas-cargar-10-kg-peso
118. Germany, France, Netherlands, Italy, Switzerland, Finland, Portugal, Belgium, and Canada, among others, have also established similar levies.

Sort of a massive Minority Report [119] with Tom Cruise in multi-tasking mode assuming that we are all guilty before the crime occurs. In fact, the digital canon applied to the analog world would mean, for example, that any citizen must pay to Traffic a fine for speeding where you buy any vehicle.[120]

In the face of the controversy, the canon was repealed by the Supreme Justice Court in 2010, and then in 2016, the High Justice Court again annulled the new legislation that transferred compensation for losses arising from piracy from the general budgets of the State (in practice, it was the same as the taxpayer paying for a crime that he did not commit).

In 2017 the Spanish government created a new order by which this time it would be the manufacturers and distributors who pay the canon and that, of course, will fall back on consumers with an increase in the final prices of their products.

Ironically, all these initiatives and associated penalties have had a miniscule impact against piracy compared to the emergence of business models such as Spotify and Netflix. In fact, one wonders how many users were really affected by the digital canon, and how many have stopped downloading movies and songs thanks to the almost unlimited access to audio-visual content offered by these platforms.

4.4. Google Tax

The most recent case of all is the approval of what is popularly known as Google Tax, which could well be called "Digital Impotence Tax".

Based on an approach by the European Commission to tax the income of multinationals in the digital economy, the government of Spain pioneered a draft bill in October 2018 under the name of Digital Services Tax, which would affect companies with a revenue of over 750 million euros worldwide and over three million euros in Spain.

---

119. "Minority Report" (2002). Directed by Steven Spielberg.
120. In Spain, vehicles pay a local circulation rate based on the engine's displacement and not exclusively on their power or speed.

The tax, finally approved in February 2020, has a particular impact on American and Asian technology companies and has already resulted in a protectionist response from North American administrations to products from some European countries. The division between partners in Europe is manifest: France has postponed the application of the levy, and other countries such as Ireland, Denmark, and Sweden have been against the introduction of the tax.

Can Spain lead a tax revolution against major technologies when the countries around it do not take the appropriate steps?

Some associations of digital companies have seen in the unilateral application of the tax a source of problems that can lead to a competitive loss of European companies. Fines, taxes, fees, and other anti-digital regulations only delay the technological growth of our sectors, thereby limiting the competitiveness of European economies while harming users with more expensive services.

Undoubtedly, with the Google Tax, a problem is recognized on a global scale, such as the existence of tax havens and the practices allowed internationally to save the payment of duties. However, technology companies are not the only ones doing it: according to a recent report by the Spanish Tax Agency,[121] of 134 Spanish companies with a consolidated turnover of more than 750 million euros, 27 pay less than 0.3% in taxes, and 16 pay less than 6%. Also, according to the World Inequality Lab,[122] the undeclared money that Spaniards have in tax havens represents 15% of the national GDP.

Spain and all EU countries should face this problem together, not camouflage it as a conflict of interest between digital giants and countries. Financial doping is a common practice in the heart of Europe: Netherlands, Belgium, Ireland, Gibraltar/United Kingdom, and especially Luxembourg have been investigated by the European Commission for tax advantages for companies such as McDonald's, Starbucks, Apple, and Fiat, among dozens of others.

---

121. *Informe País por País para multinacionales con matriz española.* (Country by Country Report for multinationals with a Spanish parent company). Available at www.agenciatributaria.es

122. Alvaredo, F., Chancel, L., Piketty, T., Saez, E., & Zucman, G. (Eds.). (2018). *World inequality report 2018.* Belknap Press.

Without wishing to justify practices that drain billions of euros from state treasuries, it is incomprehensible that this type of anachronism should be allowed. The digital economy is paying the price for the loss of competitiveness of traditional European sectors and the predatory actions of large companies.

Tirole exposed that "we must insist on a level playing field and not impose different regulations on different competitors based on an arbitrary classification and specific regulations".[123] Externalizing European frustration through a "fiscal revolution" in the digital economy, taxing income and punishing the sector of the future that can generate more competitiveness and wealth should be considered a clumsy strategy.

---

123. See: qz.com/1310266/nobel-winning-economist-jean-tirole-on-how-to-regulate-tech-monopolies/

5. THE REGULATION SPIRAL

5.1. We need efficient digital regulation

The authors of this book defend digital and technological momentum as an essential part of the development of a competitive and future economy, without which the viability of the welfare and the realization of many other social achievements would be questioned. However, this stance is not against regulation. We hope that at no time does the reader conclude that we maintain an anti-regulatory position. We'll say it very clearly: absolutely not.

The digital world is worthy of efficient and intelligent regulations, of lawyers who know its mechanisms, of faculties that teach subjects so that future legislators understand the environment in which business activity takes place, of advisors who can build bridges between the right to privacy and the exploitation of data.

However, are we moving in that direction? Is Europe securing a new generation of legal professionals capable of understanding the challenge we face as a society in the age of AI? If not, rest assured that the potential reach of disruptive new technologies will be severely restricted.

With all of the above, the authors only want to highlight the risks and costs of inefficient digital regulation that does not solve the purposes that motivate it and hinders the concurrence of digital startups on equal terms between countries in a world where technology has become the key differential element. A regulation that seems to protect analog sectors affected by digital competition more than deal with the development of our economies, with double standards and outdated or excessive bureaucratic burdens.

There are a multitude of tools and formulas to easily safeguard the anonymity of a population sample. The obstacle therefore exists when the administration understands the law in a restrictive way that generates costs for companies and makes them responsible for the attack of hackers and malware.

Meanwhile, complaints are piling up at national data protection agencies due to the latest change in European privacy regulations, with insufficient staff to deal with all the demands.

5.2. The regulation spiral and the weakness of the European digital sector

Let us return for the last time to the "right to be forgotten". What many lawyers consider as regulatory "creativity" should be considered as an impairment of the right to freedom of expression and information, which would never have been allowed if it had affected the traditional press. Rivers of ink would have flowed all over Europe until the regulations were scrapped.

However, in this case, the burden test falls on the digital world, and its European companies have neither force nor impact to impose its criteria.[124]

We must be aware that, if we do not act, a regulationist spiral is approaching, based on very shaky foundations as regards the Internet and the digital world, with a sensationalist vision or lack of understanding from many media, as if artificial intelligence was already a little less than an inescapable threat to our species, falling into other errors such as thinking that "smart gadgets" are an attack on our privacy.

However, Alexa or Google Home listening to us can save our lives thanks to the applications that detect sleep apnea, or a clock parameterizing our pulse can prevent us from a heart attack, or with facial recognition systems that warn about our state of attention at the wheel. Why is it so difficult to understand all these benefits that digital technology can provide to Europeans and enhance their leadership?

5.3. The demonization of social networks

More worrying is the attitude regarding the "disastrous" influence of social networks, especially in electoral processes.

---

124. The opposite case occurred in the United States with the SOPA, where the strength and drive of its technologies could stop its approval.

Controversial situations such as Brexit, the foul play in Donald Trump's campaign, or the Tsunami Democràtic App of Catalan independence in Spain have encouraged many politicians and editorialists, who taking advantage of the situation have deployed a frontal attack especially on Facebook, even warning of the role of these networks to promote acts of crimes against humanity.[125]

It would be stupid to deny that social networks influence society and its decisions. However, part of digital rejection lies in how they detract from the power of influence of traditional media. This was clearly seen with the victory of Donald Trump, and in the subsequent analysis focused almost exclusively on the disinformation strategy[126] or social media ad management.[127]

The "war on like" could be understood as a way to prevent hatred generated on Twitter, fake news, and radicalization… But aren't social networks a continuation of our feelings? Aren't political parties the ones that encourage disagreements between citizens? Aren't we being manipulated to a certain extent when we are guided by the editorial line of newspapers or radio stations?

We just have to go to the newspaper archives and historically analyze some headlines to realize how the unemployment figure or public debt is considered good or bad depending on the editorial line of the media and the party in the government, or the lightness with which corruption plots are dealt with.

Does this mean that we should not act on fake news covered in election campaigns, or prevent the intrusion of countries like Russia, or the fraudulent use of data[128]?

---

125. elpais.com/internacional/2018/04/12/actualidad/1523553344_423934_.html

126. theatlantic.com/magazine/archive/2020/03/the-2020-disinformation-war/605530/

127. Hilary Clinton's team signed 66,000 ads on Facebook for about $ 28 million. The Republican campaign, led by Brad Parscale, reached 5.9 million optimized ads with $ 44 million: ninety times more impressions with just twice the investment. See: bloomberg.com/news/articles/2018-04-03/trump-s-campaign-said-it-was-better-at-facebook-facebook-agrees?sref=mezxKzsV

128. elpais.com/internacional/2018/02/24/estados_unidos/1519484655_450950.html

Of course not. These actions must be severely punished. Practices that predispose society to act in a particular way adulterate the digital environment, and even democracy itself, whose basis for free choice is the freedom of truthful information. But blaming social networks massively for the illegal practices that occur in them is like judging the fire and not the pyromaniac when there is a forest blaze.

It is education, not regulation.

Manipulation, digital or analog, is carried out with treachery due to the lack of knowledge of a population, because the weakness of a democracy is proportional to the lack of education of its citizens.

Let's digitally train the population and stop hiding spurious interests that hide behind certain regulations. Although it will be impossible to prevent all cases, an educated population will be less vulnerable to fake news and algorithms that make tailored messages, and they will learn to move through the digital sphere exercising their rights in the direction deemed appropriate.

It is not regulation, it is education. Regulatory paternalism has never gotten along with the right to liberty.

6. PROPOSING A EUROPEAN TAX TO GUARANTEE FREEDOM OF THE PRESS

Faced with the regulatory excesses in Europe, with norms, sanctions, and fees induced by tax collection reasons and disguised protectionism, we want to argue other forms of defense of our key sectors, especially the press because in recent years red flags have been raised that could call into question the freedom of the media, and we should take this very seriously.

Almost all publishing groups, from major international newspapers (The New York Times, The Washington Post, The Guardian, etc.) to local ones suffer a critical financial situation or problems that are very difficult to overcome. The press has been the subject of one of the greatest disruptions, and that we can summarize as follows:

a) The entity of the recession of sales in paper format. The press business model generated solid income from the newspaper's sale and advertising. This model is in crisis in part because of the free media on the Internet with an infinity of formats: from the microblogging of Twitter and videoblogs of YouTube to initiatives like The Huffington Post.[129]

b) The disruption of the new digital advertising and its impact on the business model. The Internet, in all its extension, becomes a great platform for absolutely disruptive advertising due to the metrics to measure its effectiveness and cost. In this revolution, the traditional press is barely able to monopolize a tiny percentage either of the global network traffic or this advertising revenue.

Attempts have been made to alleviate both impacts - decrease in sales **(figure 4.7)** and advertising **(figure 4.8)** - with a continuous change in the business model. Virtual kiosks have been developed, the subscription has been strengthened, and the pages are

---

129. We cite this particular outlet to recall the disruption that its founder Arianna Huffington caused years ago to create a journalistic blog from home that surpassed The New York Times in web traffic.

flooded with so much content marketing that even readers can't clearly appreciate where the information ends and the advertising begins.

Figure 4.7. Newspaper sales in the US (million units)

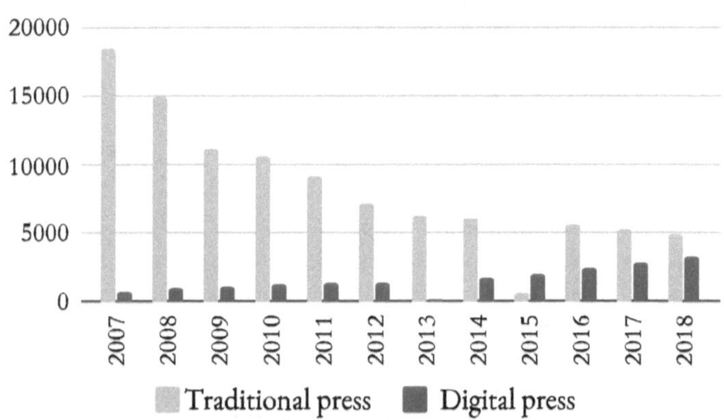

Source: Pew Research Center analysis of Alliance for Audited Media data

Figure 4.8. Advertising revenue in the Spanish press (€ million)

Source: Information Media Association

Still, revenues are collapsing, and in the last twelve years, all groups have had to make drastic cuts in costs and staff. Governments have come to the rescue through institutional purchases of advertising space in newspapers, but finally the benchmark media are being acquired by third-party companies, such as Amazon, which took control of The Washington Post, or by international funds and large corporations, losing its shareholders' visibility and transparency.

The conjuncture could not be more inopportune and dangerous for democracies, involved in radical changes of the first order such as the exaltation of extreme ideologies in Europe, the US and Latin America, disintegrating political processes like Brexit, and the lack of digital education of the population in the face of fake news.

How can we deal with this vital problem for democracies?

In recent years, one of the authors of this book, like Eisenhower Fellow, has had the opportunity to contrast with some media professionals the hard situation of the press in Europe, particularly in a country like Spain. In the medium and long term, it is hard to see a solution. The crisis in sales and advertising revenue does not seem to hit rock bottom.[130]

The press is currently raising some hope through readers' awareness of paying for closed digital subscriptions. In fact, some prestigious publications such as the Wall Street Journal, The New York Times or The Guardian have presented promising results in terms of revenue generation.[131] But in our view this solution limits and impoverishes access to quality information. The highest quality and most interesting information is hidden from the general public, while disinformation is excellent fodder for the media that live off fake news and covert interests.

On the other hand, the subscription-based model is a slow route, if a sufficient number of contributors is reached to allow the survival

---

130. We thank Javier Cremades, president of the Spanish Eisenhower, for creating the journalistic award that recognizes editors and the best media professionals.

131. The New York Times (NYT) launched the subscription model in March 2011. The newspaper now has more than four million digital subscribers and aims to reach 10 million by 2025. From 2017 to 2018, its digital subscription revenue increased by 18% year after year, up to $ 401 million according to the latest NYT annual report. Advertising revenue is already roughly halved between its digital platforms and print on paper, according to the latest quarterly report.

of the media, condemning the search for external financing, sometimes with opaque or partisan mechanisms, which can weaken the quality of journalism.

In this situation, Europe could lead a normative model that would allow solving the problem because the right to information without limitations or coercion is vital for our democracies, and we should have no qualms about defending it, whatever the cost.

Digital charges applied for years in some European countries have ensured, according to their advocates, the survival of the cultural industry and the emergence of new talents in music or film. Preserving the local culture is extraordinarily important and, although there may be reluctance in the forms of the canon, if it serves its purpose and is done transparently, then welcome.

Our proposal, along the same lines, is that countries should introduce a tax with sufficient revenue to finance freedom of the press under the best possible conditions of solvency, transparency and constitutional commitment. This tax should:

> **a) Adjust its collection volume to the financial needs of the media** to ensure its total solvency and viability without resorting to dubious funds. The regulation should prohibit any opaque fund and even the participation of political parties. A period of at least 10 years should be established to allow for a transition to a solid and sustainable digital model in the press.

> **b) Financial aid should be granted based on absolutely objective indicators which identify good journalistic practices and efficient management**, such as the number of users or the traffic generated by the body of information strictly related to freedom of the press and opinion.[132]

These aids should not be incompatible with the generation of income through the loyalty, support and commitment of readers. In fact, the ultimate aim should be the digital transformation of the sector, avoiding becoming a subsidized industry.

---

132. Avoid, for example, the generation of easy, demagogic, and populist traffic, or adding traffic to sections that, even though they are part of traditional newspapers, may have little to do with press freedom, from society notes and sports to or crosswords.

c) The realization of this proposal would requiere a high endowment of funds, which should be distributed among all sectors of the economy with a minimum contribution, or raise taxes on detrimental practices such as the consumption of tobacco or sugar, sports betting, or practices with a high environmental impact. This would be a way of correcting the diseconomies they generate.

A tax of these characteristics should also serve to distance us from the accusation that the digital economy is the great evil of the traditional press. Pretending that technology companies subsidize the weak financial situation of the press, as happens with the Google Tax, is absolutely counterproductive for future sectors and European startups.

Of course, what is outlined here is only a first idea to debate and mature given the unhealthy situation that our freedoms and democracies could go through without a free press. Moreover, this funding model could open other ways for critical industries and services for any country facing an accelerated disruption and digital transition. From universities to healthcare, to any sector that is the core of European economies.

7. PRIVACY AND CORONAVIRUS

«… the civilization of the 19th century is of such a nature that it allows the average person to settle in a world of surplus, of which he only perceives the superabundance of resources, but not the anxieties. He is surrounded by prodigious instruments, by beneficial medicines, by far-sighted States, by comfortable rights. Instead, he ignores how difficult it is to invent these medicines and instruments and ensure their future production, he does not realize how unstable the organization of the State is, and he hardly feels obligations within himself. This imbalance falsifies him, makes him believe in his roots as a living being, causing him to lose contact with the very substance of life, which is absolute danger, radical uncertainty. The most contradictory form of human life that can appear is the "satisfied master" ».

JOSÉ ORTEGA Y GASSET (1930): The rebellion of the masses.

About to close the first edition of this book [133] during 1st. lockdown generated by COVID-19, an intense debate has arisen that very well summarizes the article by Cabrol, Baeza-Yates, González-Alarcón, and Pombo (2020):[134] *Is data privacy the price we must pay to survive a pandemic?*

Surprisingly, amid the coronavirus crisis, with the infections and deaths of the most vulnerable social groups and with most part of the world population confined to their homes and deprived of fundamental rights (without freedom of movement, without the

---

133. This section was the last to be written of the first edition of this book, between April 19 and 20, 2020, in full confinement in Spain. Some of the arguments may be limited by the information available up to that moment. Nevertheless, an attempt has been made to update some information in this edition.

134. Marcelo Cabrol (BID), Ricardo Baeza-Yates (Universidad del Nordeste), Natalia González Alarcón (BID) & Cristina Pombo (BID) (2020): publications.iadb.org/publications/spanish/document/Es_la_privacidad_de_los_datos_el_precio_que_debemos_pagar_para_sobrevivir_a_una_pandemia.pdf

possibility of carrying out their work, with health diminished by the saturation of emergencies, etc.) and at risk of creating one of the worst known economic crises, passionate voices of politicians, journalists, writers, and professionals from various disciplines rise to defend the invulnerability of privacy at the cost of seeking efficient solutions to combat the pandemic.

COVID-19 has proven that the idea of privacy as a fundamental and inviolable right has deeply affected the European population. However, the consequences they have had for Europe during this time have clearly weakened rationale, logic and justification, as we expand in Chapter 11.

Some Asian countries such as China, South Korea, and (Taiwan) have used to a greater or lesser extent the geolocation of people to trace movements and control contagion. These methods, together with the ability to perform tests and other measurements, have made it possible to contain the pandemic despite facing potentially greater risks than Europe (complete ignorance of the virus, less advanced health systems, population density, etc.).

On the contrary, the European Union has made very limited use of digital resources. In Italy, France, and Spain, the impacts on death and economic and social cost have long since surpassed China, yet the use of technology that can accelerate the exit from the crisis has been limited by legal restrictions on privacy law. The impact on the economies of the old continent is expected to be so devastating that economic and financial rescue scenarios are already being projected; however, we remain suspicious of "red lines" for fear of losing hypothetical freedoms.

Since this topic is of utmost relevance and touches on the thread of what we have written so far, we would like to make the following reflections before moving on to proposed solutions to prevent European decline in the age of AI:

a) Why is there a rigid interpretation of the regulation on privacy?

It must be accepted that there is a state of opinion and sensitivity about privacy that makes any European government, even if it could propose some permissive interpretative formula, end up inhibiting itself in the use of any digital medium that violates privacy. Public agencies and legal specialists have adopted an excessive rigidity in the interpretation of privacy regulations, although contradictorily, by using legal argumentation, even in criminal law figures such as "state of necessity"[135] are established, being a cause of exemption from criminal liability.

In the early days of the pandemic we were able to read in prestigious Spanish media opinion articles alluding to the "degradation of the constitutional charter" due to the use of certain technological measures. Specifically, it was pointed out: *'The geolocation of the entire population, aimed at identifying those affected by the virus, for example, or ultimately forced confinement, would mean an alarming degradation of the quality of our Constitution', motivating 'an instinctive rejection from a moderate constitutional sensitivity'*[136].

And in other news we could read that that three hundred researchers from around the world *"warn about the danger of the systems that countries such as Germany or France are developing to track possible new coronavirus infections. …The solutions that allow reconstructing invasive information about the population must be rejected without any kind of debate"*.[137]

Unfortunately, this position is the prevailing one when it comes to making political decisions, trying to draw a line that separates the Asian "interventionist" model from the "Europe of freedoms", even if this means a crisis of historic dimensions and thousands of deaths behind us.

b) Who is managing and protecting our sensitive and personal data? Will they defend our "constitutional" right?

Opinion groups that defend privacy as an irrevocable and inviolable right have questioned the possible partisan use of our data if it

---

135. The state of necessity occurs when a subject's legitimate interests are in a state of danger and can only be saved by injury to another person's legitimate interests.

136. The Constitution under the state of alarm, Diario El País: elpais.com/elpais/2020/04/16/opinion/1587025782_733659.html

137. Hundreds of researchers warn of the danger of espionage of some tracking 'apps', El Confindencial: elconfidencial.com/tecnologia/2020-04-20/apps-rastreo-contactos-pepp-pt-dp3t-nkt-protocol-ios-android_2556627/

ends up in the hands of governments, or even that it could be used once the pandemic is over. This is despite the existence of a European Parliament, national Congresses and a trustworthy judiciary in each EU country.

During the days of confinement, it was heard in some media that European citizens fear new totalitarianisms, given our recent history marked by dictatorships, fascism or Soviet despotism. But curiously enough, we are encountering "jihadist attitudes" in defense of privacy, which, either because of technophobia or spurious interests, are causing an effect contrary to the interest they are trying to arouse with their debates, and are devaluing the defense of values that define us as Europeans.

In fact, it is hardly a matter of concern that private for-profit companies, which make a business out of data exploitation, have access to this information. But just as an intellectual exercise, ask yourselves the following questions: how can private companies be allowed to be the only ones responsible for protecting a right of "constitutional sensitivity"? Why is there no question about the interests existing between these companies and the Administrations, which regulate their activity, set their prices and even award large tenders? What guarantee do we have as citizens that companies are dealing correctly with cyber-attacks that could violate our constitutional right?

It is true that there is a regulation that severely penalizes companies that fail to comply (even unintentionally or are victims of cyber-attacks) with their obligation to safeguard data. But the existence of sanctions does not mean that there is no vulnerability, and not even the heads of state themselves are guaranteed privacy, no matter how much the Constitution protects it. Let's remember how the US, an "ally" country, spied on the telephones of 35 world leaders, as revealed by The Guardian. [138] And it was not a one-off event: the German government suspected that the cell phone of its president Angela Merkel was spied on from 1999 to the end of 2013. And like her 200 other politicians.

---

138. theguardian.com/us-news/2015/jul/08/nsa-tapped-german-chancellery-decades-wikileaks-claims-merkel

People should assume that neither the mobile network nor Internet protocols are designed to preserve anonymity or privacy. Therefore, formulating a right that is violated by the very nature and essence of technology and the rules that define it is little less than pointless gestures.

If we wanted to preserve our privacy above all else; if we value this right so much that we don't want to take any risk; if society truly understood it as something inviolable and inalienable - we would all have long since disposed of our smartwatches, car navigators, mobile terminals, etc. But no one does.

The digital economy and an absolute, dogmatic and radical interpretation of privacy are very much at odds with each other.[139]

c) Europe reaps the harvest of its sowing.

While our elders died in hospitals, and we were creating an almost unprecedented economic crisis, many specialists focused on debates and questions such as: can individual data be a public good? Do citizens have the right to freely decide whether their movements are controlled?

At the time of closing the first edition of this book, we were expectant of the outcome of the entire situation caused by COVID-19, which kept us confined for several months. However, we can already affirm that the Europe of great laws and digital lethargy reacted late and badly.

When you read this, you will surely have more evidence. Yet it is clear that despite having more developed health services and the advantage of the previous Asian experience, the number of infections and deaths in Italy, France, the United Kingdom, and Spain have far exceeded China, a country whose welfare state is still far from the European one.[140]

---

139. Are there technologies to preserve privacy or security? Yes. One is the TOR (The Onion Router), which is commonly used to access the dark web. Other alternative is Blockchain, whose best-known exponent is bitcoin. We have already mentioned that many of European efforts would have been successfully crowned if attention had been paid to this technology.

140. When we write these lines, before considering any Asian technological

Privacy was a key element in these differences in contagion. Europe, like Asia, had adequate technology, with initiatives such as the alliance between Google and Apple to use their operating systems as a contagion tracker, [141] or the many apps proposed by European technology companies to their governments.[142] However, European technological solutions had to comply with the aforementioned restrictions, resulting in totally inefficient systems.

A good example is the proposal of the "Pan-European Proximity Privacy Preserving Tracking Consortium" (PEPP-PT), [143] composed of seven European countries, which aims to promote a digital tracking solution against COVID-19 with a protocol similar to the following:

1) You, as a mobile user, **access the app store and voluntarily decide** whether to install an app or not. There is no imposition whatsoever.

2) Once installed, you must give **consent for an anonymized ID to be emitted via Bluetooth** from the device so that it can be tracked by other mobiles that also have the application without being able to find out your identity.

3) If you test positive for coronavirus, you can voluntarily send (or not) the data of people with whom you have had contact to the health authority of your country, the only receiving entity.

---

teaching, we are witnessing a media and government deployment that accuses the Machiavellian origin of the virus itself from the falsity of the data in a Chinese laboratory. Time and history will tell.

141.   apple.com/es/newsroom/2020/04/apple-and-google-partner-on-covid-19-contact-tracing-technology/

142. Excellent proposals of enormous value have been made, competitive at a global level, which we also know thoroughly. Andrés Torrubia, Aurelia Bustos, Antonio Parraga, and Elad Rodríguez developed with enormous diligence "Open Coronavirus" that offers a digital solution for monitoring, diagnosis, and containment of infections with open source.

143. esmartcity.es/2020/04/17/espana-suma-iniciativa-paneuropea-pepp-pt-impulsar-solucion-digital-rastreo-contra-covid-19

4) The health authority will **notify other users who have been at risk of contagion** by being coming into contact with you if those users provided their consent to be contacted by the health authority.

5) Finally, once the status of exceptionality is passed, all **information will be deleted.**

Now think: with so many restrictions of moderation and the obligatory willingness of citizens to preserve privacy, will this measure have any effect?

China and South Korea have shown us the real power of technology to act against pandemics. We could track the movement of infected people, know who was nearby and if they are potentially infected, alert their contacts, provide tele-assisted support to those who are sick and cannot leave home, publish maps of areas with greater risk, or simply enforce measures to control the contagion.

Europe trusts everything to an unprecedented act of extreme generosity. It has renounced the technological factor to embrace a smooth model that is insufficient. However, we can rest assured: our privacy is kept by mobile operators and telecoms, and they will never deliver it to our governments because the law that our governments make prevents it. We have certainly reached an intellectually surreal, contradictory, and Kafkaesque state.

Closing the loop

All these debates, this permissiveness or attack depending on whoever keeps our data, the idea of a return to totalitarianism, or drawing Asian societies as little less than hostages to their governments, only takes the spotlight away from another of these uncomfortable truths: the existence of covert protectionism resulting from the European digital impotence.

In the media, more attention is paid to privacy criticism because it attacks tech giants than to closing an incoherent debate. Maintaining such an exaggerated defense stance of privacy seems unreasonable when we risk thousands of human lives and hundreds of thousands of jobs.

Will it be necessary to remember that the right to privacy is subject of gossip and "trade" in TV shows? Do we blindly trust our operators and not our governments to temporarily monitor the traceability of an infection? Have we made Netflix and its Black Mirror fiction our inspiration and future reference to preserve privacy?

Without a doubt, we suffer from a false and empty dogmatic intellectual empowerment, full of witty tweets that bring us closer to the caricature of the "satisfied master" exposed by Ortega y Gasset and included at the beginning of this chapter.

Meanwhile, we observe how week after week of confinement, the European decline that gives the book its title became a reality, and we ask ourselves: what will European society look like ten years from now? What will remain of our EU? And how will its countries emerge from one of the greatest economic and social upheavals? Should we have talked about privacy or survival, about restrictions or solutions? Should we have focused on preserving supposed European "values" that only politicians seem to identify with, or on correcting an announced decline in the economy and the welfare of citizens?

Table Annex Part 1. Macroeconomic statistics

	Pop. (millions)	Nominal GDP (2017) (millions)	GDP pc (2017)	Public Debt (%GDP) (2018)	Public Exp (%GDP) (2018)
European Union	510.4	17,338.8	33,971 €	-	44.0%*
Eurozone	341.4	12,628.0	36,989 €	-	49.8%
UK	66.02	2,637.8	39,956 €	87.00%	40.8%
Germany	82.68	3,693.2	44,669 €	64.10%	43.9%
France	67.10	2,582.5	38,487 €	97.00%	56.0%
Italy	60.53	1,943.8	32,114 €	131.50%	48.6%
Spain	46.59	1,314.3	28,210 €	98.40%	41.3%
Greece	10.75	203.1	18,892 €	181.90%	46.7%
Sweden	10.05	535.6	53,294 €	40.90%	49.9%
Estonia	1.31	26.6	20,314 €	8.80%	39.5%
US	325.3	19,485.4	59,900 €	82.30%	34.8%**
China	1,339.4	12,237.7	9,137 €	47.80%	34.0%
Israel	8.712	353.2	40,559 €	61.00%	38.7%**
Mexico	129.16	1,150.9	8,911 €	54.20%	25.7%
South Korea	51.46	1,530.7	29,746 €	39.80%	20.8%**
Japan	126.78	4,872.4	38,432 €	236.40%	37.4%**

* Calculation made on 23 of the 28 EU countries
** Data refer to the year 2017 (latest year available)

	Spending on R&D (%GDP)	Life Expectancy (2017)	Unemployme nt rate (2017)	Urban population (% total) (2017)	CO2 (k.tons/m illion people) (2014)	Renewable energy (% of total consumption) (2015)
European Union	1.96%	80.99	7.60%	75.45%	6.35	16.56%
Eurozone	2.10%	81.95	9.00%	76.77%	6.41	16.08%
UK	1.66%	81.15	4.30%	83.14%	6.35	8.71%
Germany	3.02%	80.99	3.70%	77.26%	8.7	14.20%
France	2.19%	82.52	9.40%	80.18%	4.51	13.49%
Italy	1.35%	83.24	11.20%	70.14%	5.29	16.51%
Spain	1.21%	83.32	17.20%	80.08%	5.02	16.25%
Greece	1.13%	81.38	21.50%	78.72%	6.26	17.17%
Sweden	3.33%	82.3	6.70%	87.15%	4.32	53.24%
Estonia	1.29%	77.64	5.80%	68.72%	14.9	27.47%
US	2.79%	78.5	4.40%	82.06%	16.15	8.71%
China	2.13%	76.41	3.90%	57.96%	7.68	12.41%
Israel	4.55%	82.6	4.20%	92.34%	7.41	3.70%
Mexico	0.50%	77.3	3.40%	79.87%	3.71	9.21%
South Korean	4.55%	82.7	8.10%	81.50%	11.4	2.70%
Japan	3.20%	84.1	2.80%	91.53%	9.57	6.29%

2ND PART: POLICIES AND PROPOSALS FOR ACTION

CHAPTER 5: A STRONG COMMITMENT TO AI IN EUROPE

« In our business we talk about emerging technologies and how they impact society. AI is by far the fastest technology we have experienced in terms of impact and immediacy ».

PAUL DAUGHERTY. Accenture CTO and author of "Human + Machine: Reimagining Work in the Age of AI".

« People are concerned that computers are getting too smart and taking over the world, but the real problem is that they are too stupid and have already taken over the world».

PEDRO DOMINGOS, professor at the University of Washington.

If, throughout 1st Part of this book, we have addressed why Europe is not a digital leader and the reasons that have led us to this situation of delay and technological dependence, in this 2nd Part, dedicated to policies and proposals for action, we will explain why the commitment to AI[144] is the only way out of the future problems of welfare, wealth, and employment that the old continent faces. Nevertheless, there is no possible development in AI without data.

Europe is the region with the highest guarantee of data protection in the world, according to the National Commission for Informatics and Freedoms (CNIL); however, that does not mean that it is something positive in practice for society, nor that this protection is efficient for the European citizenship. Countries that are in a situation of partial protection (such as the United States, Canada,

---

144. For those readers who wish to become familiar with Artificial Intelligence, we recommend Lasse Rouhiainen's book (2019) Artificial Intelligence: 101 Things You Must Know Today About Our Future. There is a version of Lasse Rouhiainen's work in Spanish and English. Available at: amazon.es/Artificial-Intelligence-Things-Future-English-ebook/dp/B079JXCVGS

and Japan) or without guaranteeing an adequate level of data protection for their users (such as China and Australia, according to the said Commission) are the ones that are creating more companies and jobs around new technologies.

The EU in its attempt to be the digital reference in the field of regulation is trying to resolve debates that have been on the table for more than 60 years, when the first discussions on the use of machine learning techniques in military conflicts took place.[145] The result is that Europe has the most secure digital laws, and China and the US have the largest companies and unicorns in new technologies.

In this chapter, we will analyze the impact of AI in terms of GDP growth, the expected effects and scenarios in some sectors as a visualization of the potential of this technology, and how European data policy will cause a greater digital gap if left unaddressed.

---

145. Wiener, N. (1961). *Cybernetics or Control and Communication in the Animal and the Machine.* MIT press.

1. WHY CAN'T AI DEVELOPMENT BE 'JUST' AN OPTION?

1.1 Beyond 'the new electricity'

Among all the technologies with great disruptive power, AI has been postulated as the general-purpose technology (GPT) of its era.[146] A technology that can continuously transform itself, progressively diversify, and boost both productivities in all sectors and well-being in households.

Very few have been considered as general utility technologies throughout history, such as the printing press, steam engine, electricity generator, internal combustion, and recently, information and communication technologies (ICTs).[147] AI is included in this exclusive club due to its capacity for social and economic transformation, the benefits to be derived from it, and its ability to hybridize with other technologies.

The implementation of clean energy, the diagnosis and prevention of diseases, production based on future consumption expectations, the viability of the circular economy[148] and many other improvements that a short time ago would have sounded like science fiction are now realistic challenges for our scientists and companies thanks to three attributes of AI:

a) Cognitive and predictive capabilities: AI algorithms try to solve complex problems in a way that a human would, processing large amounts of data generated by connected systems (for example, sensors) to improve diagnostic, predictive, and

---

146. Brynjolfsson, E., Rock, D. and Syverson, C. (2017): *Artificial Intelligence and the Modern Productivity Paradox: A Clash of Expectations and Statistics*. NBER Working Paper No. 24001. nber.org/papers/w24001

147. Helpman, E. (Ed.). (1998). *General purpose technologies and economic growth*. MIT press.

148. Geissdoerfer, M. et al. (2017). The Circular Economy—A new sustainability paradigm? *Journal of cleaner production*, *143*, 757-768.

prescriptive capabilities.[149]

b) Ability to teach oneself and improve: Deep learning will not only allow efficient solutions to be sought but will also improve them until the optimum is found even when completely new situations arise for algorithms[150] - something that can be implemented toward any business goal, from selling more products to producing more efficiently with the least possible environmental impact.[151]

c) Ability to transmit what has been learned: Unlike humans, machines can instantly transmit everything they have learned and apply without restrictions from the cloud the skills to do or execute tasks. In just tenths of a second, algorithms learn from past versions, while it can take any of us months or years to acquire complex knowledge in languages, mathematics or any other discipline.

The AI debate

Why then is there so much media and punditry debate over AI? Why do many call it a great evolution while others approach it to a pre-apocalyptic state of the human species? Why the enormous disparity in the stakes of its development between countries?

For all these questions, Sundar Pichai, CEO of Google, has the answer: "AI is the most important thing humanity has ever worked on. I consider it a more profound change than electricity or fire"[152]. And as with fire or electricity when they were unknown to humans, something similar is happening with AI: there are those who decide to pour water on the fire, and those who act with courage, weighing

---

149. Autonomous driving is a good example of the potential of AI, which will allow machines to observe, learn, and offer suggestions or even automatic actions.

150. AlphaGo demonstrated the potential of Deep Learning with an algorithm learning from scratch, without human intervention, and in record time.

151. technologyreview.es/s/9676/el-aprendizaje-automatico-se-automatiza-si-mismo-para-que-la-ia-llegue-todos-los-publicos

152. See: emol.com/noticias/Tecnologia/2018/01/25/892636/CEO-de-Google-sobre-Inteligencia-Artificial-Es-quizas-lo-mas-importante-en-lo-que-la-humanidad-ha-trabajado.html

opportunities and dangers, seeking to join the revolutionary advances.[153]

AI has opened up a new field of action and economic transformation of our societies for which we had better keep an open mind. The scale of the impact and the speed of assimilation expected from AI and the set of disruptive technologies that enhance it is such that it must be seen as a matter of survival, and not only of competitiveness.

---

153. Brynjolfsson, E., Rock, D., & Syverson, C. (2017). *Artificial intelligence and the modern productivity paradox: A clash of expectations and statistics* (No. w24001). National Bureau of Economic Research.

2. EUROPE'S COMMITMENT TO ARTIFICIAL INTELLIGENCE

Europe, by tradition and economic history, has a fundamental role to play as an AI superpower. However, it will first have to close its technological gap, something that can only be achieved with a public, solid and ambitious strategy in the face of the pressure from the USA, China and other countries such as Israel, Canada and South Korea.

For this purpose, the European Commission has already set up an investment fund of 20,000 million euros to enhance its AI strategy. Will it be enough? Let's compare the European commitment with that of the two great technological powers.

The US bet

Despite the ideological shift between Obama and Trump, the bet on AI was positioned as a fundamental strategy to ensure U.S. economic and political leadership. The Trump Administration maintained the so-called 'American AI Initiative'[154] of 2016, which aimed to implement a joint plan from and for all national departments and agencies, seeking greater collaboration with other countries,[155] especially with Europe.

The plan includes spending on the whole of the administration and the army, which are closely linked to research, specialization, training, and standardization of processes that take AI as the basis for modernization, transformation, and disruption.

---

154. The National Artificial Intelligence Investment Plan Update Document can be downloaded at nitrd.gov/Publications/Publication Detail. aspx?pubid=97

155. Information collected on the website whitehouse.gov/ai and the breakdown of investment in research and development of the federal government in 2019: whitehouse.gov/wp-content/uploads/2019/03/ap 21 research-fy2020.pdf

By 2020 the US planned 1 billion dollars of government funding for non-military AI R&D. Also, they have more than 2 billion dollars of investment in unclassified AI projects (which leaves out an important part of agencies such as NASA, the Pentagon, or the CIA) and predictably at least 1 billion dollars planned for research in AI.[156]

The business sector and some specialists have described this investment as insufficient.[157] However, in the US, it is private investment, especially that of the technological giants, that is the engine of the advancement in AI. In 2018, they disbursed more than 8 billion dollars to finance startups linked to this technology, to which we must add the billions of dollars invested by Google, Facebook, Amazon and similar companies in their own developments.

The US universities also joined the commitment. To cite three examples of a different nature, MIT has a fund of 1 billion dollars to promote a new model of university focused on machine learning,[158] Carnegie Mellon University works with companies such as Bosch and Argo AI to create research laboratories, with budgets that exceed 10 million dollars, and Google has a 25 million-dollar fund for university research on new uses of AI.

The Chinese bet

The Asian giant has boosted its public investment in AI with impressive values. Investment expectations are 10 billion dollars until 2030, to which are added the individual initiative of each region and the raising of international funds. In total, more than 70 billion dollars were estimated to be spent only in the year 2020, framed in the "Made in China 2025" plan to lead the new technological era, and which made US experts in defense and geopolitics tremble.[159]

---

156. techcrunch.com/2020/02/07/white-house-reportedly-aims-to-double-ai-research-budget-to-2b/

157. wsj.com/articles/executives-say-1-billion-for-ai-research-isnt-enough-11568153863

158. technologyreview.com/f/612293/mit-has-just-announced-a-1-billion-plan-to-create-a-new-college-for-ai

159. military.com/defensetech/2018/07/30/china-leaving-us-behind-artificial-intelligence-air-force-general.html

The construction of the Mentougou technology park (Beijing) seeks to give dynamism to the private sector, its Achilles heel compared to the US industry. The creation of digital ecosystems from which new cases such as Huawei, Alibaba, and Xiaomi arise is key for China to be the big winner in the AI era.

The European bet

The European Commission, within the Horizon 2020 Plan, has initially arranged (2018-2020) about 2.6 billion euros of investment in robotics, big data, and another series of new technologies related to AI - an amount that is expected to rise to 20 billion in the next few years.[160]

We must also add here the individual initiatives of each country, especially those led by France, Germany, and the United Kingdom: in 2018, French President Emmanuel Macron announced an investment of 1.5 billion euros in four years in AI; months later, Angela Merkel announced an investment valued at 3 billion euros; finally, from London, the investment of 200 million euros in public-private initiatives has been proposed, in addition to complementary actions in incubators and universities that will multiply the initial bet.[161]

However, these investments are likely to be insufficient. At present, private investment in European AI is almost irrelevant compared to that of its "rivals" **(figure 5.1)**. Closing the initial gap with China and the US will require greater effort.

Also, the structural weaknesses that we have been pointing out (reduced private investment, weakness of digital ecosystems, and the segmentation of the European market) limit the indirect effects of investments made in advanced sectors.

Thirdly, the disbursement that the European Commission plans to make is not limited to productive innovation and sectors of the future. and a base that consolidates entrepreneurship, Europe runs

---

160. It is important to note that the economic collapse that the coronavirus will mean for the EU (which could exceed 30% of GDP according to some estimates) could put this type of investment at risk.

161. For example, the University of Oxford has a £ 150 million investment to develop what it claims to be the university of the future.

the risk of losing itself in R&D based on the hypotheses of the methodological, scientific and ethical debate in academia, rather than on business-driven tools. We will not deny that both approaches are necessary, but the first cannot paralyze or underfund the second.

Figure 5.1. Private investment in AI (2016) (US$ millions)

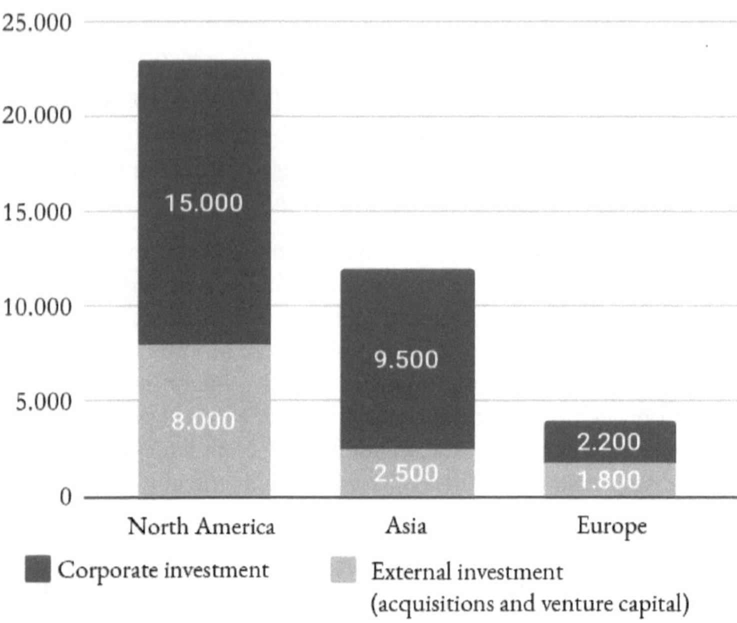

Source: Mckinsey Global Institute

Finally, the oversize that data privacy has taken in the EU could make the billion-dollar investment a superfluous expense, more intended to satisfy and feed its mature sectors than to take the definitive step towards digitization.

Europe must react and address these issues in order to no longer be a losing economy.

3. MEASURING THE IMPACT OF AI ON THE GLOBAL ECONOMY

Estimating the impact of AI on our economies is certainly complicated for several reasons. We are at an early stage in the application of the technology, without knowing which investments will be continued, which developments will end up being used massively, and whether the expectations of industrial transformation will end up being fulfilled.

Technology usually requires decades to be seen in statistics, as the Solow paradox warns, something that would merit a debate on the lack of access to data for research and how economics studies the disruption caused by technological leaps.[162]

In addition, the fact that AI is a cross-cutting technology makes it difficult to extrapolate data accurately. It is not only a matter of accounting for the effect of direct business investment, but also for those that, indirectly, generate competitiveness tools such as Google Maps, Microsoft To-Do, and IBM Cloud, among thousands of other applications that use AI for their operations.

Despite these difficulties, the large consulting firms have already produced very interesting first predictions, based on data and interviews with companies that serve as a first approximation.

First predictions

The report *Why artificial intelligence is the future of growth*[163] by Accenture and Frontier Economics suggests that economies that do not rely on AI in the next fifteen years may see their growth prospects cut by up to 50%. This effect is especially significant in the most innovative countries (USA, UK, Finland, and Sweden), while those specialized in more tradicional sectors, such as Spain or Italy, will see

---

162. See: Brynjolfsson, Rock y Syverson (2017) cited above.
163. accenture.com/t20170524t055435__w__/ca-en/_acnmedia/pdf-52/accenture-why-ai-is-the-future-of-growth.pdf

a smaller increase in productivity per worker **(figure 5.2)**. In approximates, investment in AI could mean an increase of $ 8.3 trillion in the US economy and close to a trillion dollars in the case of Germany and the United Kingdom, doubling their current growth rates.

Figure 5.2. Annual GDP growth forecast in 2035, with and without investment in AI

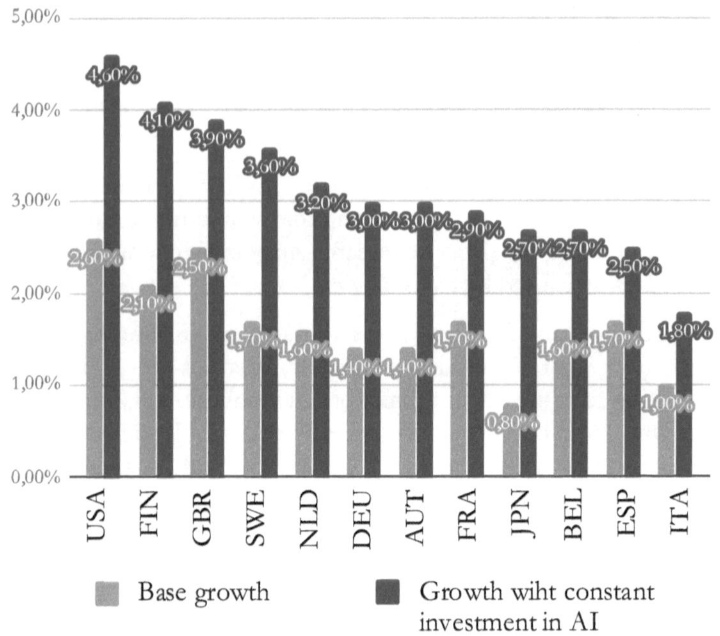

Source: Accenture y Frontier Economics

PwC, in its report *Sizing the Price*,[164] estimates a 14% increase in global wealth directly attributable to AI in the year 2030 derived from an increase in productivity ($ 6.6 trillion) and consumption ($ 9.1 trillion). The biggest beneficiaries of this boost will be those that are making the greatest effort to master technology. China will increase its GDP by 26%, which is equivalent to 7 trillion dollars attributable to its commitment to AI; in the United States, 14.5%,

---

164. pwc.com/gx/en/issues/analytics/assets/pwc-ai-analysis-sizing-the-prize-report.pdf

that is, almost 4 trillion dollars; and finally, Europe is expected to increase its wealth by 10%, or 2.5 trillion dollars. According to the consultancy, the US and China will share 70% of the total surplus generated by AI **(figure 5.3)**.

Figure 5.3: Forecasting the impact of AI on GDP in 2030

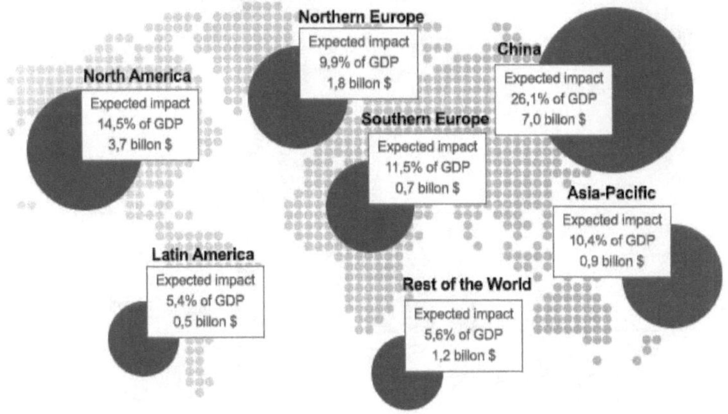

Source: PwC

Finally, *Tractica's Artificial Intelligence Market Forecasts*[165] report points out that Asian countries will be the ones to take advantage of the development of AI the most. It is estimated that in the next five years, Asian business performance derived from technology will exceed 11 billion dollars, more than double that estimated for the whole of Europe **(figure 5.4)**.

In summary, all the results lead to the Asia-Pacific area being the new technology leader, and China will win the so-called "war for AI" [166] against the US. The EU will be relegated to a completely secondary role.

---

165. tractica.com/research/artificial-intelligence-market-forecasts/
166. forbes.com/sites/cognitiveworld/2020/01/14/china-artificial-intelligence-superpower/

Figure 5.4: Business returns derived from AI by region (2015-2024) (in millions of dollars)

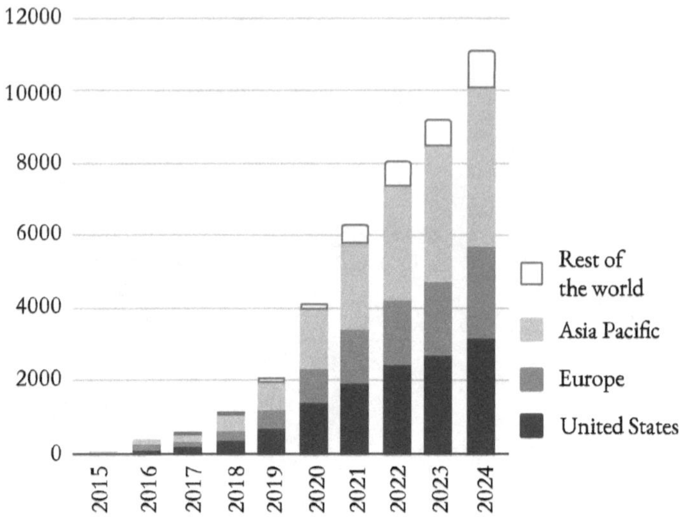

Source: Tractica

4. SECTORIAL IMPACTS OF AI

Although the founder of the World Economic Forum, Klaus Schwab, has linked the fourth industrial revolution to AI, we must not lose ourselves in the buzz and the "tailor-made" interpretations that each one wants to give of the industries 4.0[167] or digitization.

The new Revolution must be understood as the confluence of technologies of enormous disruptive power such as robotics, Blockchain, nanotechnology, quantum computing, biotechnology, the IoT, 3D printing, and of course, AI.

At this early stage is difficult to visualize a company, large or small, that can survive if it does not work on customized orders or learning about buyer trends, as Amazon and Alibaba do, or that does not learn to optimize prices based on the experience of their users, as Uber and Airbnb do, or that does not adjust product recommendations to its users, as Spotify or Youtube do.

Taking advantage of the transversal improvements offered by AI and the rest of the disruptive technologies will require profound transformations in terms of knowledge, business models, human capital, and, of course, investment. A process of change more radical than that experienced from the 90s with the appearance of the Internet

Sectorial adaptation rhythms

Not all industries know how or are able to adapt technology at the same pace. The financial and technology sectors, due to a question of competitiveness and financing capacity, are the ones that are making the greatest effort to adapt to the new technological paradigm **(figure 5.5).** Some examples include the recent acquisition of Xnor.ai for 200 million dollars by Apple, or the announcement by BBVA bank to launch an 'AI Factory' staffed with 150 professionals to improve all products where AI is a differential element.

---

167. Schwab, K. (2017). *The fourth industrial revolution.* Currency.

Future AI demand trajectory
Estimated % change in AI spending over the next three years,
weighted by company size

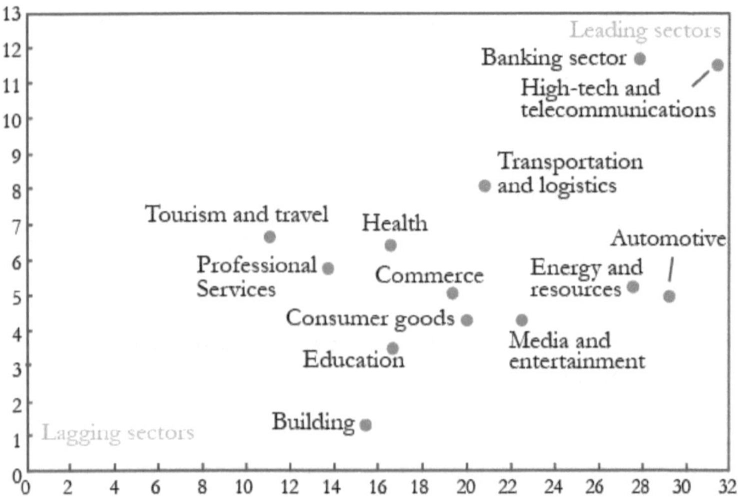

% of companies adopting any of the AI technologies in
some process of their business, weighted by company size

Source: Mckinsey Global Institute

Other sectors such as the automotive, transport and energy industries are also making a major effort, knowing that the AI-driven
transformation will be completely radical. We only have to think
about the hybridization of AI with the internet of things or 3D print-
ers to get an idea of a revolution that will be unstoppable.

Finally, the more mature industries such as tourism, professional
services or construction, are having a later adaptation than the rest,
but due more to the business base (SMEs, family businesses, etc.)
than to the lack of opportunities. Think of Airbnb, the development
of smart cities and destinations, or the number of professional tools
that already use AI to realize their capacity to be reinvented.

Understanding, therefore, that no economic activity will be
spared from new disruptive technologies, in the following pages, we

have tried to synthesize a future scenario of change in some specific industries; changes that just ten years ago sounded impossible, today seem to us a close reality, and in a few decades the new generations will probably ask how we, men and women of the 20th and early 21st centuries, were able to live part of our lives without such improvements.

i. Agriculture and the environment

Agriculture is currently one of the most capitalized technological sectors, and AI will have an impact on a multitude of aspects from robotization, monitoring, tracking and control of crops, and the optimization of irrigation, the use of pesticides and harvesting.[168]

In livestock farming, the changes generated by AI are already being appreciated, which allow increasingly efficient management with artificial vision for animal control, optimized weight control, and automated feeding systems, among others.[169]

With this, it will be possible to cover the nutritional needs of the entire planet, the natural regeneration of the land, and environmental preservation, with farms in less space, maximizing the quality of the product, or adapting production to climate change.

John Deere's computer vision prototypes that will identify weeds and growth problems in each plant show us that solutions will come sooner rather than later. In this specific case we are talking about a reduction of pesticide contamination of up to 90%[170].

The Japanese companies Sony and Cookpad have reached an agreement to adapt the crops of each area of the planet to their biological ecosystems.[171] The pilot project is being carried out in Alicante,[172] one of the areas with less rainfall per year, seeking to regenerate a land under attack and at risk of desertification. The first

---

168. news.mit.edu/2019/algorithm-growing-agriculture-0403

169. medium.com/neuromation-blog/ai-in-agriculture-49c0ea0e2b48

170. forbes.com/sites/bernardmarr/2019/03/15/the-amazing-ways-john-deere-uses-ai-and-machine-vision-to-help-feed-10-billion-people/

171. This includes the study of crops, and also of bacteria and fungi that can help plantations and the soil, for example, by fixing nitrogen from the air to soluble nitrates that act as natural fertilizers.

172. Concept tests have also been carried out in Africa and Asia.

results are surprising, and within 5 years it is expected to achieve farms maintained only with rainwater and without any type of pesticide or pollutant.

Along these lines, the Farm 45[173] project aims to create an international community of farmers, university experts, and entrepreneurs to change aggressive agriculture with the natural environment towards sustainable crops and to promote biodiversity and the regeneration of the land. AI will be an important part of studying the viability and efficiency of these new ecosystems.

IBM Watson also works with AI and IoT technologies to assist farmers in their planning, plowing, planting, spraying, and harvesting. The challenge is to increase agricultural production to supply the entire world population in 2050 without increasing the space for cultivation,[174] especially in the poorest areas.[175]

Beyond AI, Blockchain can be used to improve water management,[176] and it would even solve authentication and traceability problems for agricultural products. In Ecuador, Blockchain is already being used to know the origin of cocoa, the remuneration obtained by farmers on the final price, and to allocate a part of the purchase of the product to ecological projects.[177] A solution that could also be used by the European agricultural sector, given the problems generated by the excessive number of intermediaries and the sale below costs to which farmers are subjected.

In short, the technological sophistication of agriculture based on disruptive technologies will be one of the pillars to tackle the great challenges of humanity in the coming decades. The EU, which advocates more than any other region on the planet sustainability environmental, has a significant incentive for agriculture to develop its green and innovation policies.

---

173. farm45.io/
174. newsroom.ibm.com/2019-05-22-IBM-AI-and-Cloud-Technology-Helps-Agriculture-Industry-Improve-the-Worlds-Food-and-Crop-Supply
175. news.mit.edu/2019/empowering-african-farmers-with-data-0530
176. Lin, Y-P., Petway, J.R., Lien, W-Y. and Settele, J. (2018): Blockchain with Artificial Intelligence to Efficiently Manage Water Use under Climate Change. *Environments*, 5, 34.
177. un.org/es/card/56071

ii. Automotive industry

AI in the automotive industry will mean a radical transformation in production issues, predictive vehicle maintenance, passenger and pedestrian safety, real-time analysis of the driver's condition, and anti-theft systems.

Of all the expected changes, autonomous driving will be the one that represents the greatest transformations not only in the automotive industry but also in related sectors. In general, the transport of people and goods and the logistics of millions of companies will experience a revolution in terms of organizational efficiency, accidents, and pollution.

Indeed, the autopilot option is hardly so rare in high-end vehicles anymore. However, a generalization of the technology would allow anyone sleeping or working to make long trips while reducing road deaths[178].

The focus autonomous driving is justified, especially in Europe, given the very high rate of aging, with more than 24% of the population over 60 years of age. However, its definitive implementation will depend on two fundamental issues: technological developments and political-administrative acceptance. In both aspects, the United States and Asia already have an advantage over the European Union, the latter recreated in discussions about the capture of data from vehicle recognition systems, and the ethical debate on how algorithms select the options that inevitably lead to third-party harm. Paradoxically, as this debate on human life is extended, the numbers of road deaths increase.

Moreover, indecision in this key sector for Europe can halt the necessary development of its technologies, and in which companies such as Volvo, Mercedes, and BMW invest billions. The EU and its administrations must understand that for these and other companies to compete with China firms, or with Google or Tesla, any regulatory help that facilitates the development, testing, and data collection will be little.

----

178. The machines do not fall asleep at the wheel; they do not get confused looking at the mobile or drink alcohol; they are programmed to respect the signals and can predict accidents based on information from their surroundings.

iii. Transportation and logistics

Beyond autonomous driving, shipping and transportation logistics will suffer major disruption, especially foster by optimization. All the businesspeople of the most important logistics corporations on the planet are aware of this.

Based on the information collected from the supply chain, customers and products, companies will be able to increase their planning capacity with algorithms aimed at reducing operational costs in route management, cutting down incidents, and increasing service quality. The delivery of parcels could even be updated according to the real-time location of the recipients.

In addition, AI is present in the latest generations of robots capable of evaluating the status of packages, tracking, locating, and moving inventory within warehouses. Deep learning algorithms allow them to make autonomous decisions regarding the different processes they carry out, optimizing storage and delivery.

iv. Energy and climate change

The development of renewable energies and the substitution of polluting sources will also be accelerated by AI, which has become an ally in the fight against climate change. This technology is helping to maximize clean energy production, for example, with the movement of solar panels or the location of mills.

Moreover, the German Borderstep Institute[179] has developed predictive algorithms that allow savings of up to 25% in heating homes. And this is just a first step: in the near future, the data generated by our homes, cities or vehicles will be used to automate consumption in an optimal way, while we users are not even aware of it.

v. Banking and the financial system

To analyze in-depth the impact of the new technological paradigm in the banking sector, we would need a new book dedicated

---

179. borderstep.org/

entirely to the subject.[180] As mentioned previously, this sector is a benchmark for investment in AI, with figures only surpassed by high-tech industries and telecommunications.

Why does the bank need to make this investment effort?

- The financial sector must adapt to an economy where intangible assets are gaining weight. There will be fewer and fewer physical offices and more software.

- Algorithms are necessary to segment the banking business, optimize the profitability of investments, detect the risk of non-payment, etc.

- The bank faces important automation systems in all areas of its customer management and where AI enhances security systems (biometric authentication) or segmentation and personalization when it comes to addressing customer service.

- The sector is facing competition from fintechs stripped of superfluous expenses and with flexibility as their flagship, which do not need large amounts of capital in order to be extraordinarily competitive in very specific areas of the sector.[181]

AI and technologies such as Blockchain promise to lay the foundations for much more efficient banking, with new processes of disintermediation, authentication, traceability, autonomy, and independence - a new way of understanding the sector that could leave the big players out of the market if they are not able to adapt. Not surprisingly, some presidents of the world's leading banks have already openly said that banking entities would become software

---

180. Most of the large international consulting firms have done studies on the impacts of AI on banking and the financial system. For an example, visit: accenture.com/_acnmedia/pdf-68/accenture-redefine-banking.pdf

181. For example, the Swiss bank UBS has partnered with Amazon to incorporate its 'Ask UBS' service into Echo speaker devices with Alexa technology. And this is just the first of many moves to come in the coming years.

companies. Others even point to their disappearance.[182]

Finally, and although the race in the use of AI in banks has almost infinite possibilities, we would like to highlight the six that the web entrepeneur.com considers the most relevant:[183]

---

1. Customer service automation: The biggest savings in banking costs in the next decade will come from the automation of assistance and services. Chatbots and virtual assistants online or at ATMs available 24/7, together with an optimized user experience, will cause the reduction of millions of jobs. In the US alone, it will represent savings of up to $ 450 billion for the sector in 2030.

2. Internal process optimization: AI will also allow the automation of high-volume - low-value processes within finance companies. For example, JP Morgan has started using bots to process internal requests to the technology department, such as attempts by employees to reset their work passwords.[184] These bots multiply by 40 the tasks made by any other employee.

3. Personalization: the detailed information of clients that banks have (income, consumption, movements, place of residence, debts, etc.) will allow personalization of all their products in terms of advice, credits, savings, and pension plans with models adapted in price and characteristics to the objectives and habits of each client.[185]

---

182. In this changing scenario, less-banked countries such as Kenya or India are adopting advanced strategies for making payments with mobile devices or managing properties completely online. In more specialized countries such as Spain and Germany, progress is expected to be slow and expensive.

183. "5 Ways Artificial Intelligence Is Already Transforming the Banking Industry". See: entrepreneur.com/article/319921

184. mckinsey.com/industries/financial-services/our-insights/the-transformative-power-of-automation-in-banking

185. An example is a technological challenge organized by Banco Santander to create algorithms that optimize product customization, with a prize of $ 60,000.
See: kaggle.com/c/santander-product-recommendation

4. Security: biometric data, such as fingerprints or face morphology, are a key element of security in payments and access to bank accounts of billions of customers thanks to smartphones. Moreover, it works with any type of recognition and sensor that can register to authenticate our operations that even our heartbeats can be the biometric identity for this purpose.[186]

5. Pattern recognition and fraud prevention: AI's ability to examine massive amounts of data and identify patterns of fraud will be key to fighting the cybercrime that costs the global economy more than 600 billion dollars each year. First results are already evident: Mastercard alone has reduced fraud against its customers by 80 percent, thanks to AI.[187]

6. Operations from anywhere upon request: AI and intelligent virtual assistants (IVA) will be able to undertake other more sophisticated disruptive innovations that range from financial-stock market advice, home insurance management, and personal finances in general. It will only be necessary to give the order to our smart speaker, watch, or mobile phone to execute increasingly complex processes.

vi. Medicine and health

In Europe where health expenditure currently represents more than 15% of total public spending invested and an increasingly aging society, any initiative aimed at improving its efficiency will be key.

The expected advances in the coming years are linked to the treatment and prevention of diseases and injuries, development of

---

186. theguardian.com/technology/2015/mar/13/halifax-trials-heartbeat-id-technology-for-online-banking

187. firstpost.com/tech/news-analysis/using-ai-in-financial-fraud-detection-can-help-banks-save-unnecessary-losses-4648611.html

new drugs linked to longevity,[188] genetic computation,[189] improvement of patient management, and self-diagnosis. There are so many expected advances in e-Health (electronic processes), tele-Health (medical tele-assistance) and m-Health (applications via mobile), that again we are forced to highlight only some of them:

1. Advanced diagnosis of diseases: deep learning algorithms are enabling important leaps in diagnoses and lowering their costs. From the sum of different data sources (mappings of chemical substances, daily tests, MRIs, or even handwritten information) the algorithms are capable of diagnosing diseases such as skin or breast cancer in seconds. The algorithms will help reduce the possibility of error in the decision-making of physicians.

2. Stopping epidemics and pandemics: AI will be key to identifying the point of origin of the global pandemics that we will experience in the 21st century and will facilitate an improvement in the allocation of resources, health interventions, and reducing the spread of diseases. The case of COVID-19 and the management of China, South Korea, and Singapore are a very good proof of this.

Globalization and climate change should put us on alert, as our generation will be especially vulnerable to global pandemics. Let's use the technology we have at hand to fight them intelligently.

3. Medicines development: Many of the analytical processes involved in drug development can be made more efficient with machine learning techniques, saving years of work and hundreds of millions in investment. AI has been successfully used in all four major stages of drug development: identifying targets for intervention, uncovering drug candidates, accelerating clinical trials, and finding biomarkers to diagnose disease.

188. "The anti-aging drug that's just around the corner": technologyreview.com/s/614154/the-anti-aging-drug-thats-just-around-the-corner/

189. A genetic algorithm is a heuristic search method used in AI and computing to find optimized solutions, searching for problems based on the theory of natural selection and evolutionary biology.

4. Personalisation of treatment: patients respond to drugs and doses unequally, and AI is helping to discover which characteristics of them cause them to react differently, allowing us to personalise the choice of the least aggressive and most effective treatment based on our clinical history. Especially in the fight against cancer or organ transplants, any breakthrough in this area can mean major advances in life expectancy.

5. Prevention in real-time: the health of each patient will be constantly evaluated from the data compiled by our wearables and smart products. Bracelets that measure the pulse, trainers that count the steps, scales that store information about weight and body fat, or sensorised mattresses that measure sleep quality. AI, drawing patterns and feeding on a database of medical records, will be able to prevent lifestyle diseases.

6. Management of waiting times: Health indicators and AI will also help healthcare to better manage waiting times of patients, being able to give priority to some, and refer others to teleconsultation. The results will be impressive.

7. Improve gene editing: Our genetic code has so much information that only the most advanced analysis systems will be able to manage its modification at affordable costs. The CRISPR system for gene editing, discovered by Nobel Prize candidate Francis Mojica, represents a breakthrough in cost-effective DNA editing, with machine learning models proven to produce the best results for increasing the precision of this technique.

vii. Tourism and urban services

Tourism is a "multi-service service", and it is becoming digitized to the extent that its different subsectors function: transport, accommodation, food, leisure, and so on. AI is already part of the tourism sector when we choose any destination using the Internet, when we follow the recommendations about a restaurant in some App, in the price management of hotel rooms, and of course, in the using of Google Maps at the destination.

For decades, the digitization of the tourism sector has focused on services at origin. Tripadvisor, Destinia, Booking, and even low-cost airlines have used their algorithms to optimise routes, prices and recommendations, transforming the way we travel over the last few decades. However, the tourism revolution in the next decade will occur at destinations. Hotels, taxis, restaurants, museums, and the cities in their entirety will be the subject of profound change driven by AI and the IoT.

The first examples are in large platforms such as Blablacar, Airbnb, and Uber, capable of having clients in half the world without having any assets in their ownership. The management of millions of requests per hour in their applications and an automated system of recommendations and pricing are enough to become the largest tourism companies by capitalization and results. Compared to traditional companies, these platforms increase the productivity of the sector and reduce the need for investment in infrastructure. Moreover, the information generated could serve to eliminate tax fraud in vacation rental activities or provide security for urban transport services, a major concern in many cities around the world.

Although the debate on the so-called "platform economy" deserves a whole chapter, it is evident that in most cities, Airbnb, Uber, Cabify, and the like have not been entirely well-received. However, can European destinations afford to do without services that are becoming standards across the globe? Is there a better alternative to fight the informal economy in the tourism sector? Isn't it more advisable for a destination to have a tourist buying in supermarkets and stores than secluding oneself in *all-inclusive* hotels? Is there another solution so that those who went bankrupt during the real estate financial crisis can obtain profitability from their real estate?

Demonizing collaborative platforms and preventing their activity will *only be bread for today and hunger for tomorrow*. We must abandon the all-out war against them to seek a formula for integration into tourism ecosystems that will extract maximum performance.

viii. Other transformations that are no less important

Although we have barely shown a small number of potential transformations, the reader will already be able to get a good idea of the effects of AI integration into our economies, so many that some scientists and experts don't even dare to put a ceiling on it. Neither will we. Beyond the industrial revolutions themselves, AI will also have a great impact on our society, our public sector, the organization of our cities, and even on how we carry out any of our day-to-day tasks. Let's take a final look at some social changes that will result from AI:

A personalized and unique world for each of us: The personalization of services will extend from commerce to education. Products, be they T-shirts or math problems, will be designed specifically for each user based on their interests or needs.

More efficient public administrations: The role of AI will be very relevant in the modernisation of areas such as justice and bureaucracy. AI is already starting to be used in the management and collection of taxes, in cross-referencing data to prevent tax fraud, or in providing public services in cities in an efficient way.

Creation of smart cities and tourist destinations: The sensorization projects of our cities for decision-making and state control promise a new era of urban coexistence. The dashboards will allow automatically to optimize the operation of cities through changes in the times of traffic lights, restricting the access of vehicles to areas with high pollution, studying the state of artistic and architectural heritage,[190] or even managing alerts and recommendations to tourists to diversify the crowding of streets.

Natural Language Processing (Chatbots): The application of AI to Natural Language Processing (NLP) currently allows spectacular progress in machine translation and virtual assistance. Our current *Google Home* and *Amazon Alexa* are the first versions of systems that will incorporate more and more facets to help people with their work, health, leisure, and any day-to-day task, from driving autonomously to regulating the shower temperature.[191]

---

190. The Santa María La Real Foundation, a leader in the application of IoT to cultural heritage, can measure with sensors the evolution of cracks, the advance of woodworm in wood, or humidity and extreme temperatures and their effects on the conservation of historical assets.

191. observatorio-ia.com/alexa-ahora-tambien-en-tu-ducha

Self-taught humanoid robotics: We can't forget robotics either, with AI helping automation processes break boundaries imposed by complexity. Robots no longer work with a single assigned task; deep learning allows them to operate based on a variety of situations, and more importantly, discover how to use objects and tools to achieve their purposes by learning both from their attempts and from interaction with human beings.[192] These advances go beyond conventional supervised learning methods.

Even the limits of art are being redefined by AI. Machines are capable of recognizing anonymous works, rejuvenating actors on screen, or imitating with such quality that even experts are not able to differentiate them from the originals.[193]

Technology for social good: In short, we are witnessing an explosion of algorithms for a wide range of human progress.[194] And although we have not been able to reflect all of them, the examples are endless: earthquake detection,[195] support for disabled people,[196] high-risk decision-making,[197] advanced drug development[198] or personalized teaching of easy-to-learn gamified English.

---

192. Xie, A., Ebert, F., Levine, S., & Finn, C. (2019). *Improvisation through physical understanding: Using novel objects as tools with visual foresight.*

193. "Computer paints 'new Rembrandt' after old works analysis" bbc.com/news/technology-35977315.

194. Some algorithms are on the way to becoming real celebrities, such as GAN (Generative Adversarial Network), Back-propagation algorithm (backprop), and Perceptron. The advances in hardware of companies such as Google with its tensor processing unit in 2017 are also key. Thanks to them, and without waiting for quantum computing, the results of AI are accelerating.

195. Researchers in Caltech's seismology laboratory have made decades of earthquake research advance through simulation.

196. The AccessMap team at the University of Washington is generating interactive maps of the physical environment of pedestrian walkways.

197. Researchers like Yan LeCun are taking leaps and bounds in supervised learning that will allow machines to learn as fast as humans do.

198. Kai-Fu Lee is an American computer scientist, businessman, and writer based in Beijing. His research and applications in AI and big data are optimizing drug supply chains, reducing shortages for more than 150 million people in rural China. He is the author of AI Superpowers: China, Silicon Valley, and the New World Order.

5. THERE WILL BE NO ARTIFICIAL INTELLIGENCE WITHOUT DATA

5.1. European vision and opportunity costs

Once the prospects for the impact of AI on our sectors, our wealth and our well-being have been set out, the question arises: how ambitious is Europe's approach to the new technological era? The following extract from the European Commission's report "Artificial Intelligence: A European Perspective" gives us an idea:

> *Currently, the global competition on AI is largely between the USA and China. For the EU, it is not so much a question of winning or losing a race, but of finding the way of embracing the opportunities offered by AI in a way that is human-centred, ethical, secure, and true to our core values.*
>
> *We have many areas of strength, including excellent research, extremely rich cultural diversity, and leadership in some industrial sectors, such as automotive and robotics.[199]*

The above paragraphs imply that Europe does not deliberately compete with the US and China by focusing on its humanist vision, which leads us to a debate that does not leave the European Commission in good stead. Are they saying that they are aware of the digital gap and are not acting to correct it? Or that they have not measured the opportunity cost and the loss of competitiveness, wealth and employment that technological dependence implies?

We are not arguing that the European Union should not be faithful to its values, because in fact one of its founding objectives is to "promote the welfare of its peoples". It is therefore unacceptable to justify technological delay when it runs counter to its own principles: one does not need to be an economist to foresee the weak growth

---

199. European Commission: *Artificial Intelligence: A European Perspective* (No. JRC113826), pp. 17.

prospects that we face in the medium and long term if our technological dependence on the US increases, or if Asia-Pacific continues to gain competitiveness in Europe's most representative sectors.

The "privacy bubble" to which the EU subjects its industries will have catastrophic consequences if it is not corrected. Firstly, because data is the fundamental input of the new digital age. Its fuel, its oxygen. Without data there is no possibility of training algorithms. Without algorithms there is no AI or its derivative technologies. And without them our economies lose capacity to create jobs and wealth.

Secondly, because regulatory measures and the media scourge on privacy delay the digitization process of countries, with a progressive loss of trust by administrations and users in the services they use. Remember how the current GDPR led to sanctions against a Swedish city council for the use of facial recognition in schools, or the more than 200 million euros that the airline IAG had to pay.

In short, the European Commission's "citizen protection" approach is turning against its economic and social future, something that has been highlighted by the European paralysis in the face of the COVID-19 crisis, and the Asian speed and agility in combating the virus, supported by the technological basis of AI and big data.

We will discuss this later.

The case of DeepMind Technologies

DeepMind Technologies was a company created in the United Kingdom in 2010. Its first great achievement was the development of a neural network that learned to play video games like humans, mimicking the brain's short-term memory.[200] In 2014 the company was acquired by Google, and in 2016 it became world-famous when its AlphaGo algorithm beat world Go champion Lee Sedol in a five-game match.

The most relevant activity carried out by DeepMind, and which concerns us in this section, is that developed in the healthcare sector.

---

200. en.wikipedia.org/wiki/DeepMind#Miscellaneous_contributions_to_Google

Among other projects, the company has collaborated with Moorfields Eye Hospital to develop applications looking for early signs of diseases that lead to blindness. Also, together with the University College London Hospitals, it is investigating the creation of an algorithm that can automatically differentiate between healthy and cancerous tissues in the head and neck areas. And it is working with the UK Cancer Research Center at Imperial College London to improve breast cancer detection by applying machine learning to mammography.

But of all its developments, we would like to focus on the agreement of DeepMind with the Royal Free London NHS Foundation Trust and the Imperial College Healthcare NHS Trust. The goal was to develop new clinical mobile applications linked to electronic patient records. With them, both medical test data and alerts to manage patient care were sent to the mobile phones of medical personnel.

The application, called "Stream", was very much welcomed since the professionals substantially improved the management of specific patients, such as those with acute kidney disease. In these cases, action times are key to saving lives, and Stream accelerated the reaction to any complication in patients.

When Google acquired DeepMind, all these developments became part of the Google Health division. And then came the controversy: the British data protection system announced that this agreement betrayed the trust of the patient, considering it a violation of European and national legislation on data protection.

It was also noted that there was no legal basis for Royal Free London to share its patients' medical records with the creators of the app. Concurrently, it was alleged that there were no guarantees that patients' information would be studied only by professionals who have their full permission.

However, when we talk about saving lives, as is the case with COVID-19, would any patient object to having their history checked by more than one doctor to have a better diagnosis? Isn't the possible leakage of data between colleagues or professionals an acceptable risk when the life of a loved one is at stake?

Once again, on such an important issue, citizens should be free to make their decisions. It would be easy to ask: Do you agree to share your data for the improvement of medical research? Do you agree to have your information processed by more than one professional to improve your diagnosis? Do you agree to take the risk of your data being recorded anonymously in a cloud that has a competent security system?

Let European patients decide between the extreme safeguarding of their privacy or contributing to better health services and new research. We are capable of donating organs even to strangers. Do they really think we care that much about giving up our anonymized medical records to contribute to curing diseases?

Without undermining the right to privacy, safeguarding our data seems to be given higher priority than saving our lives. In Europe, it is legally easier to donate a vital organ such as a kidney than to share our medical records anonymously.

5.2. A new approach to the GDPR

The EU has developed a discourse and legislation on privacy from a restrictive perspective for technological development, which is unfair and inefficient for its motivational purposes. As we have already explained, any data guardian is vulnerable to information theft, no matter how zealous they are. Even the most advanced and expensive devices like iPhones are not impregnable.[201]

Therefore, threatening with certain types of sanctions, rather than helping the digital economy, compromises the future activity of any company that works with sensitive data due to the wariness of the penalties.

European data protection policy must seek to defend citizens in cases of real vulnerability. Such as when we are subject to a blatant violation of our privacy, or when we have suffered online fraud, or by acting against the black market in payment services accounts. A good example of necessary digital action occurred in August 2019 in

---

201. The Google Threat Analysis Group (TAG) warned at the end of February 2019 that several web pages had been attacking iPhone users for about two years, exploiting 14 vulnerabilities present in the mobile operating system of Apple, iOS. googleprojectzero.blogspot.com/2019/08/a-very-deep-dive-into-ios-exploit.html

Spain, when a citizen was arrested in Madrid for uploading 555 videos to a porn website of hundreds of women recorded with a mobile gadget installed on the top of a backpack, which he left on the ground next to victims in train cars or lines at the supermarket.[202] The performance of the Spanish police was brilliant, and the sanction should be severe.

However, preventing cybercrime is as complex as preventing supermarket robberies, scams, or any other non-digital fraud. Analog crimes have been with us for millennia, and only education in schools, the provision of specialized security forces, and new technologies can eradicate them. The current GDPR should serve as a criminal framework, not as a coercive and restrictive tool at the service of the traditional economy. It is not acceptable that the right to privacy conditions the development of sectors in Europe, such as healthcare, whose potential based on AI requires a lot of data and anonymized medical records.

We think that it would be interesting if a real debate were opened on the opportunity costs of the over-dimensioning the right to privacy, and that patients, families and society in general could decide on the value given to data protection when our health is at stake. Fortunately, legal professionals like Mikel Recuero[203] are increasingly appearing to question the "legal labyrinth that ends up delaying or even stopping important medical advances or new diagnostic tools."[204]

It is not about giving up our right to privacy, but about understanding privacy with a new approach based on the freedom to decide of each user in matters as essential as their financial future or their health.

---

202. elpais.com/sociedad/2019/08/21/actualidad/1566377166_355922.html

203. Researcher at the UPV / EHU Faculty of Law awarded the second prize for research by the Spanish Agency for Data Protection.

204. elcorreo.com/bizkaia/premiado-investigador-upvehu-20200204130133-nt.html

6. SOME CONCRETE PROPOSALS: DATA AND PRIVACY

To prevent the high opportunity cost derived from oversized privacy in Europe, we propose the following solutions:

1. Draw up an "Ambitious Artificial Intelligence Development Plan" in Europe as a whole, with large funding available for success stories and new startups in key strategic sectors and a plan focused on benefiting not only key sectors such as health, administration, and education but also the rest of the representative sectors of the EU countries, with AI as an engine of competitiveness and differentiating element.

The European bet on AI should exceed those assumed by the United States and China to regain lost ground. The amount of EU investment should not fall below **100 billion euros**.

2. Create a fair, efficient, and clear legal framework that encourages the use of data for the public good, facilitating and encouraging access to this data for research and establishing guidelines to minimize the risk of data leakage or transfer.

3. Support investment in open data and the construction of databases and datasets of high interest for the progress of critical sectors such as medicine, smart cities, public services, and citizen service, where AI can generate enormous benefits for the whole of society.

4. Educate citizens so that they can freely decide between the benefits, costs, and risks of sharing their data. For example, they know how to weigh whether they prefer not to share any data (such as their consumption habits) or share it with companies that offer personalized products such as Netflix, Amazon, financial institutions, or the supermarket around the corner.

5. Make it easy for citizens to exercise their right to transfer their medical or other data in well-informed environments.

6. Facilitate startups to adopt ethical codes regarding the use of AI and data without the financial cost being a barrier. Without a doubt, the economic value that the exploitation of this data has can generate the base of an entire industry and the strengthening of the digital economy.

7. Facilitate infrastructure and access to computational processing capacity for large databases and small companies.

8. Encourage and support cybersecurity positively and proactively, helping the institutions, companies, and startups that may be more vulnerable.

9. Promote in global forums a harsh international criminalization of cybercrimes, harmonizing the legislation of the countries.

10. Adjust and establish a global consensus on an international typology for cybercrime and ensure that all its features are in line with the fundamental rights of individuals.

CHAPTER 6: PROSPECTS FOR JOB CREATION AND DESTRUCTION IN THE DIGITAL AGE

« The countries with the highest robot density have the lowest unemployment rates ».

ULRICH SPIESSHOFER, President and CEO of ABB.

We are approaching a time of automation of a large number of tasks, which will particularly affect labour-intensive sectors. Europe and the rest of the world are facing an era of exponential changes that will lead us to an unknown situation. Will the new jobs created by the digital economy compensate for job destruction in mature sectors? Will a consensus on wealth distribution be reached? Will we ever need a global universal income?

It is difficult to predict, but what we know basing on many indicators is that demand for STEM (science, technology, engineering, and mathematics) skills and their hybridization with any other branch of knowledge will increase over the years, leading to a "talent war" for which the countries of the European Union will have to prepare conscientiously.

Job creation for a country that wants to maintain its level of wages and salaries will depend on the digital economy and those technologies that feed the competitiveness of mature sectors.

1. EUROPEAN PESSIMISM ABOUT EMPLOYMENT IN THE DIGITAL ECONOMY

All past generations, without exception, have faced technological progress and its impact on employment. Agricultural machinery eliminated manual labor and animal draft tasks with centuries of tradition, hydrocarbons closed coal mines, advances in telecommunications left millions of telemarketers unemployed, and more recently, advanced robotics (industries 4.0) has replaced human capital in factories in any sector.

It is what we know as "technological unemployment" - one of the study topics par excellence in economic theory since the end of the 18th century. To date, this tech unemployment hasn't led to a job apocalypse or anything like it. The agricultural revolution led to a massive global exodus from the countryside to the city, from working in the primary sector to construction and industry. Later, the industrial transformation gave way to a revolution in services, with training being adapted to the new tasks.

In the case of Spain, for example, in 1901, agriculture occupied 66.7% of the active population. Industrialization and the introduction of technologies in the sector have reduced the figure to 4.7%; nevertheless, the modernization process has multiplied GDP by 15.[205] With these data and the common good in mind, what credibility would a government have that is more concerned with the destruction of agricultural employment than with the possibilities of industrial and tertiary work? Or that did not promote an education according to the technological paradigm shift?

---

205. With the model change, most of the underemployment hidden in the agricultural sector also disappeared, generating in turn diversity and entities of public and private jobs unthinkable 100 years ago.

The effects of a disruptive change in employment

Before the computer age, machines succeeded in replacing human or animal "brute force", speeding up tasks and eliminating danger. The appearance of microchips made it possible to end millions of routine and repetitive tasks, in addition to working remotely and operating devices in unsafe scenarios.

Today AI is aiming to replace cognitive tasks of all kinds, such as identifying cancerous tumors, tracing stock market investment patterns or making new scientific discoveries.[206]

This qualitative technological leap will have consequences on employment that we could not imagine a few decades ago, as reflected in the research at the University of Oxford carried out by Carl Frey and Michael Osborne[207]. According to the paper, 47% of jobs in the US are capable of being automated with existing technology. And 90% of the rest will undergo changes so significant that they will bear little resemblance to the current ones.

Other reports such as "What's now and next in analytics, AI, and automation"[208] by McKinsey Global Institute or "The macroeconomic impact of artificial intelligence"[209] by PwC support this prediction and put labor-intensive sectors such as construction and transportation on alert. Countries like China, Brazil, Russia, India, Mexico, and Italy would be at risk of massive automation of jobs **(figure 6.1)**. In the best-case scenario, job destruction figures would be reduced to 9%.[210]

---

206. agenciasinc.es/Noticias/El-algoritmo-que-actua-como-un-cientifico

207. This is the most important work that has been done on the possibilities of job automation. See: Frey, C. B., & Osborne, M. A. (2017). The future of employment: How susceptible are jobs to computerisation? *Technological forecasting and social change*, 114, 254-280.

208. mckinsey.com/featured-insights/digital-disruption/whats-now-and-next-in-analytics-ai-and-automation

209. pwc.co.uk/economic-services/assets/macroeconomic-impact-of-ai-technical-report-feb-18.pdf

210. Arntz, M, T Gregory and U Zierahn (2016) The risk of automation for jobs in OECD countries: a comparative analysis, OECD social, employment and migration. Working papers, no.189. Paris: OECD.

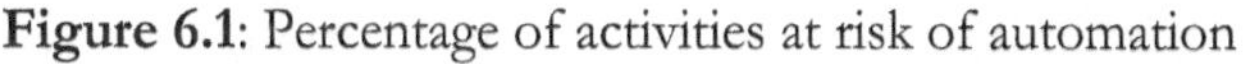

Figure 6.1: Percentage of activities at risk of automation

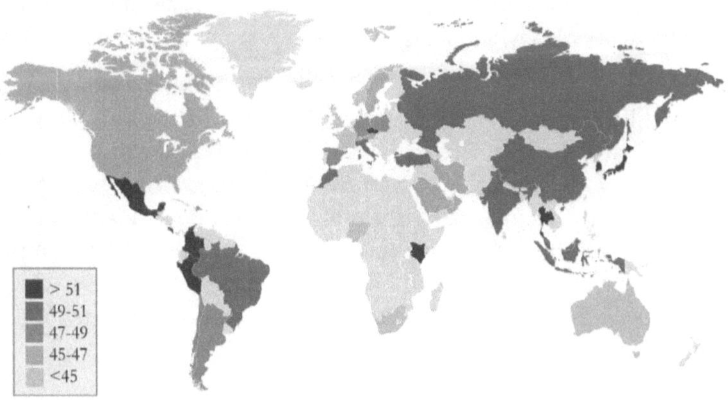

Source: Mckinsey Global Institute

Despite the different techniques used and some methodological issues that should be addressed,[211] it is necessary to highlight three key facts on which all the reports coincide:

1) AI and the rest of the disruptive technologies will cause a global employment 'shock' that will affect labor-intensive sectors.

2) The transformation will be dramatic for economies that do not adapt their productive fabric to the technological forefront.

3) New jobs will be especially associated with STEM [212] skills and technologies that fuel the competitiveness of mature sectors.

The predominant political message

In Spain, one of the countries with the highest youth unemployment rates in the EU, official statistics echo the digital talent deficit to fill the demand of the private sector. Also, the European Commission has warned of the need to fill millions of jobs in the field of

---

211. For example, Osborne and Frey derive results for 700 jobs from the analysis of just 70 work activities. One might also wonder if automated tasks will not lead to new ones that require human supervision even in the same job position.

212. Let's remember: science, technology, engineering, and math.

new technologies.[213] If the European or Spanish economy could satisfy these demands and incline its productive specialization towards the digital areas in which it lags the most, surely the unemployment data would be reduced to unprecedented figures.

Despite this, in 2017 the current President of the Spanish government published a tweet on International Labor Day (May 1) that said: *"I encourage unity to face unemployment, long-term joblessness, poverty and the digitization of the economy"* **(figure 6.2)**. We do not want to make a personal criticism or disqualify the political party: this is just a sample of entrenched and widespread opinions in European politics, which convey a very negative message to society as a whole, warning of the dangers of the digital economy.

Figure 6.2. Tweet by Pedro Sánchez

Source: Twitter[214]

---

213.   ec.europa.eu/commission/commissioners/2014-2019/ansip/blog/digital-skills-jobs-and-need-get-more-europeans-online_en

214. twitter.com/sanchezcastejon/status/859003484582158336

The discourse of a large part of European political left and right, entrenched in protectionist attitudes, shows more interest in safeguarding the present than in responding to the labor demands of the future. This approach is leading parties to distance themselves more and more from the new generations of digital workers, who do not feel protected by their legitimate representatives, with inflexible regulations that do not take into account the possibility of teleworking from anywhere in the world, or the lack of regulatory agility.

We need all political parties, without ideological distinction, to create agreements and national pacts around the digital future. Public opinion and media must also emphasize the creation of new jobs to compensate for the destruction that will inevitably occur. Digitalization must be understood as the only possibility, not as the enemy to beat.

2. TOWARDS A STEM TALENT STRATEGY IN EUROPE

All experts and international organizations agree on defining STEM skills as the basis of future professions, although we have to clarify some aspects. When we talk about professionals in the sectors of the future, we are not only encouraging our students to become scientists, mathematicians, or computer scientists but also to hybridize knowledge using STEM skills in a transversal way in any other specialty.

The best way to preserve any profession and its jobs is to reinvent them using new capacities and skills provided by current technologies. The work of cab drivers, messengers, teachers, architects, doctors, biologists, philosophers and lawyers will last for decades. However, these professionals must be aware that in a shorter period than they can imagine, they will find themselves performing tasks that are completely different from those they do today.

Doctors will coexist with AI tools capable of making real-time diagnoses to propose effective individualized treatments. Police officers will use facial recognition and automated drones to tackle imminent dangers. Teachers may be experts in enhancing the emotional intelligence of their students, reformulate their functions with more psycho-pedagogical skills and teaching techniques where gamification and personalization have more weight. Taxi drivers may have to serve as passenger assistance because cars will drive autonomously through our streets.

In this way, we can define "digital talent" as the human capital trained to participate in this transformation of the labor market. People with transversal STEM skills, who will be present and highly demanded in all professions of the productive fabric. In just two decades in the EU, the number of professionals with higher education linked to the areas of science and technology has almost tripled, with all the countries of the old continent (especially Finland, Belgium, Norway, Sweden, Ireland, and Denmark) increasing their recruitment **(figure 6.3)**.

223

In concrete figures, we have gone from less than 20 million jobs generated in technological areas in 2000 in Europe to more than 55 million today, from 14% of the active population to almost 22%. Something very similar happens in the United States, with STEM professionals receiving a salary, on average, 26% higher than other jobs.

Figure 6.3. Active population with higher education employed in science and technology areas (% of the total workforce)

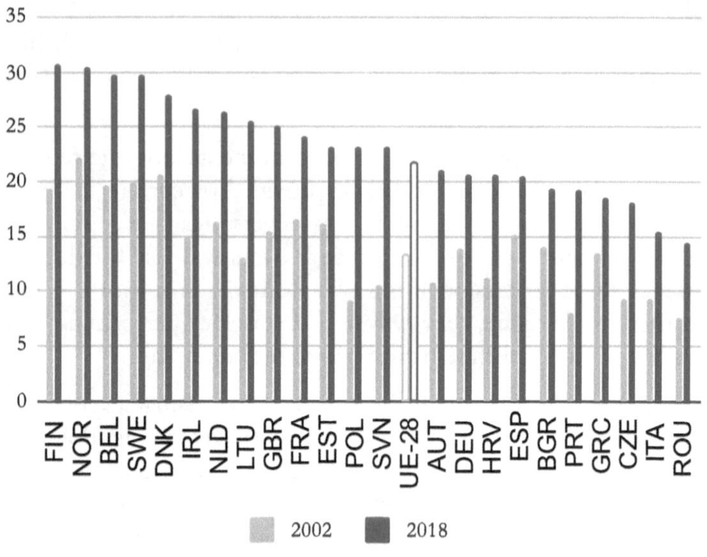

Source: Eurostat

The data leaves little room for doubt, with forecasts skyrocketing in the next five years. In the US, a growth of more than 12% per year is expected in the labor demand for computer engineers and more than 30% per year for experts in statistics and mathematics.[215] In the EU, there will be more than 7 million new jobs that will require STEM skills: enough to hire all the unemployed in the economies of Mediterranean Europe.

---

215. "STEM Occupations: Past, Present, And Future" report from the US. Bureau of Labor Statistics.

Also, Spain, the second country with the highest youth unemployment in Europe, will need to cover more than 1 million STEM jobs if it takes on the challenges of digital transformation. The Spanish National Innovation Survey warns that more than 20% of companies are unable to innovate due to lack of trained personnel, and more than 50% have no thought of promoting an innovation process, surely due to lack of knowledge of its managers of the new possibilities of the market.[216]

Faced with this inertia in labor demand, organizations such as the International Monetary Fund warned of a STEM job deficit of more than 40 million this decade. The European Commission has also shuffled in speeches the figure of 825,000 job vacancies related to computing and telecommunications.

However, this shortage of STEM professionals is not affecting all regions equally. Finland, US, Israel, Canada, and Germany have a wide availability of scientists and engineers in their labor markets **(figure 6.4)**, making the attraction of talent a spearhead of their economies. On the other hand, France, Spain, Belgium, Denmark or Italy among others show a deficit that they should try to solve as soon as possible, just as China or South Korea are doing by prioritizing their educational policies.

The subject is not trivial. The differences in the training and availability of STEM professionals could accentuate the digital and economic gap between the two Europes, and also between Europe and the US and Asia, with relevant impacts on income and employment.

It is, therefore, worth asking why those countries with the highest structural unemployment do not focus on the digital economy to promote mass hiring. If we were concerned about youth unemployment, we should stimulate the skills that will be key in future sectors and accompany them with measures to prevent the drain of talent to third countries.

---

216. National Innovation Survey, the year 2018, carried out by the National Institute of Statistics. See in the Science and Technology Section of the website ine.es.

Figure 6.4. Availability of engineers and scientists in the labor market (1: not available - 7 available)

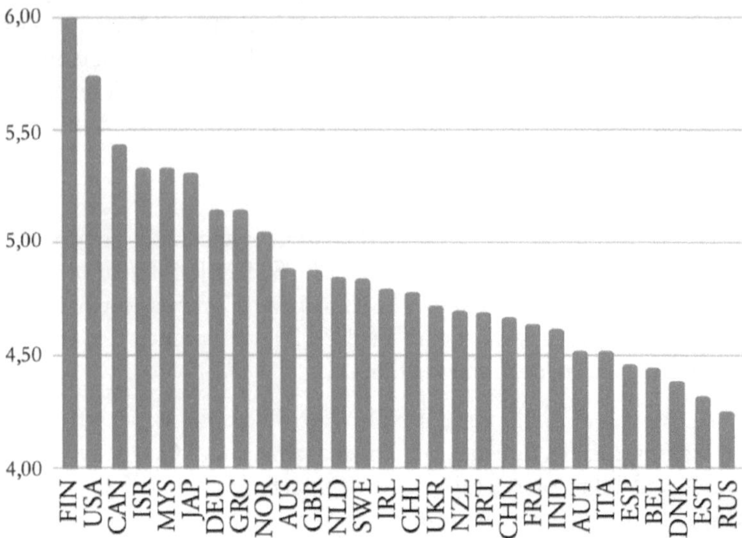

Source: World Economic Forum and the World Bank

3. EUROPE AND THE WORLD WAR OF TALENT

3.1 Bringing society closer to the new STEM

AI has opened up a scenario for the renewal of all professions, in addition to creating a large number of jobs to exploit and enhance the new technological tools. The impact of this technology will be exceptionally visible not only in the most routine and repetitive activities but also in those in which human behavior can be imitated or improved by machines.

Can someone precisely delimit the most demanded profiles for the coming years? Clearly not. It will be the market that makes the adjustments at all times. Yet, given that it is STEM skills that sustain the current technological wave, we can assure that as education systems train their students with these knowledges, the data on net job creation will be more positive.

Society must view the new technological age not as a danger but as a challenge, not as an army of algorithms ready to steal data and jobs but as the answer to humanity's challenges. Europe needs to emphasize the discourse on the digital economy to give it the recognition and importance it deserves.

The response of young people and technological specialization

Historically in Europe there has been a high interest in STEM subjects with an increase in enrollment in all its areas of study. Only architecture is the discordant note due to the real estate crisis of 2008. Germany, Austria or even Greece have a high volume of students in scientific, technological or engineering fields, with relative values even higher than South Korea, Sweden or the United States (**figure 6.5**). Portugal, Romania, Sweden and Finland also have more than 25% of STEM graduates in all disciplines.

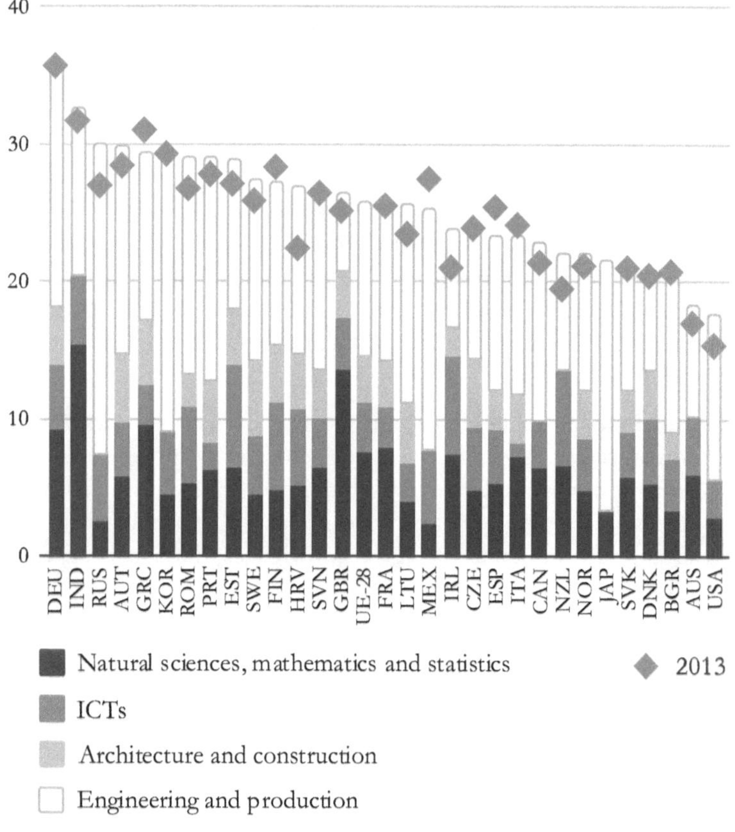

Source: Eurostat and OECD

So where is Europe's problem?

The high European dependence on traditional industries means that the contribution of scientists, engineers, and technicians to the workforce is less productive than in other countries. Remember the difference between "innovation" and "disruption" that we discussed: Europe has specialized in innovation, but not in the disruption necessary to reach technological leadership.

The companies that are revolutionizing the automotive (Tesla, Google), tourism (Airbnb), education (Coursera), retail (Amazon, Alibaba) or transportation (Uber, Didi) sectors were born far from the old continent. It is in the countries where these businesses are located that STEM skills are more closely linked to digitization.

In Europe, on the other hand, there is a greater connection with practices that do not lead to a renewal of the industrial fabric, but to a constant improvement. The existence of STEM professionals is a prerequisite, but not a sufficient condition. The interesting figures presented by some countries in STEM training, as is the case of Greece, lose strength in a context not specialized in disruption and digital economy.

3.2. The Global War for Talent

There is currently an estimated worldwide STEM talent shortage of more than 80 million, [217] which will cause a "global war for talent" [218] to recruit the best-qualified professionals to tackle the challenges of the digital economy.

In the age of knowledge, human capital is the key factor to explain the competitiveness of economies. Indeed the American historian and best-selling author Arthur Herman has already warned of an imminent crisis caused by the shortage of graduates in science and engineering in the US. Only 14% of the students are training in STEM areas, insufficient to cover the demand for employment[219]. The US response to this crisis is to attract international talent, thanks to the high salaries in the big tech companies and the possibilities for entrepreneurship in their ecosystems.

The opposite case is occurring in Israel, and especially in Canada, which are redoubling their efforts with pioneering AI training plans.[220] The result has been the relocation of large multinational technology companies to their research centers. China, although there are no official data, also seems to be doing its best. Some estimates suggest that between 35% and 40% of its university students are enrolled in STEM programs. In absolute terms, we are talking

---

217. "The global talent crunch" report produced by Korn Ferry.
218. Michaels, E., Handfield-Jones, H., & Axelrod, B. (2001). *The war for talent.* Harvard Business Press.
219. hudson.org/research/14547-america-s-high-tech-stem-crisis
220. The city of Montreal boasts the highest per capita concentration of AI researchers and students in the world: 5 per 1,000 inhabitants.

about 5 million STEM graduates per year![221] Almost twice as many as India (2.6 million), and eight times more than the United States (600,000 students) according to IMF data. The "MIC 2025" plan continues on its course to achieve technological leadership.

Europe, however, does not have a clear common strategy for attracting or creating digital talent, beyond the funding of projects under the H2020 umbrella. As we will see below, European technology companies cannot compete with Asian and American dominance, and educational plans are less ambitious than in the countries that are called to lead the new technological paradigm.

Year after year, China, Singapore, Japan, Taiwan and South Korea occupy the top positions in the PISA report in mathematics and science. Given this scenario, the EU runs the risk of becoming segmented in terms of labor and competition. And this is not a north-south divide: the Netherlands, Denmark and Belgium suffer from a deficit of STEM professionals of the same magnitude as Italy or Spain.[222]

The effort to empower our young people and professionals in STEM subjects must be traced from a correct strategy. The objective should not only be to transform conventional sectors but to converge with the most disruptive economies in cutting-edge technologies, thus responding to future job vacancies that have not yet been invented.

---

221. bbc.com/news/business-35776555

222. [222] In Spain, since 2001, the demand for university enrollment in engineering and architecture has fallen by 30.5 percent. The 2008 economic crisis disrupted the evolution, especially of the second, according to a report by Ivie. See: dx.medra.org/10.12842/INFORME_SUE_2018

4. WOMEN IN A STEM WORLD

Encouraging employment and training in AI and other disruptive technologies should be the first step for Europe if it wants to get closer to the US and China. And in this promotion of STEM talent and performance, European and national administrations must be obsessed with incorporating more women into these knowledge areas.

According to data from the European Commission, the equality of men and women in the digital industry would raise the GDP of the EU by around 9 billion euros per year. Also, it would help reduce the gender pay gap. However, we are far from parity:

- In OECD countries, only 1 in 5 IT and telecommunications graduates are women.

- In 107 of the 114 nations registered by UNESCO, the number of graduates in technical careers is less than 50%. In the EU no country shows figures higher than 45% **(figure 6.6)**.

- In Europe, the ratio of female engineers employed in high-tech sectors is 1 to 4 compared to their male colleagues **(figure 6.7)**, and only a small fraction of them achieve leadership in technology companies and research.

Countries must design imaginative and effective programs and measures to overcome the cultural gender barrier with technology. It is necessary to break down stereotypes, highlight great female leaders in STEM areas, and to change the perception of subjects such as mathematics or physics from an early age.[223]

If women do not join en masse in the construction of the new world that is beginning to be drawn and we do not eliminate the barriers that prevent them from growing professionally, their interests, desires, and needs will be underrepresented.

---

223. In Spain, only 8% of 15-year-old girls say they want to study a career related to technology, while almost 25% of boys of that age say they want to.

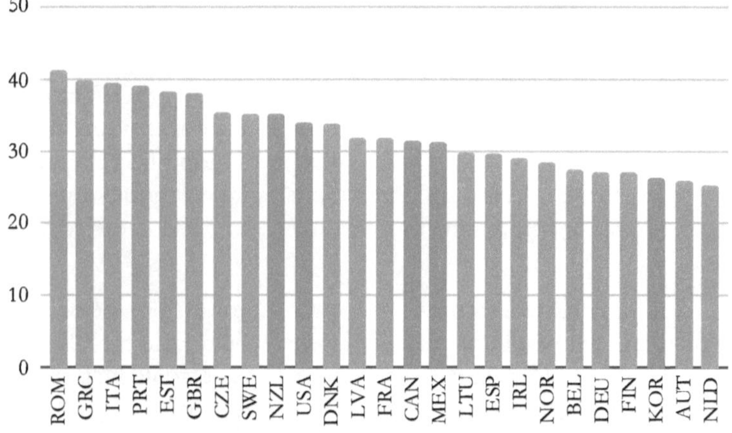

Source: UNESCO

Figure 6.7. Percentage of female engineers employed over the total and in high technology sectors

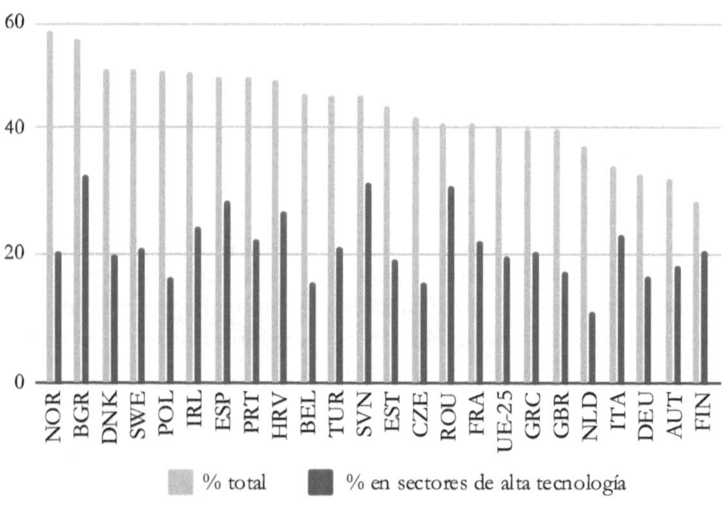

Source: Eurostat

5. THE STEM REVOLUTION REQUIRES A DIGITAL TRANSFORMATION

The study of job creation-destruction is very recurrent in the history of economic thought, from the profoundly negative initial vision of David Ricardo and Malthus ("machines destroy net jobs"), the excessively positivist idea of John Stuart Mill ("technical progress occurs slowly, and therefore its impact is minimal"), to the more realistic of McCulloh's temporal mismatch ("in the medium term the creation of machines generates more employment than such machines destroy").

Of all, perhaps the most accurate is the vision of the first Nobel laureate in economics, Jan Tinbergen: "innovation tends to raise the demand for the most qualified workers." Yet to face the era of AI and automation, it is essential to qualify the sentence: "innovation tends to raise the demand for the most qualified workers ... in the disciplines and sectors that drive such innovation."

However, measures to boost the skills of the jobs of the future will be of no use without a productive fabric that is committed to the cutting edge of technology. This is the case in Spain, where demand for IT professionals grew by 6% between 2018 and 2019,[224] a smaller increase than that experienced by occupational risk technicians (27%), crane operators (19.4%), and courier and messengers (16%). With these data in hand, we might think that it might be smarter for Spaniards to spend their time completing an analog training rather than hybridizing STEM knowledge.

The public administration must react as soon as possible in countries like Spain, where there is a high risk of losing a whole generation of people who think that they will find a professional opportunity in traditional industries rather than in the so-called sectors of the future.

---

224. elpais.com/economia/2020/01/31/actualidad/1580471100_13.html

New technologies broaden the horizon of tasks that can be automated every day, while at the same time they present us new challenges for which, if the situation is not reversed, we will not be prepared. Once again, we emphasize the same idea: in the medium term, education in the most innovative fields will be the ones that offer the best guarantees of success in the labor market.

6. SOME CONCRETE PROPOSALS: DIGITAL EMPLOYMENT

We recapitulate concrete proposals regarding employment and the labor market seen in this chapter:

1. We must maximize opportunities to create new jobs in the digital economy. The labor market will be subject to very relevant tensions and convulsions in the creation and destruction of employment. **The STEM strategy seems to be the strongest way to bet on future jobs and advanced technology sectors.**

2. The balance between job destruction and digital job creation is linked to the country's strategy. An ideal solution would consist of a country that is committed to being a powerhouse in disruptive technologies, making the most of its STEM resources – with a prior educational commitment.

3. Avoid the political syndrome "against digitization". Old Europe sees its job market in danger due to the prospects of job destruction, the entity of youth unemployment, and the high levels of population aging. The destruction of routine jobs will give competitiveness to its traditional industries, and the commitment to future sectors will generate new, more qualified, and better-paid jobs.

4. The most powerful labor policy in the digital age is education. As we will see in the next chapter, it is education policies that can revolutionize the job market and a solid strategy to lead the new era of AI and digital technologies. Only an educational revolution (computational thinking in primary and secondary schools and university employability) will allow us to confront and guarantee the huge changes that are coming.

5. Non-digitization can lead to significant job gaps between young and old, or between rigid and immovable public employees and the self-employed willing to continually reinvent themselves. And it also carries a gender gap. The non-incorporation of women into the technological areas of the economy implies a high cost both for the potential of the country and for women's own opportunities to access the best paid and most lucrative jobs in working life.

6. The incorporation of women into the technology market is a central and key aspect for any country as a strategy for the future. Remarking on the previous point, it is difficult for a country to overcome the lack of STEM capital without the full incorporation of women into the technological field. Those countries that are not efficient in incorporating policies for women will see their growth possibilities diminished.

CHAPTER 7: THE EDUCATION AND TALENT REVOLUTION IN THE CONTEXT OF DISRUPTIVE TECHNOLOGIES

« Education is the most powerful weapon you can use to change the world ».

NELSON MANDELA.

« The illiterate of the 21st century will not be those who cannot read and write, but those who cannot learn».

ALVIN TOFFLER.

If we want to confront the great challenges that the 21st century brings us, we need to prepare the society of the future with an extremely solid education, thinking about the complex problems that human beings must respond to.

How do we do it?

The American economist James Heckman[225] gives us some clues about this in his book "Schools, Skills, and Synapses"[226] in which, with econometric models, he demonstrated that educational investment in childhood is the one with the greatest cognitive impact and presents the highest rates of return. A "preventive" action that surpasses any other social activities

Stopping climate change, the management of the immense power linked to artificial intelligence, and dealing with global pandemics are examples of why we have never needed so much of this preventive

---

225. Received the Nobel Prize in Economics in 2000.
226. ftp.iza.org/dp3515.pdf

education. Avoiding the disaster that can be wrought by the "dissatisfied gods"[227] that we have become, according to Yuval Noah Harari's *Brief History of Humanity*, will only be possible if we were educated in a manner consistent with the needs and difficulties of our environment, starting from a principle of sustainability and efficiency.

In this chapter we are going to focus on the direction that education in Europe must take in order to face digitalization and the great challenges of the current technological paradigm with solvency. This involves changing and improving our education systems, boosting computational skills in primary education, obsessing over employability and efficiency in universities, rewarding creativity and talent, and motivating lifelong learning.

No half-measures.

Education also needs a healthy dose of disruption.

---

227. Yuval Noah Harari, already mentioned above.

1. EDUCATION AS THE CENTRAL AXIS OF ECONOMIC POLICY

What is the first step that countries must take to ensure the subsequent competitiveness of their economies and the well-being of people in the digital age? What should be the priority on which to start building a society of the future? How should the uncertain threats that confront us as a species in the coming decades be addressed?

Answering these types of questions can be difficult; however, any response that we give will include education as one of its key elements. Betting on educational improvement, even when the country makes mistakes, usually yields revenues. In fact, it would be difficult to find cases in which increased spending on training human capital has had negative effects.

The Nobel Prize in Economics has finally paid the tribute it deserves to education, along with entrepreneurship and health, as a key factor in the fight against poverty, at its 2019 edition.[228] It is our obligation as economists to emphasize time and again that education policy must form part of the central axis of economic policy. The training of our professionals is the basis for competitiveness, decent employment and the improvement of a country's welfare.

Digital natives

In the EU, and once the basic needs for access to education have been solved decades ago, national administrations must be aggressive and demanding in their results. Their "digital education" must

---

228. Banerjee, Duflo, and Kremer were winners of the Nobel Prize in Economics for their studies on poverty reduction by helping to develop policies and incentives to help the poorest households. Banerjee and his wife, Esther Duflo - originally from India and France, respectively, and professors at MIT - took Kremer's methodology as a fundamental basis for evaluating other determining fields in development and the fight against poverty, focusing on education, health services, and entrepreneurship.

go far beyond the mere introduction of technological devices or some isolated competencies in the students' curriculum. It must be treated as a social requirement.

An analog population in the 21st century is a society vulnerable to fake news and phishing, fragmented by the technological gap, and without equal opportunities. Educational methods, almost petrified for decades, must be revolutionized to adapt to the profiles demanded by the digital society and drive the knowledge economy.

You may think that the right steps are being taken, or even that we are exaggerating. But the fallacy of "digital natives" shows us what a society in the age of AI should not be like: young people who are born surrounded by digital tools, but who limit their time on the Internet to social networks, Fortnite and WhatsApp. They barely know the endless possibilities to expand knowledge, nor the solutions to improve their productivity, neither think how the regulations on the digital environment affect their immediate future.

1.1. Countries that are committed to digital education

Some European countries have already begun a determined immersion in digital education that will revert in the medium term in three aspects:

-   Greater leadership in technological and economic development.

-   Faster and more effective implementation of the digital economy.

-   Greater assimilation capacity of digital education and efficiency in the fight against social gaps.

Finland and the UK, as European leaders, are already instilling digital values and possibilities by introducing computational thinking in primary and secondary schools. A decision that, in addition to generating reputation in its commitment to education, becomes a great endorsement for its economy and its digital development.[229] In

---

229. genbeta.com/actualidad/finlandia-creo-curso-inteligencia-artificial-pa

the case of the United Kingdom, it has even become the best response to the uncertainty after Brexit. Japan, Israel, and South Korea have also accelerated the introduction of computational thinking in their schools and are already working on the training of the future, including specific subjects and skills in programming, algorithm design and analytical problem solving..[230]

What advantages will these measures translate into for pioneer countries pioneering digital education? Again, three concrete elements:

-   Attraction of technological investments and location of companies for which human capital is a priority. Israel and Canada are a clear example.

-   The increased digital culture will serve to overcome the deficit of STEM talent. The technological vocation will also encourage hybridization with traditional sectors. [231]

-   The danger of a digital divide by gender or social strata is minimized. Students also acquire a greater capacity for entrepreneurship and for exploiting the full potential of advanced technologies.

Reasons enough to start the debate on where education in Europe should be heading in the decade that has just begun.

---

ra-sus-ciudadanos-ahora-esta-disponible-gratis-para-resto-mundo

230. Iyer S. (2019) Teaching-Learning of Computational Thinking in K-12 Schools in India. In: Kong SC., Abelson H. (eds) Computational Thinking Education. Springer, Singapore

231. Also, become familiar with new forms of education, such as continuous training, necessary in the face of such speed and entity disruptions.

2. PERSONALIZATION AGAINST SCHOOL FAILURE: AI AND PRIVACY

Our politicians should be obsessed with school failure and drop-outs' rates. There is nothing thornier for society than to see its talent fade away and how those who should protect the retirement of their elders do not achieve a minimum training.

However, does it make sense to set common learning goals when students have different vocations or learning abilities?

Students are not robots. Some learn faster than others. A few love mathematics, some soak up the humanities like sponges, and some simply want a ball. We find boys and girls with attention deficit and others that not even Peppa Pigg[232] entering the classroom would not break their concentration.

Faced with so many possibilities, it is worth asking, shouldn't we adapt education so that each student maximizes their chances of learning? Don't our students deserve a system that combines a different kind of education with non-discrimination and equal opportunities? Our education systems must address how to prevent students from dropping out of a subject or course due to lack of motivation, difficulty or laziness.

AI can be the solution to these problems if the EU takes the initiative and the lead in the personalization of educational processes. For example, facial recognition could help to identify at what point in an explanation learners switch off and what arouses their attention the most, a continuous analysis of the results obtained by students would help to develop follow-up and reinforcement exercises for students with different abilities, and a network of anonymized data shared between centers would allow the development of learning models adapted to different sociocultural conditions.

---

232. British cartoon series for children created by Neville Astley and Mark Baker.

China has already taken the global lead in employing AI in its education, with an investment of more than \$1 billion in 2019 for that purpose. According to MIT Technology Review the results are so surprising that we should already start questioning how we humans will learn in this century or what role teachers will play in classrooms.[233] However, the same article reminds us that a differential element with respect to the West is that "data privacy is much more lax", which allows increasingly sophisticated personalized teaching algorithms to be trained.

Europe has before it a great opportunity to balance and weigh its humanist tradition and its sensitivity to rights against the great challenge of transforming an education that allows each individual to develop their capacities to the maximum. To this end, the right to an inclusive and guaranteed education must be prioritized over an exaggerated privacy.[234]

---

233. See: technologyreview.com/2019/08/02/131198/china-squirrel-has-started-a-grand-experiment-in-ai-education-it-could-reshape-how-the/

234. We thank Jesús Conill, Professor of Moral and Political Philosophy at the University of Valencia for his teachings in the debate: "Artificial Intelligence, privacy, intimacy. The opportunity cost of technological delay". ÉTNOR Foundation Conference at TJ OST webpage: ost.torrejuana.es/inteligencia-artificial-inteligencia-artificial-privacidad-intimidad-el-coste-de-oportunidad-del-retraso-tecnologico/

3. COMPUTATIONAL THINKING IN PRIMARY AND SECONDARY EDUCATION

Given the predicted shortage of professionals with STEM skills, the first response must urgently be given in primary education, teaching our children to play and learn with the language of technology. Let them turn it into their ally to enhance their creativity and the efficiency of the tasks they will perform in the society around them.

In a generalized way and to date, educational programs have gradually incorporated technology subjects in schools and institutes, but without giving it the importance it deserves. Since the 1990s, when very basic computer classes (mainly Microsoft Office) were incorporated, the approach has barely changed. Today a student learns to work in the cloud and to relate to the digital environment, but subjects on robotics or the design of algorithms hardly have a place in extracurricular tasks in very few schools.

Computational thinking goes far beyond simply working with computers or learning code. It seeks to develop the ability to solve problems and design systems using fundamental computer science concepts (modeling and decomposing problems, processing data, creating algorithms and generalizing them). A subject designed for anyone, not just computer scientists or engineers, to take advantage of the benefits of disruptive technologies applied to any activity or job.

Let's see what advantages the implementation of computational thinking brings[235]:

---

235. See: Seow P., Looi CK., How ML., Wadhwa B., Wu LK. (2019) Educational Policy and Implementation of Computational Thinking and Programming: Case Study of Singapore. In: Kong SC., Abelson H. (eds) Computational Thinking Education. Springer, Singapore.

245

- **Mathematics and technology that is friendly for all:** learning from a very young age weakens cultural barriers and the traditional dread that mathematics and technological training arouse in children and young people.

- **Encouraging STEM vocations** corrects the vocational deficit of engineers, mathematicians, computer scientists, and scientists in general.

- **Promoting the inclusion of women in the technological field:** would alleviate the total shortage of STEM professionals in absolute terms and help reduce the wage gap between men and women.

- **It favors the disciplinary hybridization of technology with any sector:** doctors, biologists, architects, lawyers, or economists must know how to take advantage of the infinite potential of computing, the exploitation of big data, or tools such as deep learning to overcome any professional challenge. Or, quite simply, to work efficiently in multidisciplinary teams.

The task of implementing computational thinking is of critical urgency. If the EU wants to catch up with China and the US in the digital race, it is essential that sterile partisan debates that provoke spiraling educational reforms are put aside. Appropriate steps must be taken to provide schools with facilities and resources, to train teachers in new areas of knowledge, and to provide sufficient hours in the learning schedule.

In addition, our governments must accompany this proposal with a host of policy shocks, which will correct the STEM skills deficit as the first generations of students trained in computational skills emerge from primary school. Until we can see the first results, we must continue our efforts by creating conferences and congresses in universities, training cycles for companies with public funds, and especially by creating an open, online and quality educational offer in digital skills.

Furthermore, we believe that educational competencies should be homogenized at the European level, [236] with flexibility for each country, but preventing that due to ignorance, mistrust or ideological bias, a government can take away the strength of digital education, creativity and scientific knowledge from the school curriculum. with flexibility for each country, but preventing a government, through ignorance or mistrust, from taking strength away from digital education and scientific and creative skills to give it to other ideologically biased subjects.

---

236. Although an attempt has been made to cover this task with the Bologna Process at the university level, we should not ignore the mistakes made. For example, the program of the European Higher Education Area (EHEA) in practice penalizes the ability of universities to respond to specific demands of their environments diligently and flexibly.

4. CHALLENGES FOR EUROPEAN AND U.S. UNIVERSITIES

« We spend a lot of money training university students who then go directly to unemployment ».

EDUARDO SERRA. President of Everis Spain.[237]

Our concern about the challenges and necessary changes in higher education goes back a long way. For more than a decade the authors have been talking about University 2.0,[238] the digital revolution, and, in general, about the "university of the future".[239]

The entity and intensity of the changes in the current technological paradigm require facing what the role of the universities should be. The university system has become a heavy elephant, with a privileged intellect, but excessively departmentalized and bureaucratized. The current times require it to be like agile gazelles, capable of pivoting according to the rapid changes taking place outside the academy.

Universities, aware of their deficits, seek to adapt to the transformations required by the knowledge society and disruptions in the labor market. However, the pace is not enough, according to at least three indicators:

1. The aforementioned deficit of STEM professionals, which shows the lack of adjustment between labor supply and demand.

2. The wage gap between those who have completed higher education and those who have not is narrowing, as can be seen in the United States, Korea, Norway, Sweden, United

---

237. alicanteplaza.es/eduardo-serra-nos-gastamos-mucho-dinero-en-formar-universitarios-que-luego-van-directamente-al-paro

238. Andrés Pedreño: The challenges of the university 2.0. See: nuevarevista.net/destacados/los-retos-de-la-universidad-20/

239. Andrés Pedreño: The University of the future. See: euroresidentes.com/empresa/innovacion/la-universidad-del-futuro-prospectiva-y

Kingdom, Germany, Japan, France, and Spain **(figure 7.1)**. Although there are still differences,[240] we are likely witnessing a change in trend, with non-university specialization gaining ground over higher degrees.

Figure 7.1. Wage differences between graduates and workers with secondary education (NI = 100)

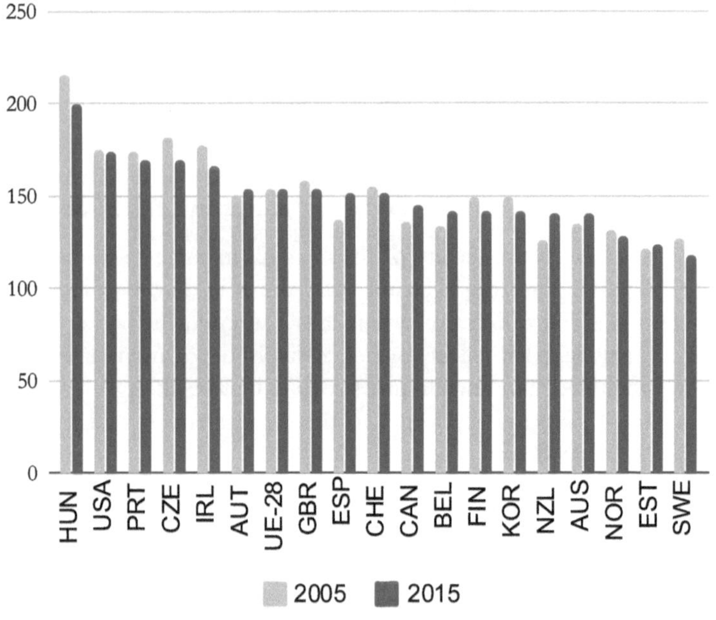

Source: OECD

3. The mismatch between university training and labor demand in countries such as Spain, Greece, Austria, Italy, and even Germany **(figure 7.2)**: the result is a difference between the activity performed and the salary according to the worker's qualification of more than 35% in average both in the US and in Europe.

---

240. Especially in specialized areas in traditional and primary sectors.

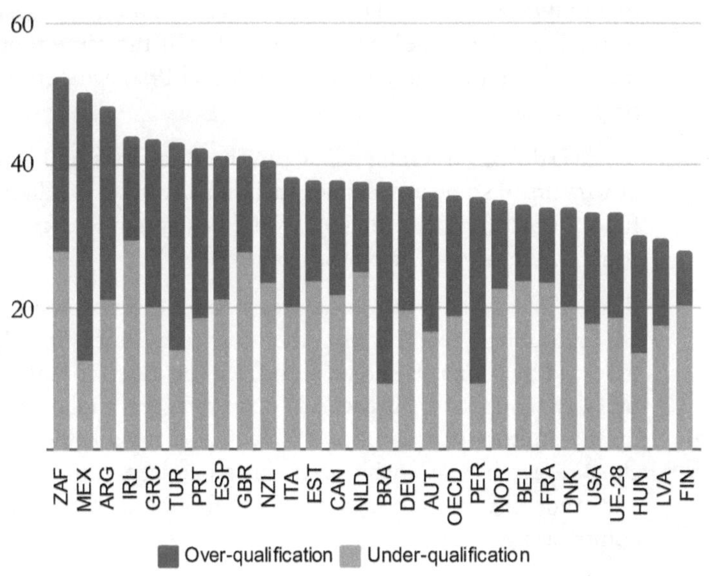

Source: OECD

In view of the above, it is worth asking: what changes must the university system face in order to correct its inefficiencies? What is failing in the university adaptation to the digital era?

4.1. Doubts in the U.S. university system

There is no doubt that the U.S. university system is by far one of the best in the world. A network that includes the leading universities in innovation such as MIT, Stanford or the California Institute of Technology (Caltech), as well as the excellence of the Ivy League[241]. However, we should not forget that these are accompanied by other universities of lesser prestige and financial capacity, creating a dual system.

The strength of the U.S. university system can be seen in three key aspects:

---

241. *Brown, Harvard, Cornell, Princeton, Dartmouth, Yale, Columbia y PennU.*

- A very close relationship with companies and digital entre-preneurship, without forgetting academic talent. Its major universities are the cradle of Silicon Valley and the largest technology companies on the planet, but at the same time they incorporate a large number of Nobel Prize winners as professors.

- An overflowing funding capacity. The donations and endowments of some universities such as Harvard ($38 billion fund) or Stanford ($26 billion) would be enough to acquire some of the largest European banks.[242]

- Research leadership in critical areas. American universities are undoubtedly contributing the most to advances in AI, followed by China, as can be seen from the index compiled by Glev Chupilo[243] (**figure 7.3**) or in a recent publication by the authors of this book [244]. It is also remarkable the close research relationship that exists between companies and academia, often motivated by collaborations with large companies.

---

242. Only five banks in all of Europe had a market capitalization of more than 38 billion euros in 2020: Banco Santander, BNP, ING, Intesa San Paolo, and BBVA.

243. The index was made based on 2,500 publications presented at the 2017 Conference on Neural Information Processing Systems (NIPS) held in California, the most prestigious in the world for AI research and which attracts the interest of 8,000 attendees.

See methodology at: medium.com/@chuvpilo/ai-research-rankings-2019-insights-from-neurips-and-icml-leading-ai-conferences-ee6953152c1a

244. Peretó-Rovira, A., Moreno-Izquierdo, L., & Pedreño-Muñoz, A. (2020). Un índice para medir la apuesta de los países por la inteligencia artificial: el caso de España y el papel del País Vasco. Ekonomiaz: Revista vasca de economía, (98), 26-53.

Figure 7.3: Top 32 leading global AI research organizations (NIPS Conference publications)

Pos.	Organization (country) - points	Pos.	Organization (country) - points
1	*Google* (US) 167.3	17	ETH (Switzerland) 27.0
2	Stanford (US) 82.3	18	*IBM (US)* 25.8
3	MIT (US) - 69.8	19	Washington U. (US) 24.0
4	Carnegie Mellon (US) 67.7	20	INRIA (France) 23.2
5	UC Berkeley (US) 54.0	21	EPFL (Switzerland) - 22.3
6	*Microsoft* (US) 51.9	22	Peking U. (China) - 21.6
7	Oxford U. (GB) 37.7	23	Toronto U. (Canada) - 21.4
8	*Facebook* (US) 33.1	24	Harvard (US) - 19.2
9	Princeton (US) 31.5	25	Duke (US) - 18.7
10	Cornell (US) 30.9	26	New York U. (US) - 17.7
11	Georgia Tech (US) 30.1	27	Cambridge (GB) 15.1
12	UT Austin (US) 29.9	28	KAIST (S. Korea.) 14.8
13	U. of Illinois (US) 29.4	29	Technion (Israel) 14.6
14	Columbia (US) 29.2	30	UC San Diego (US) 14.6
15	Tsinghua U. (China) 28.4	31	Wisconsin U. (US) 14.4
16	UCLA (US) 27.2	32	**Amazon** (US) 14.3

Source: medium.com/@chuvpilo/

Mismatches in the U.S. system

Despite its world leadership for more than a decade in the US, a part of society and the productive fabric linked to technology are demanding changes in higher education. The most advanced university system in the world, in the country that leads the way in cutting-edge technologies, that fosters Silicon Valley and the gestation of the largest technology giants, is failing to respond diligently to the needs of the digital economy.

How is it possible? The answer is found in an educational perfect storm summarized in three points:

1. Traditional U.S. university offerings are too slow to adapt to the needs of the economy.

It is becoming increasingly difficult to adapt the training offered to the changing demands of the digital labor market. In this context, other more flexible forms of learning such as Massive Open Online Courses (MOOCs) are emerging, which are capable of competing with the most prestigious educational institutions on the planet. We will talk about this later.

2. There is a bankruptcy of the US college student loan system.

Student debt has reached a colossal 1.6 trillion dollars,[245] more than the value of the GDP of Brazil, Canada, Russia, or Spain. This student indebtedness, beyond the purely financial problem, indicates the difficulty of repaying loans even after finding employment.

University degrees are losing value, and higher education is no longer always associated with high salaries. A few years ago, studying for an MBA or another master's degree was synonymous with finding a high-paying job quickly. Today many companies rely more on the skills of open training.

3. The founders and leaders of many digital giants did not finish their university studies, like Bill Gates and Paul Allen (Microsoft), Steve Jobs (Apple), Mark Zuckerberg (Facebook), Michael Dell (Dell), Jack Dorsey (Twitter and Square), Arash Ferdowsi (Dropbox), Jan Koum (WhatsApp), Evan Williams (Blogger and Twitter), and Larry Ellison (Oracle).

Some entrepreneurs argue that "on-demand training", open innovation, networking, and the dissemination of knowledge in collaborative environments have contributed more than university campuses to promote entrepreneurship, creativity, and disruption.

---

245. theguardian.com/us-news/2019/jun/24/student-debt-us-elections -explained-bernie-sanders

Looking for solutions to an uncertain future

How are universities responding to this lack of flexibility, the mismatch with the labor market and competition from new learning methods? Surprisingly, in this situation of change, leading universities such as Stanford, Harvard and MIT are consolidating a model based on open and massive knowledge, contrary to their elitist traditions. With their experimentation, rather than transforming, they are seeking to reinvent the role of universities in society.

Still, experts like Harvard Business School Professor Clayton Christensen predict that up to half of all American universities could close or at least declare bankruptcy within the next decade. Moreover, Moody's estimates that dozens of institutions (one in five small private universities) will face a dangerous scenario in the coming years[246] due to a decrease in income since the financial crisis of 2008, an increase in expenses, and the drop in the birth rate of American families.

Perhaps the digital reinvention of education, as the big universities are anticipating, will be their lifeboat.

4.2. Inaction and aging of the European university system

It is urgent that we in Europe become aware that the concerns and problems of American universities also affect us, even to a greater extent. Perhaps our digital backwardness, the welfare system and the predominance of public universities mask the perception of European problems. But there are elements that alert us to an unflattering situation. These are the following:

-   The financial situation of European students, where it is comparable, is no better than in the United States. The average student debt in the British university system (the most similar) is $55,000, compared to $37,000 in the US. [247].

---

246. cnbc.com/2019/12/03/the-other-college-debt-crisis-schools-are-going-broke.html

247. Source: yaleglobal.yale.edu/content/student-debt-rising-worldwide

European public and "free" systems also have deficiencies. Although the cost of enrollment is very low for students, university graduates in Sweden complete their higher education years with an average of $20,000 in debt used to cover their living expenses. In Norway, the average debt is $25,000.[248] To this must be added the public spending that they generate and that is shared by all citizens in taxes.

- Youth unemployment rates in Europe are structurally higher than in the US and China, especially in the southern economies.

- There is a lower productive relationship between universities and companies, with the differences in technological patents mentioned above. The contribution of research to society in terms of wealth generated or jobs created is not valued, nor is the entrepreneurial activity of the teaching staff facilitated.

Academic incentives, especially in economies with little industrial tradition, come mainly from publication in scientific journals, which have little reach outside the university environment. In Spain, the excessive fever to increase scientific publications costs almost 100 million euros a year in journal subscriptions alone[249] - ten times more than in Germany or Finland. And Latin America is copying this model.

A paralyzed system.

The European economic, political, and university systems seem to have lived in the last decade in an atmosphere of conformism, relaxed in its comfort zone. The enormous cost of digital delay has hardly been perceived, and the system, too conservative, has not sufficiently encoraged the promotion of employability and

---

248. OECD and Government of Spain. Overview of Education 2014: OECD Indicators. oecd-ilibrary.org/education/panorama-de-la-educacion-2014-indicadores-de-la-ocde_eag-2014-es

249. elconfidencial.com/tecnologia/ciencia/2018-02-16/revistas-cientificas-suscripciones-millonada_1522586/

entrepreneurship. Surely the positive evolution of the economy since the 2008 crisis has had a lot to do with it. Both income and the labor market showed a solid recovery, instilling a message along the lines of "Europe is doing well" **(figure 7.4)**. However, the COVID-19 crisis and the problems that many countries have had in adapting to distance education, in addition to the economic disaster, have brought us back to reality.

Figure 7.4. Economic and unemployment evolution in the European Union before COVID-19

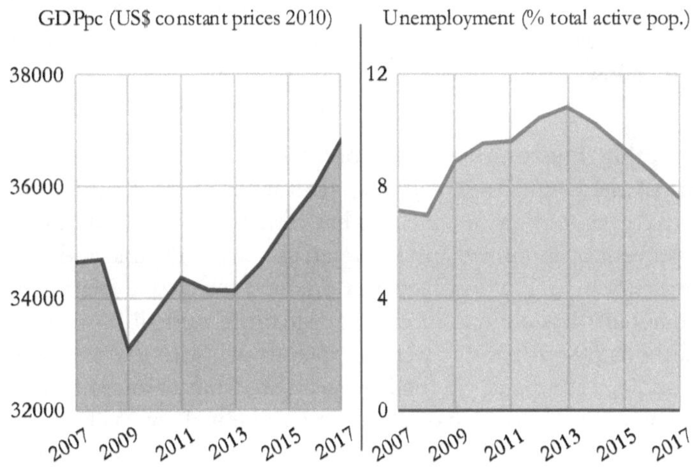

Source: World Bank

Part of the problems mentioned could have been anticipated and resolved with the entry of young teachers to the faculties, who would speed up the digitization of the system. An early commitment to new educational models based on gamification and hybrid methodologies, combining face-to-face and distance learning, would have eliminated all concerns about the quality of teaching and the achievement of learning objectives during confinement due to the coronavirus.[250]

---

250. The so-called 'flipped class', in which the theoretical sessions are available on the internet and students come to the centers for debates and practical activities, has been advocated by experts for more than a decade; however, few are those who practice it.

However, the financial problems derived from the 2008 crisis prevented progress in the recruitment of new professionals. And when hired, new professors and researchers have had to endure low salaries and uncertainty about their future even after obtaining their doctorates.

The workforces of many European universities are very old. A high percentage of its professors, with extraordinary teaching and research experience, are reluctant to explore new methods in line with the digital world and its disruptions. And the same happens in decision-making positions, with managers that do not foresee that the future of the academy surpasses their analogical vision of reality. However, science teaches us that only constant experimentation allows us to approach the best solutions.

In this situation (financial problems, lack of regeneration, unemployment, and indebtedness), European universities should have considered above all else what their contribution should be to prevent or minimize any future crisis. A new flexible and open university model, with objectives oriented towards social impact and not just academic. A model that will make it possible to answer questions that affect our welfare, such as: why are there no large technology companies in the European economy? How should we deal with the digitization of employment? How do we make access to knowledge more flexible and open to equalize training opportunities for all citizens?

However, beyond the necessary fight against public cuts in education after the 2008 crisis, in all this time there has hardly been any serious and profound debate on the transformation of the university model. Trapped in its outdated structure and with a little relationship with the companies in its environment, the European academia is in a delicate situation, but lacking the financial impetus of the major American universities and the public commitment to disruption that prevails in countries such as China and South Korea.

5. OPEN LEARNING AGAINST THE UNIVERSITY BUREAUCRACY

« The right thing to do was to adapt to the circumstances ».
FRANZ KAFKA. *The process.*

« In Spanish universities to buy a pen there is a civil employee doing paperwork that costs 40 times more than the pen ».[251]
MARCOS MARTÍNEZ. Stanford University.

5.1. The end of university bureaucracy

Europe is going to need its universities to bridge the technology gap with the US and China. Both have more funding capacity, more disruptive companies, and in some cases a greater tradition of promoting innovation than the old continent. Therefore, the EU should focus on fostering a unique executive intelligence, with more attitude and obsession for talent creation and the employability of its young people.

Is it happening? Sadly not.

Bureaucracy is a virus that affects more and more educational areas, complicating everything from simple administrative tasks such as visiting teachers or changing the name of a subject, to others of greater importance such as accreditation processes or the creation of new disciplines.

The promotion made by the European Commission and the governments to address new scientific challenges also collides with a tangle of bureaucratic procedures that violate the very principles that motivate the calls for application. So much so that European universities have specialized teams in applying for funds and grants

---

251. 'This is how the bureaucracy suffocates the Spanish University.' Article published in El Mundo (10/16/2019): elmundo.es/papel/historias/2019/10/16 /5da5ddfcfdddffca848b4609.html

for researchers. Departments, organizations and professionals who deal exclusively with filling out the documentation and coordinating meetings, and who take up a significant part of the budgets allocated to research.

Consequently, and in the face of the discouragement of numerous researchers, a large part of the public funds end up in proposals of limited relevance and future viability. Projects created to sustain structures of professionals dedicated to soliciting projects, in which it is more important to fulfill the curricular dossier than the social impact of the research.

Due to these situations, some think, not without reason, that universities and educational evaluation agencies need very radical reforms, induced by the needs of an increasingly digital society.[252]

A clever solution would be, for example, to value researchers by a scientific curriculum fully traceable with existing digital tools. Funding could be awarded directly and objectively based on the impact of published articles, money raised in previous projects, theses directed, training hours or extracurricular activities. Evaluation and monitoring would not focus on the application process, but on the delivery of research results.

If the European university system wants to start a revolution, it must begin by putting an end to a perverse bureaucratic system, which is not only unwarranted, but also threatens the value of free competition, our time, our intelligence and especially our patience.

5.2. The competitiveness of MOOCs

Higher education, whose traditions are as old as the millenary University of Bologna, must also be susceptible to disruption. Universities need to rethink their traditional presence-based teaching

---

252. Let us suggest that instead of national agencies to approve degrees for all universities, an institution specialized in foresight be created, which will help to determine in advance what will be the sectors of the future and the technological leaps that young people will face.

With this capacity, our universities would be giving greater prominence to AI or deep learning from very different scientific perspectives (computing, economics, law, neuroscience, marketing, engineering, biology, environment, or medicine in general).

models in order to promote alternative educational methods that encourage hybridization between areas of knowledge.

Open education platforms (MOOCs) such as Coursera, Edx or Udacity have anticipated the response that could be expected from academia, and have responded with diligence and low cost to the shortage of human capital in highly demanded areas such as data science or digital marketing.

Faced with the bureaucracy and tedious processes to create new courses, the founders of these platforms, who are or have been professors at universities such as An-drew Ng (Coursera - Stanford) or Sebastian Thrun (Udacity - formerly Stanford), have proposed educational offerings that are not only highly demanded by companies, but also anticipate this demand. Those who are trained in these new lines of study, some of which do not exist in the universities themselves, have enormous competitive ad-vantages. So much so that they even promise to return the money for the training if the students do not find a job.[253]

These platforms, in terms of student volume and impact, can have an enormous effect on our educational systems. Just think that the first MOOC in history - a course on AI organized by Se-bastian Thrun - counted 160,000 students from more than 200 countries in a single term. It would take a university professor more than a thousand years to reach that many students!

Could this alternative educational model be replicated in Eu-rope? It seems difficult, to be honest. In the US, it has been the universities themselves that have turned to open education, raising tens of millions of dollars in different rounds of funding for its implementation. Aware of the technological possibilities, it is the educational centers that do not want to be left out of future train-ing alternatives.

Away from the sterile debate on whether or not MOOCs will replace face-to-face classes, Stanford, Harvard, and MIT decided to research and experiment on this educational disruption, learning and obtaining valuable data on the dynamics of their students and

---

253. insidehighered.com/news/2018/03/16/udacity-ends-pledge-stu-dents-get-hired-or-get-their-money-back

the labor market. Future changes in teaching and administration at major American universities will be influenced by this information.

This effort on the part of the university system has been finely complemented by the major North American technology companies: Microsoft has promoted online training through the Linkedin network, which implies an almost perfect fit between curriculum, traceability of acquired skills and impact on the labor market; IBM, through cognitive class, provides free materials on data science and Artificial Intelligence; and Grow with Google offers a wide repertoire of open training that covers entrepreneurship, programming and web analytics.

Prestigious digital firms whose courses are always well received in any job interview.

Where is Europe in MOOCs?

Only the British Future Learn, promoted by the Open University, seems to follow in the American trail, thanks to the support of other major universities such as Oxford, Cambridge and Leeds, which provide courses. In the rest of the continent, the lack of institutional support, funds, and understanding of the business model have deprived promising projects of being able to compete in the open learning market, and thus to provide the educational system with a much-needed agility.

European universities and public administrations must understand that MOOC platforms, in order to be competitive, must not be born from them, but driven by them. They must provide them with sufficient flexibility to respond to the dynamism of our society and encourage teachers and students to feed and update themselves with thousands of hours of available training.

Let's think about the advantage that our educational systems would have from enjoying an unlimited knowledge base with which to hybridize. Think how the system would be enriched with an open model of universities contributing content., the amount of training resources that students could have had during the confinement caused by the coronavirus if we in Europe had encouraged MOOC training years ago.

There is still time.

6. A UNIVERSITY MODEL FOCUSED ON EMPLOYABILITY

The speed of the changes observed in previous chapters, especially in employment, must be sufficient to motivate a necessary change in our educational systems.

Prior to the financial crisis of 2008, the tertiarization of the economy generated a very significant volume of jobs in the European economy, providing a rapid professional outlet for the growing number of university graduates. Traditional labor-intensive jobs (tourism, construction, and non-innovative manufacturing) and the job placement capacity of the public sector, with countries such as France, Greece, the United Kingdom and Spain exceeding the ratio of one civil servant for every four employees, made up most of the labor demand.

The American and European educational systems responded quite well for decades to the social and labor needs of their time, with changes that occurred gradually and companies that could innovate linearly and without leaving a reasonable comfort zone.

Today the situation is quite different. This time, urgent changes are demanded, with exponential growth technologies such as AI, big data, and the internet of things, and the associated digital transformation processes. Therefore, we are going to need an educational system based on flexibility, diligence, and speed to respond to real needs without losing excellence, rigor, or reputation.

We must ensure that all our degrees receive a good dose of data science, algorithm construction, and other knowledge rooted in computational thinking. There is a need to reform entire degrees such as journalism, advertising, economics, and medicine in the face of the changes coming to their sectors. Newspapers are closing, fintech is reinventing the financial system, and AI promises to diagnose better than the most reputable doctors. However our university degrees, except for the incorporation or reformulation of some subjects, continue to teach programs almost identical to those of decades ago.

Neither universities nor governments are heeding the call for help from business[254]. A serious disconnection that leads to the disillusionment of our productive fabric, unable to find enough talent, and to the depression of the millennial society, with a perspective of receiving the minimum wage almost perpetually. A concern that is already a trend in the USA, which is beginning to be echoed in the UK, the European country with the best universities, and which will soon become a matter of state for the rest of the old continent.

Obsessing over college employability

The change we want for universities requires quick and efficient responses focused not so much on current labor demand but adaptation to future employability. What kind of employability are we referring to?

As a first stage, it would be interesting to move from a traditional concept of employability based on "the of an individual to be sought after by companies to work in them" to a more refined and current one: employability as "the real and potential added value that an individual can contribute to the competitiveness of companies".

How to get the European university system to achieve great advances in employability would take us several chapters, so let us refer you to the article "The Digital Society and Employability"[255] that discusses it at length. Nevertheless, we would like to give some hints on how universities should articulate themselves from this new concept of employability focused on competitiveness and productivity. Specifically, this would be done on the following bases:

---

254. An interesting exercise for faculties, directors of training programs, and teachers is to dissect a simple startup from their environment. Dialogue and study how it behaves, the needs of future companies, and how it will be a possible career opportunity for young university students.

We have done it. It is striking that many startups demand professionals for specific positions that they cannot fill.

255. Andrés Pedreño: "The Digital Society and Employability" nuevarevista.net/economia/la-sociedad-digital-y-la-empleabilidad/

1. Professional excellence and training in the skills necessary to compete in today's global economy.

2. The **real hybridization** - not overlapping - of knowledge, especially computing, with any other discipline.

3. The **capacity for entrepreneurship** as an engine of proactivity and creativity.

4. The need to correctly **assimilate** relevant and **disruptive innovations**.

5. The **ability to foresee**, with university studies based on the identification of knowledge and skills linked to the sectors of the future.

The conclusion is that the implementation of policies that favor employability may seem complex. Nevertheless, perhaps simple formulas can be adopted that respect university autonomy and its capacity for self-governance as much as possible. That would be the case of policies that index employability objectives - well measured - with financing incentives: public investment in collaboration with private companies, monitoring the hiring of young people, and an enormous social return in terms of the labor market, wealth, competitiveness, and potential growth.

7. SOME CONCRETE PROPOSALS: EDUCATION AND EMPLOYMENT

We recapitulate the concrete proposals regarding employment and the labor market discussed in this chapter:

---

1. Introduce computational thinking in primary and secondary education, with the explicit purpose of familiarizing our students with this type of language of our time.

2. Hybridize all fields of knowledge with **computational thinking,** so that doctors, biologists, architects, lawyers, physicists or economists can take advantage of the potential of computing, the exploitation of big data, and tools such as machine learning or deep learning.

3. To clearly and effectively measure university employability, differentiating between sub-employability and employability.

4. Reward, incentive, and provide budgetary support to universities and **teachers that increase the employability of university graduates**, without exhausting bureaucratic procedures.

5. Promote the incorporation of young talent into universities and improve their economic status in academia with renewed criteria and incentives.

6. Make the educational offer more flexible so that universities can respond to the potential demands of the labor market.

7. Respect university autonomy and the presumed maturity of university institutions but prioritize **support** for good practices and incentives to improve employability.

---

8. Streamline administrations and eliminate the high bu-reaucratic burden faced daily by university professors and researchers, who spend more time filling out documents than preparing the professionals of the future. This is an irritating factor and alien to the digital era.

9. The European labor market should be a highly mobile talent stream. If a single European digital market is pursued, student and professional mobility programs that allow European to study and/or work in at least 4 or 5 different countries should be encouraged.

10. Create a new digital culture and training among senior managers and entrepreneurs of large European companies and a vision that weighs the ability to look into the future.

In addition, in the short term, a set of urgent measures related to the need to increase the number of STEM resources would be worthwhile. We specify them as follows:

1. Educate to lose the fear of mathematics and computing. Labor markets will need specialists in STEM skills, be they lawyers, sociologists, biologists, or teachers.

2. Promote quality professional -not university- training related to STEM, with shorter cycles and a well-defined curriculum based on market needs.

3. Encourage the incorporation of women into university STEM degrees. Paradoxically, in a country like Spain, large technology companies such as IBM, Google, Facebook, Fujitsu, Siemens, Amazon, Microsoft, and HP are run by women who create a great public image. It would be necessary to project much more among current young women these personalities, together with that of successful female tech entrepreneurs.

4. Support for express training following the model of advanced digital ecosystems such as Silicon Valley. These programs provide training in the basic subjects most in demand by companies for immediate incorporation into the workplace.

5. Online training aids, such as SPOCs (Small Private Online Courses), short and low-cost online MOOCs, and unlimited places that allow many young people to be trained in any subject. Universities should collaborate with private companies and administrations for this purpose. Google has been a pioneer in this field, and together with universities has managed to train in recent years more than 2.5 million students across Europe in digital subjects that are in high demand in today's job market.

CHAPTER 8: ENTREPENEURSHIP AND STARTUP SCALABILITY ISSUES

« Where there is a successful company, someone once made a brave decision.»
PETER DRUCKER.

« If your work can be done by a computer, get another one. If your job can be done by a robot, find another one (...) If your job doesn't bring meaning, find another. If your work can be digitized, find another .... And if after looking for it you can't find it, create it, invent it. »[256]
RAMÓN SAMSÓ.

In Europe, brilliant ideas are flowing at the same pace as in the rest of the world. Young and not so young talents from Germany, Sweden, France, Greece or Spain are able to imagine solutions and applications as powerful as Uber, Airbnb or Twitter. So why don't European startups reach the size of American or Asian ones? Why do Googles and Facebooks exist in California and not in Europe?

The key is scalability, in the ability of companies to mature, grow, and evolve without losing flexibility. And this is something that does not depend only on businesspeople and entrepreneurs, but especially on their environment. That the digital economy has so far failed in Europe is clear. The transformation of our production model and the modernization of a society should not be measured in the volume of investment in R&D, not even in the number of scientific papers, but in terms of employment and wealth generated by the cutting-edge sectors.

---

256. Ramón Samsó (2009). *El código dinero* (The money code). Obelisco Editions.

That is where the European digital impulse policies have been totally inefficient, or even counterproductive. Although more startups are emerging in Europe every day than in Asia, very few become "unicorns" or benchmarks in their sectors. The big European tech companies, the ones that are supposed to shape the future of our economies, are still 20th-century companies. Some of them with more than a century of life.

1. EUROPEAN IRRELEVANCE IN THE TECHONOLOGY INDUSTRY

If the digital economy has taught us anything, it is that talent and technology can often make up for the lack of financial resources and even government support. With few employees but a disruptive attitude, many companies have been able to reach global markets, generate millions in revenue, create thousands of jobs and even reinvent an entire sector.

However, for this to happen, startups must be integrated into ecosystems with factors that boost their scalability. Factors that are born of very ambitious policies, yet in Europe seem to remain with little incentive to implement an "entrepreneurial spirit" that is both necessary and insufficient.

The European failure in high innovation industries can be seen in three classifications that are worth highlighting:

- **Technology companies by market capitalization:** only the German SAP would enter as a representative of the EU in the select club of twenty technology companies with a market valuation of more than \$100 billion. The dominance of the North American and Asian multinationals in the industries of the future is absolute and growing **(figure 8.1)**.

The average age of the major European technology companies, most of which are over 50 years old, is also noteworthy. Some of them are even centenarians, as a result of the privatization of their telecoms, which we have already mentioned.[257] However, in China and the US their technology leaders are predominantly young, almost all of them born after the 1980s. Only exceptional cases such as Samsung or IBM predate that date, although their continued reinvention is beyond doubt.

---

257. Deutsche Telekom, Orange, Telefónica (1924) and Swisscom.

Figure 8.1. Companies by market value in sectors of the digital economy (2019)

Company (Year Founded)	Region	Main Sub-sector	Value (x $ 1000 million)	Financing ($ millon)
Microsoft (1981)	US (Was.)	Software	1040.34	1
Apple (1994)	US (CA)	Electronics	934.05	6,200
Amazon (1996)	US (Was.)	e-commerce	887.50	108
Google (1998)	US (CA)	Services	817.83	36
Facebook (2004)	US (CA)	Messaging	524.09	2,300
Alibaba G (1999)	CH (Zhejiang)	e-commerce	454.98	8,900
Tencent . (2000)	CH (Guang.)	Services	397.92	76,800
AT&T Inc (1983)	US (TX)	Telecom.	255.75	nd
Samsung E. (1969)	Corea del Sur	Electronics	241.83	nd
Verizon Com. (2002)	US (NY)	Telecom.	234.49	30,100
Taiwan Semic. (1987)	Taiwan	Electronics	207.38	nd
Intel Corp. (1968)	US (CA)	Electronics	206.18	2.5
Cisco Systems (1987)	US (CA)	Telecom.	201.19	2.5
Oracle Corp (1977)	US (CA)	Services	178.93	nd
China Mobile (1997)	Hong Kong	Telecom.	172.63	nd
SAP SE (1972)	EU (Ale.)	Services	146.53	1.300
Adobe Inc (1982)	US (CA)	Software	139.66	nd
Netflix (1997)	US (CA)	Entertain.	132.70	3,100
Salesforce (1999)	US (CA)	Services	126.05	64.4
Paypal (1999)	US (CA)	FinTech	122.99	217
IBM Corp (1911)	US (NY)	Services	118.60	nd
Texas Instr. (1991)	US (TX)	Electronics	114.77	nd
Broadcom Inc (1993)	US (CA)	Electronics	109.07	nd

REST OF MAJOY EUROPEAN TECHNOLOGIES				
ASML Holding (1984)	EU (Hol.)	Electronics	91.99	nd
Deutsche T. (1995)*	EU (Ger.)	Telecom.	79.11	nd
Vodafone (1983)	EU (RU)	Telecom.	48.80	nd
Orange (2013)**	EU (France)	Telecom.	40.10	nd
Dassault Syst. (1981)	EU (France)	Tecn. 3D	37.36	nd
Telefónica (1924)	EU (Spain)	Telecom.	35.14	nd

* Deutsche Telekom is the result of the privatization of the Deutsche Bundespot agency, created in 1947.

** Orange is the transformation of Postes, télégraphes et téléphones, a French public communications agency created in 1879 and later renamed France Telecom.

Source: own elaboration from Financial Times and Crunchbase

- **Global leading emerging companies:** in the last decade, only eight European companies have ranked among the 100 startups with the highest market capitalization, in a list once again led by the US and China **(figure 8.2)**.

  Although there are companies capable of outstanding local markets and even consolidating their business model in other European countries, there is usually some American startup that lead the sector worldwide. And it is not surprising that in the long term European digital companies will be acquired by their U.S. or Asian rivals, something that has been repeated on numerous occasions.

Figure 8.2. Leading startups that went on the stock market since 2010

Company (Year Founded)	Region	Main Sub-sector	IPO value (x1000 million of $)	Financing. (millions of $)
Facebook	US (CA)	Messaging	18.4 (2012)	2,335
Spotify	EU (SW)	Entertainment	9.2 (2018)	2,755
Uber	US (CA)	Mobility	8.1 (2019)	24,712
Xiaomi	CH (Beijing)	Electronics	4.7 (2018)	3,447
Meituan	CH (Beijing)	Services	4.2 (2018)	8,334
Snapchat	US (CA)	Messaging	3.4 (2017)	4,898
Lyft	US (CA)	Mobility	2.3 (2019)	4,912
iQiyi	CH (Beijing)	Entertainment	2.2 (2018)	3,005
Twitter	US (CA)	Messaging	1.8 (2013)	1,460
Rocket Int	EU (Ale.)	Incubator	1.7 (2014)	2,249
Pinduoduo	CH (Shan.)	Elec. Sales	1.6 (2018)	1,700
Zhong An	CH (Shan.)	Fintech	1.5 (2017)	822
Pinterest	US (CA)	Messaging	1.4 (2019)	1,466
Yandex	Rusia	Analytics	1.3 (2011)	16
Mercari	Japón	Elec. Sales	1.2 (2018)	116
Delivery H	EU (Ale.)	Delivery	1.1 (2017)	2,593
Ping AG	CH (Guang.)	eHealth	1.1 (2018)	900
Tencent M.	CH (Guang.)	Entertainment	1.1 (2018)	910
Adyen	EU (Hol.)	Fintech	1.1 (2018)	266
Chewy	US (FLO)	Elec. Sales	1.0 (2019)	451
Zynga	US (CA)	Entertainment	1.0 (2011)	866
NIO	CH (Shan.)	Mobility	1.0 (2018)	3,899

OTHER EUROPEAN STARTUPS				
Zalando	EU (Ger)	Elec. Sales	0.6 (2014)	467
Home24	EU (Ger)	Elec. Sales	0.6 (2018)	155
Funding C	EU (RU)	Fintech	0.3 (2018)	422
HelloFresh	EU (Ger)	Delivery	0.3 (2011)	367

Source: own elaboration from Crunchbase

- **The number of unicorns:** finally, the EU also languishes in
the matter of *unicorns*, that is, companies that without a market
capitalization have an estimated market value of several hundred million euros.

In a global ranking, there is no European unicorns among the
25 with the largest estimated market capitalization, and there
are only five among the top 100 **(figure 8.3)**. This is a truly
worrying indicator since these startups are a true reflection of
how regions are able to create companies and jobs for the future.

How do the EU and its countries intend to guarantee the
growth of their economies in the coming years without companies
in sectors of the future? How are their productive fabrics going to
be transformed without benchmark high-tech companies that provide innovation to the rest of the sectors?

Figure 8.3. Top unicorns by funding (not yet going public) since 2010

Company	Region	Main Sub-sector	Financing to date (millions of dollars)
Ant Financial	CH (Zhejiang)	Fintech	22,000
The We Company	US (Nueva York)	Real Estate	12,800
Grab	Singapur	Urb. Mobility	9,100
JD Digits	CH (Beijing)	Fintech	4,800
Airbnb	US (California)	Travel	4,400
Lazada Group	Singapur	Elec. Sales	4,200
Ola	India	Elec. Sales	3,800
Chehaoduo	CH (Beijing)	Urb. Mobility	3,300
GOJEK	Indonesia	Delivery	3,070
Lu.com	CH (Shanghai)	Fintech	3,015
Inspur Cloud	CH (Shandong)	Services	2,900
SenseTime	CH (Beijing)	Artificial Intellig.	2,600
Kabbage	US (Georgia)	Fintech	2,400
Tokopedia	Indonesia	Elec. Sales	2,400
ofo	CH (Beijing)	Delivery	2,150
DoorDash	US (California)	Delivery	1,970
Instacart	US (California)	Delivery	1,900
Lianjia	CH (Beijing)	Real Estate	1,800
View	US (California)	IoT	1,800
Avant	US (Illinois)	Fintech	1,770

LEADING EUROPEAN UNICORNS			
Deliveroo	EU (UK)	Delivery	1,530
Transferwise	EU (UK)	Fintech	772
N26	EU (Ger)	Fintech	682
GetYourGuide	EU (Ger)	Travel	654
Babylon Health	EU (UK)	eHealth	635

Source: own elaboration from Crunchbase

2. THE SCALABILITY DIAMOND IN THE DIGITAL ECONOMY

2.1. Scalability factors in successful ecosystems

To find the factors that enhance business scalability in the digital economy, we have first tried to synthesize three key aspects that concur in the ecosystems where the large technology companies of our time emerge.

They are as follows:

1. Entrepreneurial culture and financing: Silicon Valley has defined an integrated structure where entrepreneurs and attracting talent are key. A large market where tech giants and emerging companies coexist and interact, where incubators and accelerators help to create an environment that favors professional networks and the sharing of ideas.

This is how financing has been generated that differs from that existing in conventional markets, where even universities participate.

2. Efficiency of public administrations and efficient regulation: flexible regulation favorable to business creation is essential to explain why the US, Estonia, Ireland and Israel have become hubs for attracting talent.

Fostering a regulatory environment that encourages disruption is essential in the early stages of technological leaps. Excessive bureaucracy and legal frameworks that do not favor the digital economy lead to insurmountable competitive losses.

3. Gazelles against elephants - flexibility and ability to embrace change and disruption: University rigidity and its limited capacity to respond to the rapid changes demanded by society and companies can burden an entire generation of entrepreneurs and businesspeople. The academic system must attend to the characteristics of the economic environment and update its control and evaluation systems.

The best American universities have been leading open learning models for years, characterized by their agility and flexibility, such as the MOOCs of Coursera, Udacity, and Edx, as mentioned above. The university analog medium must be supported by the digital medium, not be a brake on new trends.

2.2. The Digital Scalability Diamond

Building on the previous three elements, we have ventured to structure five drivers of enterprise scalability **(figure 8.4)**.[258] These factors are bureaucracy and ease of starting a business, entrepreneurial culture and business knowledge, access to finance, attraction and retention of talent, and the company-university-sector relationship.

You will notice that this tentative model is inspired by Michael Porter's well-known *"competitiveness diamond"*,[259] undoubtedly the most important reference for the competitive study of regions.

---

258. This model, arising from the experience and previous knowledge of the authors, will be duly contrasted in future research.
259. Porter, M. (1990). *The Competitive Advantage of Nations*. New York: Free Press.

Figure 8.4. Drivers of competitiveness and scalability of companies in the digital economy

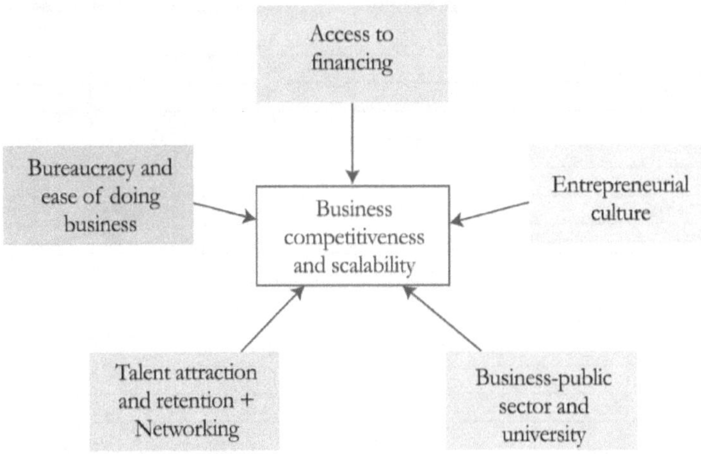

Source: own elaboration

i. Bureaucracy and ease of doing businesses

Inflexible and efficient administrations are a real drag on the creation of companies and wealth, with costs that are measured in billions of dollars for the global economy. Specifically, in the United States, a loss of 3 trillion dollars a year is estimated: 17% of its total wealth.[260]

Although there is no specific data for Europe, this figure may be even higher, using the OECD indicators of ease of doing businesses as a proxy variable. These show that in the Eurozone it takes, on average, twice as many days as in the US to start a business and three times the initial investment **(figure 8.5).**

---

260. Hamel, G., & Zanini, M. (2016). Excess Management Is Costing the US $3 Trillion Per Year. *Harvard Business Review*. hbr.org/2016/09/excess-anagement-is-costing-the-us-3-trillion-per-year

Figure 8.5: Ease of starting a business by country

	Days to start a business	Cost to start a business (% pc income)	Procedures to start a business
United Kingdom	4.5	0.0	4
Ireland	5.0	0.1	3
New Zeland	0.5	0.2	1
China	8.6	0.4	4
Norway	4.0	0.9	4
United States	5.6	1.0	6
Estonia	3.5	1.1	3
Greece	12.5	1.5	4
Israel	12.0	2.8	4
Eurozone (average)	9.84	3.6	5.2
Spain	12.5	4.0	7
Germany	8.0	6.7	9
South Korea	4.0	14.6	2
Mexico	8.4	16.2	8

Source: World Bank Doing Business Indicator

How does the lack of efficiency of the public sector contribute to the scalability of startups? In addition to being a psychological barrier, the greater the administrative obstacles, the less time spent generating wealth and jobs. The contradictory, slow and cumbersome regulations, the time-consuming process of obtaining licenses, or having to leave the workplace to carry out administrative procedures are discouraging and almost desperate reasons for any entrepreneur.

This feeling is even worse when it comes to startups, whose differential is creativity and agility to survive in an extremely competitive global environment.

Below we present some of the obstacles faced by businessmen and entrepreneurs in our environment due to the inefficiency of some public administrations. We leave a space at the end for the readers to incorporate their own.

1. Impediments to the international mobility of talent, such as the rigidity of visas or residence permits.

2. Complexity in the procedures for applying for public funding or subsidies, with confusing communication in relation to aid for the digital sector.

3. Restrictions on licenses to open a digital business in some locations.[261]

4. High taxation even before making profits.

5. Archaic professional categorization and deductible expense headings poorly adapted to the expenses of digital startups.

6. Outdated tools and inefficient information on tax issues, which even require physical presence to resolve formalities.

7. Payment terms to companies by public administrations are too long, which causes many companies to be unable to compete.

8. The public agencies do not have up-to-date databases that are freely accessible to companies, and usable open data is conspicuous by its absence.

---

261. Digital activity, unless it is associated with other activities that generate problems, is harmless enough to be located in any city center, tourist environment, renovated buildings, etc.

ii. Entrepreneurial culture

Much of the success of digital ecosystems have depended on an entrepreneurial culture rooted in society. A mix of interest and motivation to carry out their own innovative and disruptive projects, and the willingness to use and share knowledge and advanced tools that provide competitiveness. All this is in an environment that favors the effective support of universities, investment funds and public administrations.

Europe hardly had a strong entrepreneurial culture until the economic crisis of 2008. The very harsh consequences of the recession, with very high youth unemployment rates and the brain drain, especially in southern Europe, meant that entrepreneurship became almost the only solution for creating jobs and wealth.[262]

Although the entrepreneurial culture is a very difficult factor to measure, if we are guided by feelings, it is clear that Europe is somewhere between necessity and recognition. References such as Steve Jobs, Larry Page, Bill Gates or Elon Musk have been occupying the pages of newspapers while generating an entrepreneurial vocabulary and culture. However, no entrepreneurs of the same fame or prestige have emerged in Europe. Do they not exist? Or is it that they are not given the attention they deserve?

One way or the other, what is clear is the difference in the capacity to create start-ups between the United States and the European Union. Taking as a reference only the data between 2018 and 2020 **(figure 8.6)**, this almost unbridgeable gap can be seen: in the U.S. almost 9,000 new startups were founded (2.4 per 100,000 inhabitants), 35% of the planet's total, and in the EU 6,000 (1.07 per 100,000 inhabitants), 24% of the total.

Only the United Kingdom (2.7 startups per 100,000 inhabitants) and Ireland (2.10) can match the figures for the United States as a whole, although they are far behind the world's major entrepreneurship benchmarks. In New York State, more than 15 new

---

262. The reader would be surprised by the number of students who have told us in our years as teachers that they wanted to be civil servants without having a clear vocation of public service. Having a stable job, whether they like the role more or less, was attractive enough to devote their most creative years to preparing an opposition.

startups per 100,000 inhabitants were created between January 2018 and December 2019, in Massachusetts more than 50, and in California an incredible 315. Three hundred times more than the EU average!

Figure 8.6: Global distribution of emerging companies (startups) created between 2018 and 2020

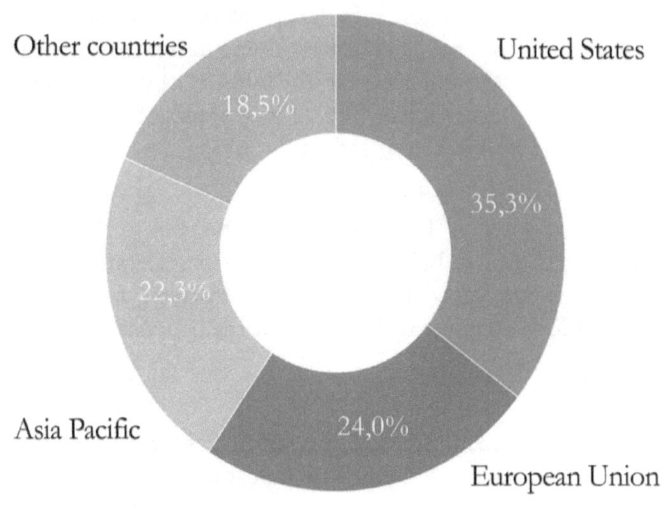

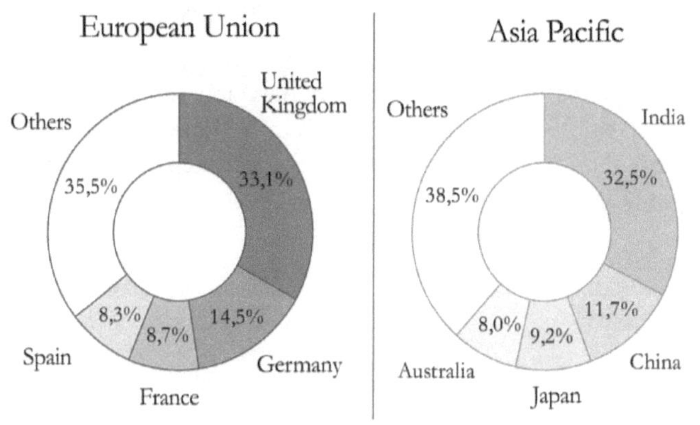

Source: own elaboration from crunchbase.com

In the Asia-Pacific area, there are 5,600 new startups in a period of growth and expansion for their economies. That is 0.12 new start-ups per 100,000 inhabitants, almost ten times less than the EU average. Not even South Korea, one of the most technologically outstanding countries, reaches the levels of business creation of Mediterranean Europe.

This situation is the result of two key elements, one sociological and the other strategic:

- The Asian population is in the process of industrialization, with a high volume of citizens residing in non-urban areas, in some cases, without access to the internet or digital tools. For example, China still has 40% of its population living in rural areas, and in the case of India it is 66%.

- The creation of technological leaders capable of competing globally, such as Tencent, Alibaba, Samsung, Xiaomi, and Ant Financial, is being promoted. That generates a lack of dynamism in the Asian region; nevertheless, it is making it possible to compete with the big North American technology companies.

Even so, in recent years, acceleration has been observed to achieve greater agility in the technological industrial fabric, especially in South Korea. From Seoul, measures are being promoted that involve a direct injection of more than 20 billion euros, as well as tax exemptions for venture capital to promote the creation of new start-ups.[263]

Although the differences between Asia and the U.S. are currently very significant, if this trend is consolidated in the rest of the region, Asia will have taken another giant step towards dominating the digital era.

---

263. koreatimes.co.kr/www/biz/2017/11/367_238700.html

iii. Access to financing

The financing capacity of European companies is much lower than those of the United States and China. In gross terms, investment in venture capital[264] in the two great technological powers is ten times greater than in Europe. These differences can be seen even more clearly when we divide the US economy into states (**figure 8.7**): California, New York and Massachusetts invest more individually than the sum total of all the EU countries. In the case of California, the figure is five times higher than the investment effort of Europe as a whole.

Figure 8.7: Volume of investment in venture capital (millions of dollars) (2017)

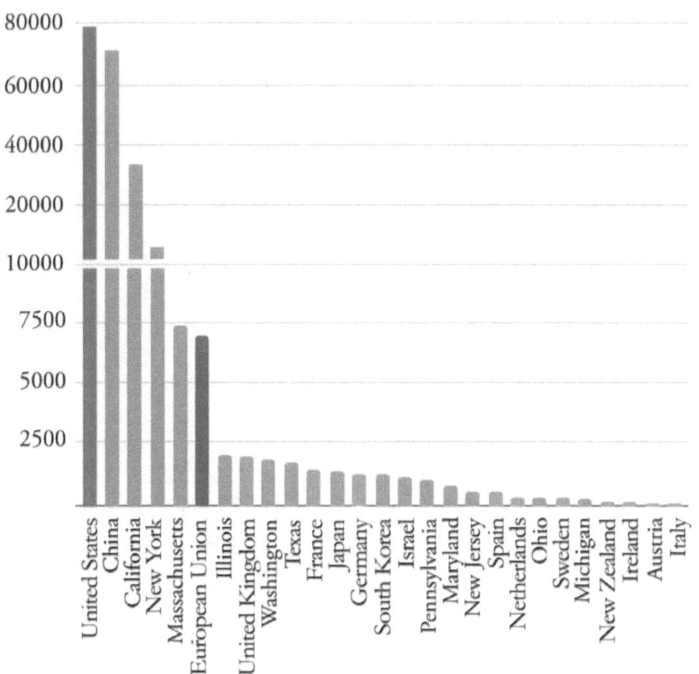

Sources: OECD, Preqin, and CBInsights

---

264. Por inversión en capital riesgo se entiende la inversión en el capital social de empresas privadas -que no participan en la bolsa, ya sea para su constitución o su desarrollo y expansión.

In relative terms, an average of $11 million per startup has been invested in California per year since 2017. That is five times more than in France, eight times more than in Germany, nine times more than in Spain, and ten times more than in the average of the EU **(figure 8.8)**. Japan, South Korea, Israel, and New Zealand also show figures that are higher than the European average, although it is China, with more than $50 million invested per startup, that truly threatens an unprecedented irruption of technological giants.

Figure 8.8: Investment in venture capital in relation to the number of newly created startups (millions of dollars, 2017)

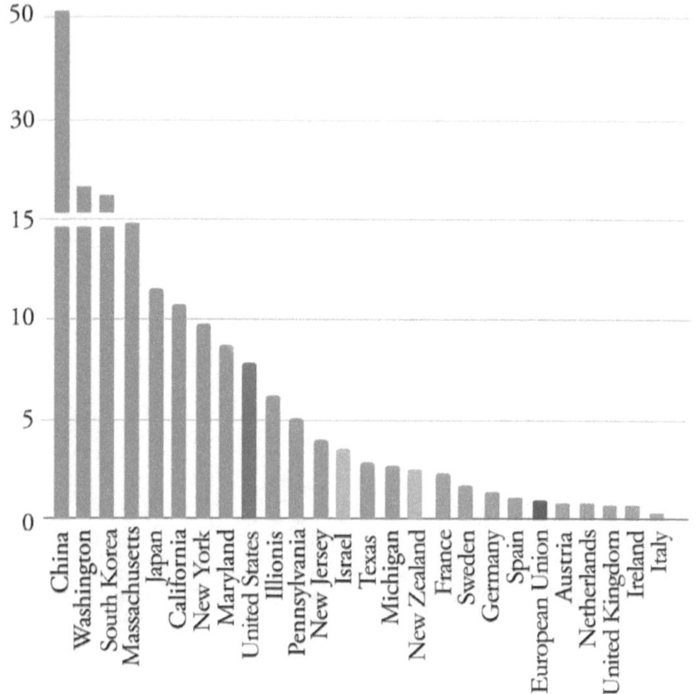

Sources: OECD, Preqin, and CBInsights

It should also be noted that in the Asia-Pacific region, 70% of the total venture capital is intended for companies in telecommunications, internet, and software sectors for users and companies.

The US, with greater diversification, reaches 60%, and the average of the European Union remains at a lagged 45%.[265]

These numbers reinforce some of the conclusions of the previous section: the business tradition of Asian countries derives in a lower entrepreneurial drive compared to the US and Europe; however, their access to credit allows the relatively few startups that emerge to compete in global markets with greater capacity than their Western counterparts.

It is urgent for Europe to increase investment in digital startups, and not just at launch. We cannot fall into the error of understanding business financing as the first impulse to create projects, but it must also accompany expansion, communication, and innovation plans which are essential to gain global competitiveness.

iv. Attracting, retaining, and exploiting talent

We have previously associated "talent" in the digital economy with professionals capable of promoting the benefits derived from AI, IoT, Blockchain, or any other emerging technology in their jobs and society. That is, those who specialize in STEM skills or who can hybridize them with other areas of knowledge such as business development, law, architecture, or biology.

In order to improve competitiveness, most technological economies firmly commit to the massive incorporation of talent into their companies. In Israel and South Korea, more than 75% of the scientists work in private companies; in the US and Japan, this figure exceeds 70%. In China, in a clear upward trend, it has already reached 60%.

In Europe, only Sweden (66%), the Netherlands (60%), France (60%), and Germany (59%) show encouraging results of scientific integration into the labor market. On the other hand, in Spain (37%), Portugal (33%), Greece (30%), Lithuania (28%), and Latvia (18%), the situation is almost dramatic for their scientists, who hardly find employment outside the universities **(figure 8.9)**.

---

265. Information extracted from different reports prepared by Invest Europe, Preqin, and PWc.

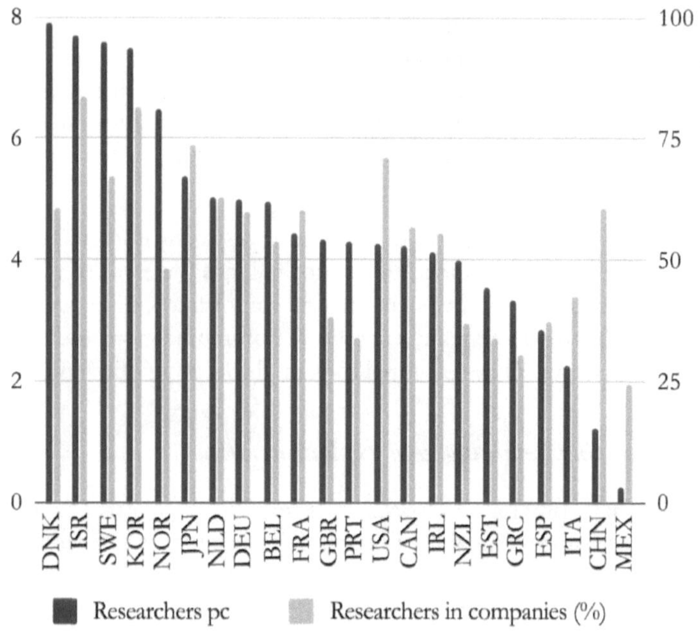

Figure 8.9: Researchers per capita and percentage of researches with their main activity in the private sector

Source: UNESCO and the World Bank

This high dependence of European science on its universities presents two serious problems that we have already commented on previously:

- Greater interest and pressure to publish articles in scientific journals than to promote advances that generate wealth and employment.

- A brain drains in other countries given the shortage of research places in universities and the higher salaries of private companies.

In this sense, some European institutions are making very commendable efforts to attract and retain digital talent; however, the European Union must provide funding and clear leadership to these projects. In particular, we would like to highlight two successful initiatives:

ICREA (Catalan Institution for Research and Advanced Studies): ICREA is a foundation created in 2000 and jointly promoted by the Catalan Government and the Catalan Foundation for Research and Innovation (FCRI).

Inspired by the French National Research Center, it works closely with universities and research centers to promote a regional research system by attracting international talent and creating research groups in new lines of study.

The ICREA has made it possible to place Catalonia in the fourth position in attracting funding aid from the European Research Council (ERC), accounting for 56.6% of all funds granted to Spain. A total of 26.5 million euros in 2016 and only 1% goes to ICREA researchers themselves. Per million inhabitants, only Switzerland, Israel, and the Netherlands achieved better results.

ELLIS (The European Laboratory for Learning and Intelligent Systems): the most recognized researchers in Europe have been the promoters of platforms such as CLAIRE (Confederation of Laboratories for Artificial Intelligence Research in Europe)[266] and ELLIS (The European Laboratory for Learning and Intelligent Systems),[267] trying to curb the diaspora of European brains in AI in the face of aggressive Chinese and American private job offers.

Specifically, the ELLIS expert group, a non-profit organization, has launched a project to develop 17 research units in different cities in 10 European countries (plus Israel). ELLIS has been ahead of the EU itself in the strategy to create new talent, attract it, and prevent its flight, a priority objective for any region that wants to lead the economy of the future.

---

266. claire-ai.org/
267. ellis.eu/

ELLIS is also identifying problems that limit the emergence of talent and novel applications in AI in the EU, such as the obstacles of universities for their scientists to collaborate with companies or create their own[268] or the bureaucratic burden that robs researchers of their time to work.

v. Relationship between companies, universities, and the public sector

Universities and the public sector play a crucial role in the well-being of society, giving priority to social research that is not always covered by companies. Curing diseases, protecting the environment, or national security are good examples.

However, we must not shy away from the honest debate that we raised previously: universities and research centers dependent on the administrations should not capitalize funds whose social profitability is usually marginal. The public sector should not compete with the private sector on R&D, but rather serve as a boost to wealth and employment. Without them, it will be impossible to continue financing new research through taxes.

The United States, Israel, and emerging Asian countries (China, Malaysia, and Singapore) have well understood the necessity of this relationship. Universities collaborate with companies, resulting in the publication of patents and registries, which in many cases end up being an element of economic impulse **(figure 8.10)**.

---

268. venturebeat.com/2019/12/27/probeat-google-only-updated-android-distribution-data-once-in-2019/

 Relationship between patents and university-company collaboration

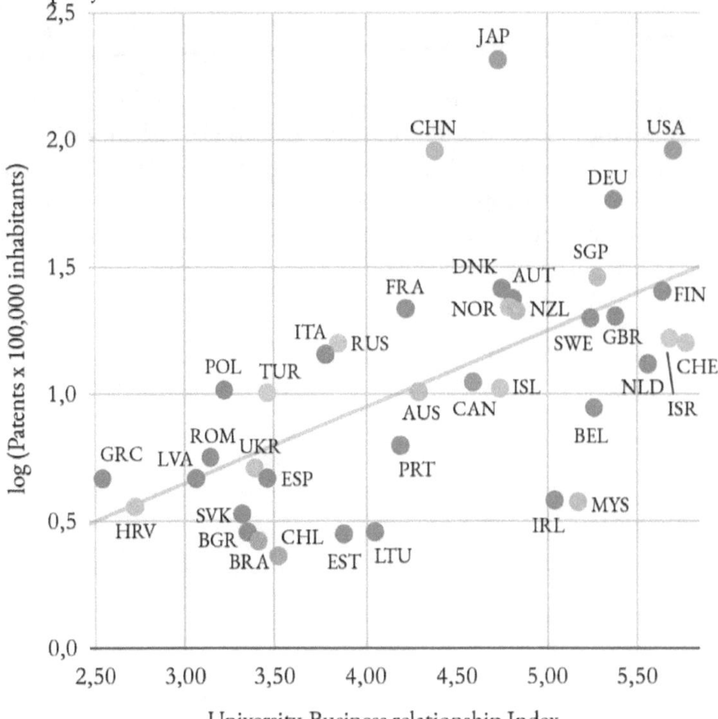

Source: World Economic Forum and the World Bank

This positive relationship also occurs in countries such as Germany, the Netherlands, Finland, and Sweden, albeit with a specialization in older sectors, as we have already mentioned. However, the countries of southern and eastern Europe lag far behind, with a poor relationship between the public sector and business that is worth studying. Purely from experience, we dare to venture two hypotheses of why this happens:

- Researchers and universities are not getting the right signals to incentivize technology transfer to businesses, even at the most basic levels of research.

- Companies do not aspire to be the engine of disruption or

lead it, but to use technology as a means of survival. Symptoms of the weakness of an overly conservative business ecosystem.

To reverse the situation of European lethargy, especially in the Mediterranean area, it will not be enough to allocate more funds to innovation or the cohesion of its regions. Instead, structural reforms must be proposed in universities and a new type of technology-based companies must be promoted, capable of exploiting the efforts made by public institutions.

3. THE FULL CIRCLE OF ENTREPRENEURSHIP TO OVERCOME LACK OF SCALABILITY

«Work hard. Have Fun. Make History.»
JEFF BEZOS.

«Good is the enemy of great. »
JIM COLLINS[269].

3.1. Does Europe have the ingredients for entrepreneurship?

In recent years, much of the old continent has jumped on the entrepreneurship bandwagon. Large companies from traditional and innovative sectors, local and regional governments, universities and training centers... have all invested in accelerators and spaces for co-working and co-living.

And this is not only happening in cities like London, Berlin, Paris, Madrid, and Rome. We also see it in smaller cities such as Dublin, Bristol, Lisbon, Alicante, and Helsinki, or in the most exotic places like the Canary Islands and Aras de Los Olmos.[270]

We have imported from Silicon Valley the ability to declare war on the comfort zone and overcome the stigma of failure. We have understood the importance of pivoting thanks to the lean canvas method. We attend and participate in meetings like Tech and Beer, or Friday Tech fever. Collaborative communities and professional networks have been built to boost self-employment. And we even test methodologies like AGILE or sprint design.

---

269. Collins, J. (2016). *Good to Great: Why Some Companies Make the Leap and Others Don't*. Instaread.

270. A Valencian mountain village of fewer than 300 inhabitants and whose digital commitment has allowed it to lead indicators such as wifi on the streets or the number of digital rural entrepreneurs in IoT.

Although much remains to be done, this whole movement is appreciated in terms of investment, both public and private, with the emergence of business angels, institutionalized venture capital funds, and a growing international investment in European projects.

The impetus of young people

The entrepreneurial culture is perceived in young people: of course there is hope in Europe!

The new generation of entrepreneurs and students sees the capitalism that existed in North America in the mid-20th century, so vividly portrayed in The Irishman[271], as something remote and almost a fiction. They also shy away from the traditional sectors of speculative capitalism responsible for the 2008 crisis. On the contrary, they identify with the new entrepreneurs of the 21st century and uphold Stephen Covey's "win-win" code of ethics [272] or the highest personal self-demands of Jim Collins.

In Europe, an ideal of creativity and effort is spreading increasingly among those who are self-employed - an impulse supported by the harshness of the economic crisis, the high attendance at public places, and the exhaustion of mature sectors. Many have lost their fear of risk. They participate in global challenges such as Google Hash Code or NASA Space Challenge when they are not working on ideas and technologies called to change the world.

The full cycle of entrepreneurship

Despite theoretically having the necessary ingredients for entrepreneurship, Europe suffers from an absolutely worrying absence of unicorns and globalized digital companies **(figure 8.11)**. It seems that the old continent has stagnated in the first step of "encouraging young people". The EU and the institutions interested in promoting entrepreneurship must go beyond theoretical models or motivation. They must be participants in the

---

271. *The Irishman* (2019), directed by Martin Scorsese.
272. Covey, S.R. *The 7 habits of highly effective people*. S&S Publishers.

creation of a "complete entrepreneurship cycle", which will accompany entrepreneurs until they achieve relevant success.

Figure 8.11. The volume of unicorns in each region of the planet (the year 2020)

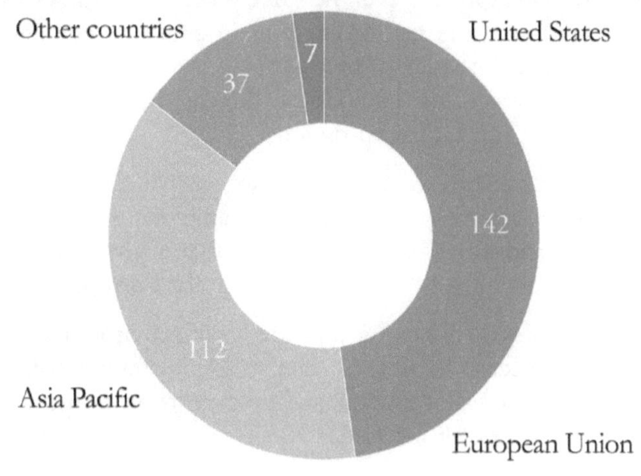

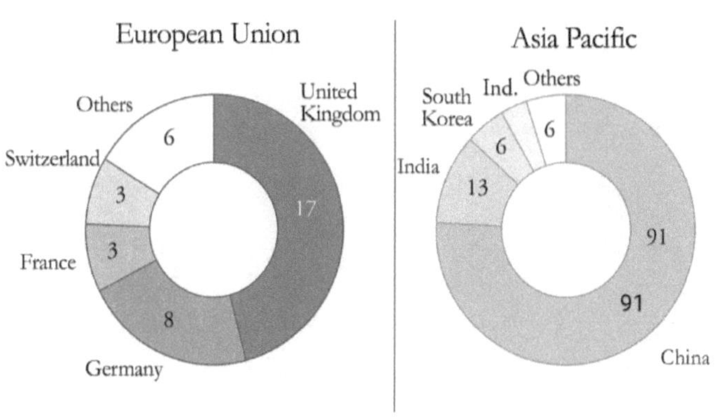

Source: cbinsights.com

The great challenge for the EU and most of its regions is to generate a digital ecosystem that is not a burden to the scalability of our startups; environments where the young and not-so-young people perceive that their ideas will be able to become a reference one day thanks to the support of society, universities and public administrations.

If this environment is not provided with sufficient resources, the entrepreneurship programs and motivational talks that are repeated in online courses, on websites and on Youtube can be empty, contradictory and even negative messages. Without a conducive ecosystem, the risk of creating an emerging company by putting at stake the assets of professionals is too high, and the result is a shortage of companies that is not corrected by methodologies and start-up programs.

European society cannot fail its young people. Our institutions must move away from insubstantial and ambiguous discourses to take a real stand. Let's get rid of the idea that in any garage in the world, ideas can grow to become billion-dollar startups.

If companies do not connect properly with environments characterized by access to finance, talent, administrative efficiency, support in all phases of growth, and efficient regulations, they are condemned to a death foretold.

4. WHAT WE NEED TO DO TO SCALE UP TO THE SAME LEVEL AS THE U.S.

4.1. Changing the discourse of the Europe of confusion

European policymakers need to calibrate their actions and speeches very carefully if they really want the digital economy to take hold.

Is Google a demon that comes to steal our data, or is it the company that allows us to communicate, move around cities, or get information for free? Is Microsoft a company that abuses its monopoly power, or is it the company that allows Bill and Melinda Gates to do more for developing countries than any cooperation program in the world? Do we really prefer a model in which our large companies (automobile, oil, construction) are the most polluting, or do we choose to bet on those that will respond to the challenges of humanity? If European entrepreneurs had ideas as brilliant as they are beyond our borders, then why is the EU once again staying on the sidelines of the new generation of digital companies?

These are questions that we must ask a large part of our political spectrum, although our hypothesis to answer them is that we live in the "Europe of confusion". Our leaders, lacking critical references and without a real common goal since the fall of the Berlin Wall, are aware of the relevance of the digital economy, but are afraid to abandon the traditional sectors that support employment. The institutional commitment to a change of model is too lax, the European Union is not pushing hard enough, and no one is willing to tell voters, including civil servants, that we must make major adjustments to prepare for the future.

It is significant, for example, that in the last general elections for the government of Spain, with the second highest unemployment rate on the continent, none of the five candidates for the presidency once uttered the word "digital" in the televised debates[273]. Or that when talking about technological applications to fight the coronavirus, more attention was paid to the violation of privacy rights than to the lives that could be saved.[274]

Although efforts are made to overcome recent barriers such as business-phobia, or the stigma of business failure, there is still an evident gap in the social recognition of the entrepreneurs between Europe and the US. Often there is an attempt to segment and differentiate between entrepreneurs and business people as if they were two different realities. The former is associated with creativity, the internet economy, and projects that are more closely linked to society. The second term, unfortunately, is linked to the traditional economy, and within it a highly speculative model.[275]

However, it is up to public administrations to put an end to this differentiation. They must do their utmost to fight corruption and tax evasion, with strong sanctions and controls, eliminating from the equation those businessmen who effectively take advantage of the weaknesses of the system. The financing of our welfare state lies in the compliance of European companies with their tax obligations. And just as there are sanctions, a culture of recognition is required that invites the continuous generation of new startups and the commitment to boost their scalability.

All the weaknesses exposed so far, such as the deficit of actions to drive AI, the anti-digital regulatory tangle, and the powerlessness to develop tech giants, are perceived by university students.

---

273. Although they kept focusing their efforts on reducing the quota of freelancers for a few months

274. 20minutos.es/opinion/coronavirus-y-la-lopd-los-datos-contra-el-virus-20200330-4210270/

275. We will not deny that it was precisely the speculative and irresponsible behavior of a significant portion of businesspeople that led to the economic crisis of 2007. It could be understood, although we will not defend it, that in certain political circles, a "caste" has come to be considered the business structure, given the behavior of some of its representatives, especially the ones with the most power. However, ignoring the prominence of companies and their entrepreneurs in a market economy as generators of wealth and employment is very dangerous.

In our 4th year "Economics of Globalization" course in the Economics degree at the University of Alicante, we used to ask how our students thought Google would be today if its founders, Larry Page and Sergey Brin, had been two students in Spain or another European country.

And the conclusion was always the same: all the milestones of the technological giant - today Alphabet - would have been diminished in Europe by difficulties and insurmountable problems to such an extent that Google, Amazon, Apple, or Facebook would have been impossible. Or they would have been small companies at best if they had been incorporated in Europe.[276]

Someone should propose this same exercise in the European Commission and draw the appropriate conclusions.

4.2. What goes wrong with scaling up

The scale of change driven by the digital revolution is so gigantic that it scares us that Europe does not have global technological benchmarks. A simple glance at how the market capitalization ranking has changed over the last two decades is enough to see this. It has gone from a panorama dominated by banks, pharmaceuticals, and energy companies, to a situation in which among the ten largest companies, seven are technology, with five American (Apple, Google, Facebook, Microsoft, and Amazon) and two Chinese (Tencent and Alibaba) **(figure 8.12)**.

---

276. Without the intention of following the exhaustiveness of the class exercise on Google's growth, we leave some questions that we ask the students. Would the library of a European university have commissioned a job to organize its information through an online search?

Would a European university have allowed its search engine (BackRub) to host and operate on its servers?

Would they have effortlessly found (in 1998) someone in the tech industry to give you a check for $100,000?

Would they have had enough qualified talent to develop their technology for scalability?

Would its listing on a European stock market have been successful in 2004 after the recent hangover from the dot.com crisis?

Would the acquisitions that today make up Google's "technology and product ecosystem" be possible? (...)

Figure 8.12. Global ranking of companies by capitalization ($ billion) (in bold, digital companies)

Company, country, and market capitalization (1997)		Company, country, and market capitalization (2019)	
1. General E. (USA)	223 mm $	1. Microsoft (USA)	904 mm $
2. RD Shell (HOL)	190 mm $	2. Apple (USA)	895 mm $
3. Microsoft (USA)	162 mm $	3. Amazon (USA)	874 mm $
4. Exxon (USA)	158 mm $	4. Google (USA)	818 mm $
5. Coca-Cola (USA)	151 mm $	5. Berkshire H (USA)	493 mm $
6. Intel (USA)	150 mm $	6. Facebook (USA)	475 mm $
7. Nippon T (JAP)	145 mm $	7. Alibaba (CHN)	472 mm $
8. Merck (USA)	121 mm $	8. Tencent (CHN)	440 mm $
9. Toyota (JAP)	113 mm $	9. Johnson&J (USA)	372 mm $
10. Novartis (CHE)	105 mm $	10. Exxon (USA)	342 mm $

Source: Pwc.

This trend is also being accentuated with the coronavirus crisis, with technology companies increasing in value while traditional companies stagnate or even collapse. In September 2020, for the first time, the value of US technology companies exceeded the capitalization of all European stock markets.[277] And the differences will increase as current technologies, even more disruptive and in which Europe still does not stand out, unleash their full potential.

If Europe wants to consolidate its ecosystems and grow with the US dimension and ambition, it should try to remedy the following differential aspects, some of which have already been addressed:

a) A non-existent European digital single market: Despite programmatic declarations for decades, in digital terms, Europe is a patchwork of overlapping markets, with no real cultural or business common ground, far from a single market of 500 million inhabitants.

---

277. https://www.cnbc.com/2020/08/28/us-tech-stocks-are-now-worth-more-than-the-entire-european-stock-market.html

Europe had to wait until May 2015 for the Juncker Commission[278] to announce the creation of the "Digital Single Market" integrated into the Europe 2020 framework. However, the most relevant approaches in digital matters have been on regulatory issues that even limit its development.[279]

The UK, for example, has always felt digitally closer to the US, India or Australia than to continental Europe. And Spain has more links with Latin American countries than with Central or Eastern Europe.[280]

b) Over-regulation and bureaucracy in the EU: Startups do not understand bureaucracy from a digital logic point of view.

It is even said that a technology company that wants to expand in Europe will need more lawyers and jurists than the sum of professionals in the rest of its departments.

c) The public sector as a client discriminates against small startups: Public administrations discriminate in their contracts in favor of large technology and service companies.

Innovative public procurement does not take into count startups, which are doomed to non-refundable public subsidies or co-investment. Curiously, the large auditing and technology companies end up subcontracting to small companies that cannot bid for public projects to perform services.

d) The corporate social culture is not as friendly as that of the United States: European social recognition of its companies is much more limited, despite the enormous advances in the matter.

The non-futile discrimination between entrepreneurs and business people is not a minor issue. There is a lot of talent who, for reasons of social status prefer to dedicate their effort to sit in a public entrance exam or exercise professional activities in

---

278. eur-lex.europa.eu/legal-content/… /?uri=celex:52015DC01 92
279. See Chapter 4.
280. Cities like Madrid or Barcelona have become the gateway to Europe for most Argentine, Mexican, and Colombian startup. See: news.crunchbase.com/news/how-spain-attracts-latin-american-startup-look   ing-for-growth/

large companies rather than becoming an entrepreneur.

e) A university system that must be even more committed and linked to entrepreneurship: European universities must support entrepreneurship and technology-based companies to a greater extent and effectiveness. University talent must be a permanent flow between companies and research centers, and not be isolated at the academic level, where the social impact is less.

f) European digital ecosystems of small size and relevance: International talent requires spaces in which to interact, where investment and technological innovation can accumulate. With a few exceptions, the large European cities, too influenced by their traditional economic structure, have not yet consolidated a completely decided commitment to the digital economy.

g) The predominance of financing based on conventional criteria: The absence of funds in Europe for entrepreneurship compared to other countries is combined with the lack of professionalism of the existing investment funds. Some are obsessed with the "exit"[281] or with openly intervening in the management of the company, setting aside its visionary creators to give it a more classic approach.

---

281. The exit is the strategy that some investors implement when establishing their investments. Through the exit, they hope to recover their investment plus a capital gain at a given time.

5. SUCCESSES AND WEAKNESSES OF EUROPEAN ENTREPRENEURSHIP

5.1. A model based on copy-paste

The disadvantages that limit the scalability of European startups have one of their clearest corollaries in access to financing. Since 2000, only 15 European companies have reached financing of more than 1 billion euros, along with the 60 US companies and more than 40 Chinese ones. Uber, Ant Financial, Didi, and Tesla raised more than 15 billion euros in their financing rounds. Uber in fact exceeded 20 billion.

No European company has ever come close to these records. The ceiling on the old continent seems to be stuck at 3 billion euros (reached by OneWeb, Spotify, and Delivery Hero), lower than those achieved by other American and Chinese startups such as SpaceX, Airbnb, NIO, Snapchat or Lyft.

We might think venture capital investment is not everything, and even more so in the digital economy. It is partly true: Facebook barely reached 2 billion in funding before becoming the giant it is today, valued at more than 500 billion euros. And Microsoft, the most surprising case, barely raised a million dollars before its IPO. However, we cannot ignore that in a global market in which technological competition has intensified so much, not having a large working capital that allows for rapid growth is a serious risk. Technology companies not only compete with startups in their field but also against the rapid transformation of digital giants, which seek to position themselves in almost any new lucrative sector: music, travel, shopping, leisure, etc.

For this reason, some European accelerators have specialized in "copy and paste" companies in their portfolios, with the real objective of facilitating the absorption of their firms. They reproduce successful ideas that are starting to become a reference in other markets, exploring new applications, or looking for a niche in regions where the original is not dominant, but without a real ambition of global leadership. Projects that could even technically surpass the original ones and adapt better to the idiosyncrasies of their regions but which, given the disadvantages mentioned above, are unable to achieve the scalability of the leading US or Asian startups to compete with them. Here are some examples:

Tuenti, the Spanish Facebook: Tuenti became one of the most successful social networks in Europe thánks to its presence in almost all Spanish-speaking countries, although it was a complete unknown outside of Spain and Latin America.

When in 2011, they celebrated reaching 10 million users per month, Facebook had more than 700 million. This lack of scalability explains why Telefónica acquired 85% of Tuenti for 70 million euros, while News Corporation paid 600 million dollars for MySpace, and Facebook reached 80 billion euros on its first day on the stock market. Given the stagnation and competitive disadvantage posed by European privacy laws to other social networks[282] in 2012 Tuenti closed its servers.

Xing, German-style Linkedin: Xing is the most important professional social network in Europe. Both in terms of the number of users (16 million) and a positive and growing income statement.

However, Xing is heavily dependent on the German-speaking market, with more than 60% of its users coming from Germany, Austria and Switzerland alone. Hence, while Xing's current valuation is estimated at 2 billion euros[283], Microsoft valued Linkedin at $26 billion in its acquisition, which is 50 times the number of Xing users.

---

282. Statement from one of the founders in the UNIMOOC training course for entrepreneurs. youtu.be/-Pzzk7baT-g

283. Estimated based on what the Hubert Burda Media group invested for the acquisition of 50% of Xing.

> *DailyMotion from France to compete with Youtube:* DailyMotion, the French video-streaming platform, has had a more global expansion (in fact, most of its audience is in the United States), although by figures it is very far from YouTube.
>
> Dailymotion receive an estimated average of more than 40 million visits per month, while YouTube is close to 5 billion. These figures influence its market value: Vivendi bought Dailymotion from Orange in 2015 for just under € 300 million, while Google paid $1.3 billion for YouTube nine years earlier.
>
> The current market value of Youtube would be around $40 billion, although we doubt that Alphabet/Google is going to part with one of its most precious assets.

These "imitations" do not only occur in the European market. China also has its own Chinese YouTube (Yoku), its own Chinese WhatsApp (WeChat), its own Chinese LinkedIn (Tianji), and even its own Chinese Pied Piper.[284] However, the greater scalability of the Asian digital market allows them, as in the case of the US, to foster Big Bang disruptors. These are companies that, by applying disruption to a product or its processes, are capable of rendering traditional companies in an international sector unable to react.[285]

Uber, Airbnb, Didi, and Netflix have reached that status of Big Bang disruptors, and are able of competing head-to-head with the big tech companies such as Google or Amazon in their niche. Something that Spotify, the only major European disruptor, has also achieved.

5.2. Some benchmark European startups

Andrés Torrubia, one of the most prominent entrepreneurs we know - and whom we have been lucky enough to interview on

---

284. See: *Silicon Valley*, HBO (Season 5).

285. Downes, L., Nunes, P., 2014. Big Bang Disruption: Strategy in the Age of Devastating Innovation. Penguin, y Trabucchi, D., Talenti, L., & Buganza, T. (2019). How do Big Bang Disruptors look like? A Business Model perspective. Technological Forecasting and Social Change, 141, 330-340.

several occasions - often says that cemeteries are full of great brilliant ideas. 'Executive intelligence' is more important than the brilliance of the concept, he says, especially in such a complex global competitive environment.

For this reason, we want to highlight below some European startups that with a lot of effort and, despite the difficulties, have managed to be a benchmark in their respective markets. Hopefully, they can serve as an inspiration to new generations of entrepreneurs.

i. Spotify

Sector: Music Streaming
Fundadores: Daniel Ek and Martin Lorentzon
Countrys: Sweden
Financing: 2,500 million euros
Approximate market value: € 25 billion

Spotify is the most notable success story of the European digital economy. The Swedish startup, a pioneer in the music streaming service with the agreement of the record companies, revolutionized the music market with an open system under subscription.

With more than 100 million users between premium and free, Spotify records exceed those of its natural competitors such as the French Deezer or Tidal. However, technological giants also have set their eyes on the music market: Apple Music, Youtube Music, and Amazon Music.

Spotify has worked on expanding utilities such as lyrics, podcasts, concerts, and especially the use of AI to customize results and recommendations. [286]

---

286.   forbes.com/sites/bernardmarr/2017/10/30/the-amazing-ways-spotify-uses-big-data-ai-and-machine-learning-to-drive-business-success/#3d2d45a04bd2

ii. BlaBlaCar

Sector: Collaborative Transport
Founders: Francis Nappez, Frédéric Mazzella, Nicolas Brusson
Country: France
Financing: € 445 million
Approximate market value: € 1.2 billion

BlaBlaCar is the world's largest carpooling social network. Present in 22 countries and with more than 500 employees and 85 million users, it is an idea that changed the way of traveling and with unquestionable advantages: less pollution, efficiency and profitability in the use of assets, accurate information for travelers and drivers, and greater flexibility of schedules and destinations.

Many other companies have tried to compete in the segment (such as the Spanish Amovens, the Israeli Gett, or the German Wunder Mobility), although again it is the threat of giants such as Uber (UberPool) or Google (Waze) that can destabilize the market and lower the valuation of the French leader.

iii. Zalando

Sector: Clothing trade
Founders: David Schneider, Robert Gentz
Country: Germany
Financing: € 465 millon
Approximate market value: € 11 billion

The story of Zalando meets all the clichés of the romantics of entrepreneurship: a couple of friends, a crazy idea, and a prototype created in a student flat that became an office headquarters, product warehouse, and logistics point, with its founders personally delivering shoes all over Berlin.

In 2010, two years after its founding, it was already operating in Germany and three other countries. Currently, 17 European countries have full access, with a turnover that exceeds 5,000 million euros per year thanks to its extensive catalog of brands and the commitment to exclusive firms of their creation.

Zalando is undoubtedly the most prominent European case in the sector, but not the only one: others such as the British Asos or the Spanish TradeInn also seek to become a benchmark in the clothing market, seeking a specialization that sets them apart in a market globally dominated by Amazon.

iv. Wallapop

Sector: Second-hand trade
Founders: Agustin Gomez, Gerard Olive, Miguel Vicente
Countrys: Spain (2013)
Financing: € 40 - 140 million
Approximate market value: € 500 million – 1 billion

The largest European second-hand buying and selling startup was born in Barcelona as one more project among other initiatives that aimed at the same market niche. Milanuncios and Segundamano.es were already operating with great success in Spain, but Wallapop also targeted the markets of the UK, France, and the United States.

Wallapop is a unique case, closer to North American experiences than European ones. Without a clear-cut business model, it managed to raise several million euros in funding rounds based solely on its potential user growth, as did WhatsApp, Facebook, Google, and Twitter.

The appearance of Wallapop and other more specialized European companies such as Vinted has been a breath of fresh air, as well as breadth in the market that benefits users.

v. Telegram Messenger

Sector: Messaging
Founders: Nikolai Durov, Pavel Durov
Country: United Kingdom
Financing: € 1.7 billion
Approximate market value: € 5 billion

Born to challenge the dominance of WhatsApp, Telegram incorporated notable differences that place it as one of the communication tools preferred by technology experts, such as multiplatform access and better encryption and security.

Although with 200 million users it is quite far from WhatsApp and its 1,500 million users, the diversification of Telegram and its technological cleverness is proving most interesting. In addition to working with an open API, in 2018, the messaging company launched the Telegram Open Network, a Blockchain platform associated with its cryptocurrency, Gram. With it, Telegram users will be able to make completely secure transactions in a matter of seconds.

In the first round of private investment, Grams was sold for nearly $1.7 billion. Currently, the Gram can already be bought and sold in any cryptocurrency market, ahead of *libra,* the digital currency devised by Facebook.

vi. Transferwise

Sector: Financial Services
Founders: Kristo Kaarmann, Taavet Hinrikus
Country: United Kingdom (2011)
Financing: € 700 million
Approximate market value: € 3.5 billion

Transferwise is one of the major European fintech benchmarks. The platform has managed to enable its 5 million users around the world to make international payments, send and receive money in any currency, and invest in currencies and cryptocurrencies. All this transparently, from a single application, and with lower fees and margins than traditional banking services.

Transferwise is not alone in this revolution. Others such as the also British Revolut, WorldRemit or Monzo, or the German N26 threaten the operating space of the large banks of the old continent.

A space that could shrink even further if the big technology companies such as Google, Facebook, Apple or even Amazon continue to increase their interest in services such as payments or purchase financing... although this will also be to the detriment of this new young and digital European bank.

313

vii. Rovio Entertainment

Sector: Video Game
Founders: Jarno Vakevainen, Kim Dikert, Niklas Hed
Country: Finland (2003)
Financing: € 75 million
Approximate market value: € 300 million

The complicated video game sector is marked by the Asian compass, with the Japanese platforms Nintendo and Sony as major benchmarks, followed by the notable efforts of Microsoft Xbox and, more recently, Google Stadia. Although projects such as the Spanish Smarch ZEl are beginning to be heard, the old continent has derived in the creation of games its most realistic options to achieve notable results in the virtual entertainment sector.

Of all the companies dedicated to this, Rovio has been the great European hope in the last decade. Its game Angry Birds allowed the Finnish firm to lead all the revenue rankings up to that moment, being the most downloaded application in 2010 and 2011, and with a spectacular rebound in 2015 that took the company's share price to € 1 billion.

Several sequels to the famous game, two movies, a television series, and much merchandising later, the company lives a complicated moment. The fierce competition with North American and Japanese games (Candy Crush, League of Legends, Pokémon Go, ...) without finding a new franchise with which to repeat the success of Angry Birds has made a dent in their revenue volume.

6. SOME CONCRETE PROPOSALS: ENTREPRENEURSHIP AND SCALABILITY

We recapitulate to action specific proposals for entrepreneurship and scalability:

---

1. Understand the entrepreneur and place him at the center of the action. Recently José Almansa, one of the greatest experts in Europe in shaping innovation spaces, proclaimed the "end of innovation and the beginning of the era of the innovator"[287] or disruptor.

Let's focus policies on them: talent, training, entrepreneurial culture and relevant and real facilities to boost business. A country that wants to exploit its full potential in the digital era must look to its entrepreneurs and attract the most talented to its territory.

2. Create a great entrepreneurial culture and enhance its value in society. The risk of not doing so is very high: the flight of the best European talents to the US or even the UK, which outside the EU could be postulated as a digital "free zone" in fiscal and regulatory terms.

---

287. That is the title of the latest book by José Almansa, a pioneer when it comes to introducing coworking spaces throughout Europe (the Impact Hub system) and reinvented it in Loom Houses with new contributions around the concept of community and collaborative work.

3. Europe must embrace and support the enthusiasm and idealism of young entrepreneurs, accompanied by measures to close the circle of entrepreneurship. The society and public administrations must create a correct culture concerning entrepreneurship and its ethical codes, but not abandon the entrepreneur in the early stages of the process.

4. Governments should be obsessed with the scalability of businesses. They must be equipped with everything that defines good international ecosystems and that explains scalability, such as a powerful digital market, endowment of specific financial means, availability of qualified STEM human resources, suppression of discouraging, costly, and inefficient deregulation, private R&D, etc.

5. Public administrations must help by acquiring technology for small companies and not only with subsidies and aid. It is necessary to end the discrimination of public procurement of innovation. Innovative public procurement must come out of its ostracism.

6. Improve the efficiency and digitization of public administrations in business creation procedures, staff hiring, invoicing, and access to grants and credits. In general, enhance the awareness of public administrations towards companies and entrepreneurs.

7. Create a legal framework that encourages digital development and especially the most important disruptive technologies. Encourage the deregulation or the suppression of inefficient regulations regarding data, privacy or intellectual property that place Europe at a disadvantage compared to other parts of the world.

8. Attend to the real needs of human capital and training of digital companies. Vocational training and universities must be much more proactive in improving the employability of their graduates, identifying with a sense of prospect the potential needs of companies. Of course, they must update many obsolete titles in the field of the digital revolution.

9. Promote and help business networks and associations. Collaborative work, sharing knowledge, carrying out alliances between companies, promoting platforms for joint use. There is a new digital business culture that Europe must understand and promote.

CHAPTER 9: DIGITAL ECOSYSTEMS – IN SEARCH OF THE EUROPEAN MODEL

« The art of life lies in a constant readjustment to our surroundings. »

OKAKURA KAKUZŌ

If Europe wants to correct its loss of economic relevance, it will need digital ecosystems. Creative environments where talent as a fundamental input drives the "disruption industry", new technological advances and companies called to reinvent economic sectors. The EU has been searching for its own Silicon Valley for decades, yet India, China, and Israel have been more successful in that endeavor.

In this chapter, we will first identify why Europe has failed to make its technological hubs worldwide references. And finally, we propose entrepreneurial "smallholdings" as one of the indigenous solutions most deeply rooted in the European reality, which will serve to provide the EU with a digital base with which to begin to be competitive on a global scale.

1. THE 28 SILICON VALLEYS

The creation of a true European digital single market in the 1990s could have been a turning point in the EU's technological and economic momentum.

In this hypothetical single market, economic specialization probably would have been maintained, with Spain leading the tourism sector, Germany consolidating its historic industrial advantage, or the United Kingdom standing out in the financial sector. However, it would have been easier to have technology hubs of international relevance, probably in the most innovative regions of the north. These regions would attract talent and funding, and then atomize renewal and competitiveness throughout Europe.

That is not a minor concern since the size of the markets in the US and China is an essential part of explaining the scalability and success of their startups. Yet the existing single European "market", which as we have already noted has been largely regulatory in nature, has hardly solved the European digital divide, nor has it promoted a change in economic policy.

Europe's fragmentation is reflected in its digital ecosystems. The US and China have concentrated all their disruptive efforts in a few areas: San Francisco, Boston, Shenzhen, and Shanghai are the benchmark regions to seek funding, study at the best universities, or enhance synergies. In turn, they feed the rest of the regions with qualified personnel and advanced services.

In Europe, each country competes to create the new Silicon Valley, whether in Berlin, London, Barcelona, or Copenhagen, despite the dissimilarities of these cities with respect to the consolidated digital ecosystems, which will be mentioned later. Because Europe's failure in the internet economy began with not understanding that digital development does not depend solely on the millions invested but also on talent, flexibility, and scalability.

In contrast, the *Silicon Waldi* of Tel Aviv (Israel), Bangalore (India), and Pangyo (South Korea) have become neuralgic centers of entrepreneurship and disruptive technologies. With less media noise but with a commitment to concentrating talent and investment, its results have been extraordinarily good compared to the attempts of European capitals. Only London, with a special emphasis on fintech, could be considered as a benchmark digital ecosystem in the old continent **(figure 9.1)**. Tallinn, the capital of Estonia, is another example of good practices.

Figure 9.1: Global distribution of Artificial Intelligence startups (countries and ecosystems)

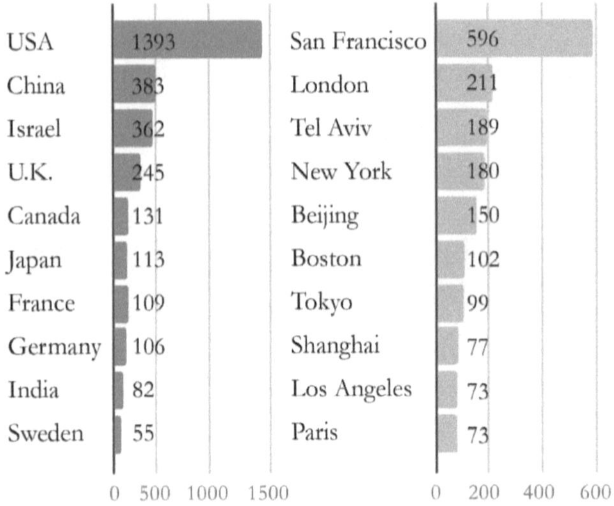

Source: Asgard and Roland Berger (asgard.vc/global-ai/)

2. TALENT AND DISRUPTION AS THE BASIS OF A NEW MODEL

2.1. Let's admit that the paradigm of competition has changed

When we talk about ecosystems, we like to refer to an idea in which all parts interact in a harmonious process that fuels creativity, innovation, and disruption of a region; nurtured by a critical mass of talent from large companies and startups, with mobility between them, with entrepreneurs who have failed in their projects and end up contributing their vision to large companies, and professionals who leave top positions to found their startup.

For this reason, policies for creating a European ecosystem must go through two essential axes: attracting and training talent for its incorporation into the sectors of the future, and finding a differential element to be able to re-engage belatedly but with guarantees in the new digital sectors. To this end, European regions should be strengthened with policies in three directions already pointed out: an educational transformation that focuses on computational thinking and STEM, an intensification of the university-business relationship fostering employability; and the creation of an entrepreneurial culture that attracts funding.

If the EU were to get involved in this strategy with sufficient funding and commitments, the old continent could begin to consider leading very important areas of the digital economy. However, even if the European Commission does not take the appropriate steps, countries, regions, and their local governments should begin urgently to draw up strategies for the construction of digital ecosystems to close the technology and business creation gap between European regions.

A good example of the kind of actions we refer to can be found in the interview in Bloomberg magazine with the entrepreneur Johaness Reck, founder of the emerging company GetYourGuide, present in 150 countries and which has raised close to 500 million euros of financing. [288] Johaness warned about how in most of Europe (except Portugal, France, and the United Kingdom), employees have to face high taxes for the transfer of shares or the distribution of profits, while in the US, companies promote workers' participation. That motivates many US professionals to continue betting on small projects, seeking to be part of the new WhatsApp, which after the acquisition by Facebook, distributed 40 million euros to each of its 55 employees.

"It's not even that I am disappointed — I am angry, really angry", Reck pointed out in the interview. The ignorance of European politicians regarding the entrepreneurial world is favoring a concentration of talent in large companies and not in projects like theirs, clipping the wings of the regeneration of the digital economy. The success of future Europe depends on embracing the new paradigm of competition, which encourages collaboration and a win-win relationship that makes it attractive for talent to land and stay on the old continent.

2.2. Israel, a case study

Israel has become a surprising success story. The continuity and ambition of its active economic policies around the attraction of talent, education, and financing constitute a very interesting guide for any country in the world.

Its growth has been well orchestrated since the transformation of its productive sector, which goes far beyond military spending. After years of promoting its R&D policies, Israel is currently the country that invests the most in innovation over its GDP in the entire OECD, with 90% of its expenditure destined for future sectors, surpassing the 70% of its total industrial production for high-tech industries.

Thanks to this commitment, and despite its small size (just under 9 million inhabitants) and the geopolitical instability of the

---

288. "Why It's So Hard for Startups to Create Wealth in Europe". Bloomberg Magazine, October 2, 2019. bloomberg.com/news/features /2019-10-02/why-it-s-so-hard-for-entrepreneurs-to-get-really-rich-in-europe?sref=mezxKzsV

region, Israel has become the promised land of talent and startups. It is the second country with the most startups in the world (more than 4,000) and the third country (after the United States and China) with the most technology companies listed on the NASDAQ,[289] and its digital ecosystem (Silicon Waldi) houses the headquarters of large technology companies such as Intel, IBM, Cisco Systems, SAP, Philips, Hewlett-Packard, AOL, and Microsoft.

The Israel Innovation Authority[290] is a good example of pro-activity and policies to promote innovation. Among multiple support measures, there are programs such as Tnufa to help companies in testing concepts and R&D, with incubators that serve as the basis for new companies, talent recruitment programs to found their startups in Israel, and entrepreneurship programs for students of any age.

In addition, a very wise relationship between companies and universities has been strengthened. The private sector finances research projects and the creation of new startups based on patents, and universities enhance human capital in line with the digital economy. Israel is the country with the highest rate of engineers in the world: 140 per 10,000 inhabitants.

This holistic commitment to the sectors of the future, with policies on education, talent attraction and efficient regulation, is also having positive effects on its labor market. In the last two decades, the unemployment rate has gone from 11% to 4%. On the contrary, Spain has gone from 10% to 15% and Greece from 9% to 18% in the same period.

The entire process of Israeli economic transformation can be read in detail in the best-seller[291] "Start-up Nation: The story of Israel's economic miracle" by Dan Senor and Saul Singer, which

---

289. It has more companies listed on this market than the sum of Spain, Italy, France, Germany, and the Netherlands. See: tentulogo.com/israel-la-tierra-prometida-para-las-startups-en-el-mundo/

290. innovationisrael.org.il/en/

291. In 2010, Start-up Nation was ranked fifth on The New York Times bestseller list. It also made The Wall Street Journal bestseller list.

helped to consolidate the country's image as a world-class international technological benchmark.

Encouraged by the success of Israel, Spain and France tried to emulate the idea after Start-up Nation. However, promoting the digital economy goes beyond a brand or a logo: it requires active policies that streamline business research and development, constant support for its technology sector, and a seamless commitment to education and talent. And this is something that has not yet been achieved in European countries.

3. AN OPPORTUNITY FOR THE ECONOMIES OF THE SOUTH

3.1. The natural environment of the digital economy

The digital economy has always moved away from large industrial and financial urban centers. New York, Chicago, Los Angeles, Detroit and Houston were the most important cities in the US in the digital smallholding must be valued for what it represents in Europe. It is not the ideal ecosystem format. However, neither is a replica of Silicon Valley. Professor Daniel J. Isenberg warns that not even Silicon Valley can recreate another Silicon Valley.[292]

In the 80s and 90s. San Francisco and Boston were medium-sized cities that made entrepreneurship easier thanks to their quality of life, lower costs and the involvement of universities such such as Stanford, Harvard, and MIT.

Asians have also understood - on their own scale - that the massification and concentration of the traditional economy and a high cost of living are not good ingredients for the development of future sectors. Shenzhen and Bangalore have been established as large technological centers of China and India, instead of large cities such as Beijing, Shanghai, Bombay or Delhi.

The digital economy seeks its own spaces where there are no brakes on disruption, and a higher cost of living predisposes to the consolidation of emerging companies negatively. That is why it is practically impossible for many startups to set up in northern Europe, where there is most innovation. In a city like Oslo the average salary is almost 40,000 euros a year net per worker, in Copenhagen more than 37,000 euros, in Stockholm or London more than 36,000 euros[293], to which must be added the cost of office rent, travel or social life.

---

292. Isenberg, D. J. (2010). How to start an entrepreneurial revolution. *Harvard business review, 88*(6), 40-50.

293. numbeo.com/cost-of-living/region_prices_by_city

Decades ago, in the construction of common socio-economic spaces in Europe, it would have made sense to develop the internet economy in these capitals - as Dublin did. However, at present, we must move away from the idea of replicating the new Silicon Valley in large cities. In fact, not even Silicon Valley could ever create another Silicon Valley, as Professor Daniel J. Isenberg warns.[294] The ecosystem created in San Francisco is impossible to match in Europe's technological and industrial capitals **(figure 9.2)**.

Figure 9.2: Represented critical mass of European digital ecosystems compared to the San Francisco area.

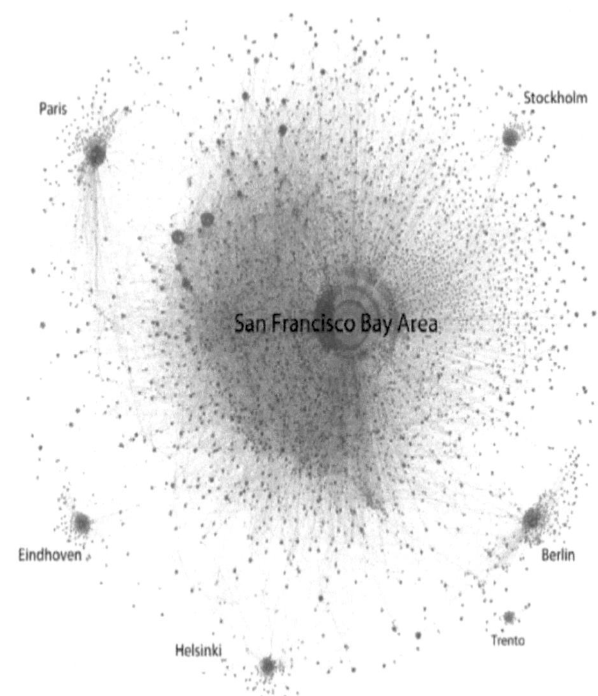

Source: What can you adopt from Silicon Valley?[295]

---

294. Isenberg, D. J. (2010). How to start an entrepreneurial revolution. *Harvard business review*, *88*(6), 40-50.

295. Presentation by Antonio Hyder. ost.torrejuana.es/que-puede-adoptar-alicante-de-silicon-valley-antonio-hyder-ftf/

However, the search for well-being and quality of life on the part of entrepreneurs does give a comparative advantage to average cities in southern countries such as Spain, Greece, Portugal, and Italy. The Mediterranean area also has an enviable quality of life due to its climate, culture, natural environment, infrastructure, and quality education systems, so much so that digital nomadism has made some of their cities fashionable in recent years.

3.2. A question of survival

More than an opportunity, in southern Europe the commitment to a productive transformation is beginning to be a necessity.

The lack of an entrepreneurial culture has led to a total lack of job security with the financial and real estate crisis. Youth unemployment rates of over 50% were reached, with young people anchored to seasonal work, insecurity or civil service examinations at a time of cutbacks. And once again, COVID-19 is threating their economies and their welfare to a greater extent than in the rest of Europe.

If Spain, Italy, Greece, and Portugal want to take advantage of their quality of life to project themselves as hubs of reference, they will have to make changes as important as those described in the previous pages: ease of attraction of entrepreneurs and STEM professionals, access to financing, educational adaptation, administrative agility,…

We would like to believe that southern Europe can play a relevant role in the digitization of the EU. That an exciting collective effort will be made so that the Mediterranean regions can become accomplished international benchmarks in the digital economy and join, from where no one expected, the major European centers of economic and financial power.

4. A EUROPEAN MODEL: DIGITAL SMALLHOLDINGS

4.1. The digital treasure of Europe

Throughout its territory, Europe hides treasures in the form of startups that are not as mediatic or cited as Spotify, Vinted, or Blablacar. A digital economy supported by talent, sometimes without incubators or accelerators. Without funding or with hardly any aid. Startups that are making their way through the traditional economy, often far from the spotlight of Berlin, Paris, London, Barcelona or other major cities.

It is the "digital smallholding": geographical areas where groups of small technology startups emerge, driven by entrepreneurs in the most "heroic" conditions, with almost no support and no comparative advantages, but with digital success rates much higher than those expected in these territories. Nevertheless, the limits to scalability explained in the previous chapter prevent these projects from becoming unicorns. Given their small size, they tend to be diluted among the aggregate statistics, falling into anonymity even in their immediate environment.

Because of the opportunity it represents in the transformation of the European productive fabric, the digital smallholding must be highlighted. It is not the ideal ecosystem format, but it has an enviable own identity. The economic and cultural diversity of Europe is a virtue that neither the US nor any Asian country has. Europe has the possibility of fostering different digital ecosystems around sectors as varied as specializations exist in each of its regions. However, first, it is necessary to converge technologically towards the countries that are ahead of us.

Digital smallholdings can help us to find potential technological hubs of global relevance in Europe. And once located, provide them with an environment and the right tools to see how their startups develop their full potential.

4.2. Patterns in digital smallholdings

In our closest environment, we have been able to work and learn from leading companies in one of the many digital smallholding in Europe. From this experience, we can extrapolate some conclusions and working hypotheses that emphasize why these ecosystems must be discovered and promoted, and can also help to detect new smallholdings in the rest of old continent. They are as follows:

a) **They generate talent in the face of a lack of opportunities.** Without having the resources of the large European capitals, in the digital smallholdings companies show enormous talent and competitive potential, capable of internationally succeeding when they have the opportunity.

b) **Adaptation to financing that is not even "family, friends, and fools":** Lack of means causes the personal performance of the entrepreneur to be the differential factor. No-cost is the alternative to low-cost. However, when projects scale abroad, they are highly valued and tend to successfully access financing through investment.

c) **Success stories emerge without incubators or accelerators.** In the absence of incubators or accelerators, and with universities that tend to be less "own" than in digital ecosystems, startups seek to create their collaborative networks or communities.

d) **They recognize and identify scalability issues.** Many startups serve as a vanguard in identifying obstacles to economic development. In smallholdings, there is usually a point where scalability becomes practically impossible due to a lack of human resources, financing, or knowledge. If the ecosystem does not correct these deficits, the only way out is through business relocation, external funding, or acquisition by another company.

e) **They promote changes in the administrations.** With little recognition, startups that form a smallholding can rarely access relevant public aid, nor do they have the possibility of accessing concept commissions or Innovative Public Procurement.

To this must be added the absence of a single digital market in Europe or the bureaucratic obstacles to access innovation funds. It is not surprising that many entrepreneurs consider that large technology companies products such as Adwords, Adsense, open-source platforms, and MOOC courses have been more decisive in the success of their projects than the administrations themselves.

However, it is precisely the development of digital culture and the appearance of these companies that can serve to change the mentality necessary in European administrations.

In short, smallholdings present a great opportunity for Europe, but work must be done to correct their weaknesses. Perhaps the best solution is a logical division of functions. The European Commission and its states should focus on scalability, and regional and local member should focus on entrepreneurship and the generation of startups.

Europe must analyze and delve deeper into the areas and small ecosystems where digital business networks are developing. From them, a European model will probably be born that better adapts to our structural characteristics and the idiosyncrasies of each region.

4.3. New valuable spaces: the case of Alicante

The province of Alicante (In the region of Valencia city, Spain) is one of these spaces defined as digital smallholdings with surprising digital talent. Its case can serve as an example and help other territories to find factors that drive wealth and job creation through digitization.

Located in southeastern Spain and with 212 km of Mediterranean coastline, Alicante is known for its quality of life and its tourist attraction. It has one of the best-connected international airports in Europe. With flights to more than 150 cities, it gives life to its coastal cities (Benidorm, Torrevieja, Altea, Jávea, Denia, etc.), once small fishing villages and today benchmarks of European sun and beach tourism.

In addition to tourism, the Alicante economy is oriented to manufacturing industries (footwear, toys, textiles, food, etc.) and especially to construction and real estate activity. For this reason, the economic crisis that began in 2008 was a harsh setback for the area from which it has not yet recovered.

Theoretically, in this picture, so characterized by an analog economy and some speculative practices, there was little room for digital evolution. However, as happened in Jurassic Park with dinosaurs that supposedly could not procreate, "digital life made its way."

The individual and almost isolated workplaces of the entrepreneurs[296] began to be channeled into networks to deepen and find solutions about the projects.[297] The universities with concrete projects also began to promote an entrepreneurial culture.[298]

Alicante currently has a very extensive and varied group of digital companies. A number of surprising success stories (Adsalsa, Orizon, Binomio Ventures, Grupo Verne, Roi Up, From The Bench, Tutellus, Fixr, Sun and Co, Clave-i, Sonneil, Recursos en la Red, 1MillionBot, etc.), which are the trigger for an association like AlicanTEC, whose purpose is to support the development of the digital economy and the sectors of the future in this territory.

Luckily for Alicante, all the effort made by digital startups points to a happy corollary. The province is experiencing a boom in the attraction of digital nomads, private sector initiative is replacing the lack of accelerators, and big companies and startups in associations such as AlicanTEC and Timur are generating a very engaging collaborative economy mentality. In addition, the region is moving away from a total and worrisome political and business ignorance, to towards a growing interest that has converged into very diverse projects led by the regional government and local organizations.

---

296. For many years without coworking spaces, until in 2016, when ULAB opened the first alternative to the classic offices in the area.

297. The Hacker Club created by Andrés Torrubia and Eduardo Manchón made it possible to build a base of contacts and relationships to exchange valuable information.

298. To highlight the Scientific Park of the Miguel Hernández University, which incubates, accelerates, and houses some startups with very interesting paths.

These are the first decisive steps for a region in southern Europe, which had little chance of becoming a benchmark in the technology industry, to transform into an economic specialization driven by cutting-edge sectors. Nonetheless, there is still a long way to go.

The following are some of the startups and projects that are part of the smallholding of Alicante:[299]

Panoramio (Callosa del Segura, 2005), founded by Eduardo Manchón and Joaquín Cuenca in the province of Alicante with fewer than 20,000 inhabitants: a web platform that exhibited geo-referenced photographs on Google Maps of places or landscapes created by the users. In July 2007, Google acquired Panoramio for $ 8 million and integrated it into its Google Maps service. It was one of Google's first purchases in Europe and the first in Spain.[300]

Trymedia (El Campello, 1999), founded by Andrés Torrubia and his cousin Alex in a coastal town in Alicante provof less than 30,000 inhabitants. The startup after a round of fundraising in New York, moved to San Francisco. Trymedia was conceived as a technological gaming platform that allowed creators to control their work and charge for their distribution. The company Digital Word Services of the Bertelsmann group obtained a license for its use. Macrovision acquired Trymedia for $34 million in July 2005.

Energy Sistem (Finestrat, 1995), founded by the Sánchez brothers (Julio, Salvador, Alfonso, and José Luis) in a town of fewer than 7,000 inhabitants. It was the first company to launch an MP3 player in Spain, and progressively became the leader in several categories such as headphones, speakers, and bluetooth sound towers. From there, they pivoted to smartphones, tablets, and eReaders. It has about 200 engineers in Alicante and 2,000 workers in China.

299. It is a selection from members of non-profit association AlicanTEC, which brings together 252 technology companies in the area. A few success stories have been selected from the more than 40 cases that might be worth mentioning. alicantec.com/casos-exito/.

300. cbinsights.com/research-google-acquisitions

Mis-recetas.org (Alicante 2010), founded by Rebecca Rippin and Andrés Pedreño, it was a recipe-sharing platform dedicated to home cooking. It was a spin-off of euroresidentes.com, a site that was the leader in traffic in Spain with 20 million unique users per month through the study of Google's positioning algorithm. It was awarded the Europe Adsense Google award in Dublin in 2011. In 2015, the Japanese unicorn Cookpad acquired mis-recetas.org and established its headquarters in Alicante for its expansion in Europe and Latin America (Cookpad currently has 100 million users and is already in 70 countries).

Planeta Huerto (Muchamiel, 2011) founded by brothers Alfonso and Pablo Sánchez, developed its know-how around Google's AdWords niches. And with this, it achieved the success of e-commerce specialized in ecological and sustainable products, with a catalog of more than 35,000 products and more than 200,000 clients from Spain, France, Italy, and Portugal. Its turnover rose in 2017 above € 9 million, without accelerators, business angels, or investors. The Carrefour group, through its subsidiary Greenweez, bought Planeta Huerto in October 2018 for an undisclosed sum.

MedBravo (Sant Joan, 2014) was founded by Aurelia Bustos, oncologist, computer scientist, and expert in AI, and awarded by King Felipe VI with the Order of Civil Merit for her work on the application of AI methods in the fight against cancer. Her startup MedBravo is a service that facilitates access for cancer patients to appropriate clinical trials for each case through a digital network of hospitals in coordination with doctors and clinical researchers.

Hawkers (Elche, 2013) founded by four young people: Iñaki Soriano, Pablo Sánchez, and the brothers Alejandro and David Moreno. In just four years, it became the third world brand in its sector and a leader on the internet for its social media marketing and its ability to identify opportunities in the Facebook algorithm. In 2014, they invoiced more than € 15 million and the following year, € 40 million. In 2016, they raised € 50 million in an investment round, becoming an international benchmark in digital marketing.

Rive Technology (University of Alicante - MIT, Massachusetts, 2006), founded by Javier García Martínez, it is specialized in nanotechnology applied to catalytic and separation processes used to refine oil, chemical products, and biofuels and for purifying air and water. It obtained 80 million dollars in various investment rounds. Since 2012, catalysts have been used in several refineries in the US, increasing their production. From the laboratory of the University of Alicante, Javier García continued to transfer technology until the chemical giant Grace bought Rive Technology in June 2019 for an undisclosed amount.

Lucentia Lab (Alicante, 2015), founded by a couple of professors from the University of Alicante, is an EBT that emerged as a spin-off of UniMOOC, a pioneering Massive Open Online Courses platform in Europe after Sebastián Turn's experience in the US. Lucentia brings together several top researchers in Spain on big data and AI, such as Mario Piattini (National Computer Science Award), Manuel Marco, and Juan Carlos Trujillo. They have been the architects of the construction of the "Google Activate" platform in Europe, which has enabled online training in digital skills for more than 2.5 million users.

Ellis Center for Artificial Intelligence (Alicante, 2019) promoted by Nuria Oliver, a telecommunications engineer from Alicante, Ph.D. from the Media Lab of the Massachusetts Institute of Technology (MIT), Chief Data Scientist at Data-Pop Alliance (Harvard and MIT), and former Microsoft researcher in Redmond. Nuria is one of the leading experts in AI in Europe, with more than 15,000 citations for her scientific articles. She is known for her work and patents on computational models of human behavior, AI, human-machine interaction, mobile computing, and big data for social good. This center created in Alicante supported by the Valencian regional government to attract talent in artificial intelligence is the only ELLIS node-unit for the whole of Southern Europe.

5. TOP-DOWN AND BOTTOM-UP MODELS FOR THE DEVELOPMENT OF DIGITAL ECOSYSTEMS

The case of Alicante is not isolated. Despite a traditional specialization of the Spanish economy, different areas of the Mediterranean, from Figueras to Algeciras, have been able to work on the configuration of very remarkable initiatives. The great attraction that this region gives to be the "European California" means that high-value spaces have emerged, even with the location of the headquarters of large international companies that have seen their advantages.

The Spanish Mediterranean has benefited from the entrepreneurial culture that since the economic crisis of 2008 has spread throughout Europe. A decade ago, not only was the stigmatization of failure, but there were hardly any references to encourage young people to became entrepreneurs. Even in Barcelona or Madrid, the largest cities in Spain, it was hard to identify communities of entrepreneurs with a relevant critical mass.

At present, with structures already more consolidated, we can detect very different strategies and results depending on whether the ecosystems have been driven by the public administrations or by companies. To better understand these differences, it is interesting to use the top-down approach (driven by the administrations) and the bottom-up approach (driven mainly by small companies). These two methodologies do not necessarily have to be opposed to each other and it would even be advisable to combine them in order to successfully promote digital ecosystems.

5.1. Top-down approaches

Barcelona

In the last 20 years, the Catalan capital has generated activity and cultivated an image that has positioned it as an international reference in digital matters. A model of government involvement and good practices that end up yielding a fruitful top-down model.

The 22@Barcelona[301] district emerged as a very early and pioneering commitment to the year 2000 by the Barcelona City Council, in a process of uninterrupted modernization. The investments in infrastructures that the city received as the organizer of the 1992 Olympic Games were followed by those of the Barcelona World Forum event.[302] And with 22@Barcelona, 200 hectares of industrial land in the Poblenou neighborhood were transformed with modern spaces rehabilitated "for the strategic concentration of knowledge-intensive activities."[303]

In Barcelona, the concept of the ecosystem to which we have been referring here was captured very well: "a space where the most innovative companies coexist with universities, research, training, and technology transfer centers, as well as housing, facilities, and green areas". With the strategic development of five sectoral clusters (Media, ICTs, Energy, Design, and Medical Technologies) it anticipated the trend of subsequent years.

With this formula, Barcelona supporting technology companies, creativity, networking, attraction and retention of talent and access to innovation. The results were not long in coming. Since 2001, more than 4,500 new companies have been located in the city, such as Yahoo! R&D, Facebook, Amazon, Casio, eBay, Mediapro, Microsoft, Sanofi-Aventis, Groupalia, Capgemini, Schneider Electric, Vistaprint, and Indra, among others, giving rise to more than 56,000 jobs.

The rest of the political and economic agents were also up to the task. An excellent example was the scientific and research policy promoted by ICREA, to which we have already referred, to attract international talent, one of the most profitable investments by far from the Catalan government. The World Mobile Congress was a corollary of the success of 22@Barcelona.[304]

---

301. Also known as District22@ or simply 22@.
302. es.wikipedia.org/wiki/Parque_del_F%C3%B3rum
303. es.wikipedia.org/wiki/Distrito_22@
304. MWC Barcelona is the largest technological congress organized by

Even so, this model - and its large European, state, regional, and local investments - has not been enough to establish Barcelona as a great digital benchmark in Europe compared to other capitals such as Berlin, Paris, London, and Dublin. Even Madrid has a comparable digital fabric. Currently, the instability of the political situation in Catalonia also makes the future of Barcelona as a technology center uncertain.

On the one hand, the hypothesis of leaving the EU could have advantages in terms of the creation of new regulatory frameworks, which would promote the development of the digital economy as in the case of the United Kingdom, or even with the invention of free space with outstanding tax incentives. However, outside the Union, the permanence of companies that take the community environment or Spain as a reference operating market is at risk.[305]

The lack of political and economic stability in southern European countries and regions can be a very worrying element in the medium-term task of building a relevant European digital ecosystem. Catalonia is an example.

Málaga Valley (Andalusia Technology Park)

Another top-down case within the Spanish Mediterranean has been that of "Málaga Valley", with a decisive support at governmental level. Although investment has been much lower than that of Barcelona, its impact have been extraordinarily relevant, demonstrating the competitiveness of medium-sized cities with a high quality of life for the digital economy.

The Malaga City Council, the University of Malaga, the regional government and the Spanish civil society (Club Málaga Valley),[306]

---

the international association GSMA. In 2019 it brought together more than 109,000 professionals with impacts on the city that exceeded 470 million euros.

305. In fact, in the last two years, the continuity of the World Mobile Congress itself has been questioned in the media, and the leading banks in Catalonia (CaixaBank and Banco de Sabadell) have located their headquarters in other parts of the Mediterranean, specifically Valencia and Alicante.

306. The Malaga Valley e-27 club was an initiative of a group of presidents of companies in the telecommunications and information technology

motivated to create a digital ecosystem of European reference taking Silicon Valley as a model, have generated in the last 20 years a technological environment in one of the most disadvantaged regions of Europe in terms of economic development.

The outcome has been very beneficial and relevant for the city and its university. Its commitment to the digital economy has enabled Malaga to establish itself as the economic capital of Andalucía (a territory with 87.2 thousand km^2 and some 8.5 million inhabitants), surpassing the regional capital, Seville. The province of Malaga is the only one with a positive interprovincial migratory balance in Spain every year since 1988, which shows its success in attracting population and retaining residents. Not even Madrid has achieved that.[307] Malaga currently attracts almost 25% more population than Seville, even though the Andalusian capital concentrates the regional government headquarters.

According to a study carried out by Deloitte, the Parque Tecnológico de Málaga (Andalusian Technology Park, known by its initials PTA), is one of Andalusia's greatest assets in the generation and transfer of technology to the territory, as well as a lever for the creation of value in the environment. Inaugurated 25 years ago, it has placed its city as a digital leader, with more than 19,000 jobs distributed among some 700 companies and a total impact that would reach up to 10% of the employed population of the

---

sectors of Spain to turn Malaga into the European Silicon Valley. The club organized events such as Málaga Media Happening, a meeting between traditional companies in the audiovisual sector and those dedicated to new information technologies. The club includes representatives from Telefónica, France Télécom, Alcatel, Ono, Yahoo!, HP, IBM, Nokia, Vodafone, PRISA, Vocento, businesspeople such as Martín Varsavsky, and local institutions and companies such as the University of Malaga and the old Unicaja. Active members of this club were renowned names such as Pedro Moneo, Jason Pontin, Chin Ryan, Kathleen Kennedy, Francisco.

307. "The combination of economy and climate has allowed it to attract more than 524,000 people from the rest of Spain in the last three decades. On the contrary, only 411,000 people have emigrated to the rest of the provinces. That leaves a positive balance in favor of Malaga of more than 113,000 people. The population gain has been so intense that it has ousted Seville as the main destination in Andalusia."

See: elconfidencial.com/economia/2019-09-29/exodo-urbano-espana-migraciones-malaga-sevilla_2240195/

province of Malaga, which is about 2% of total employment in Andalusia.[308] The Park contributes up to 8.65% of the GDP of the Malaga province directly and indirectly. At the regional level, that means up to 1.71% of GDP.

Without a doubt, the great success of the PTA has been its ability to attract foreign technology companies such as Neueda, Solviteers, Ciklum, ITRA, Ebury or The Workshop, as well as the well known Oracle Corporation (its second most important operations center after Dublin), Accenture, TDK, Adif, Accra West, Ericsson and Huawei.[309]

5.2. Bottom-up approaches

Alicante, Valencia, Murcia and Baleares[310]

The rest of the Spanish Mediterranean – Comunidad Valenciana, Baleares, and Murcia - follow what we could identify as a bottom-up model. It is the model of digital smallholding already studied, and that, as we said, arises from the ashes of the real estate and financial crisis.

In these regions, the roadmap for future growth set by their governments was based almost exclusively on tourism and events, real estate and other activities unrelated to the digital world.[311] The

---

308. muypymes.com/2018/02/16/pta-silicon-valley-malaga

309. Local talent has been concentrated around the Park, expanding internationally with indigenous companies such as Aertec, Airzone, Ingenia, and AT4Wireless (bought by the German Dekra). The BIC Euronova incubator covered the birth of most of these local companies. Called by its wealth-generating capacity, many Spanish professionals see PTA as a place to develop their careers or start their businesses.

310. We will focus on the case that we know best, Alicante, with some references to the rest of the cases.

311. Examples of this analogical strategic initiatives in the Valencian Community are La Ciudad de la Luz, Terra Mítica, and events such as the Volvo Ocean Race and Formula 1.

At the same time, it stopped promoting other projects such as the Alicante-Elche-Santa Pola triangle of the Investors Club or the MedPark of the University of Alicante. Murcia and the Balearic Islands, on a smaller scale, also followed a very similar policy of promoting the traditional sectors and, at times, too linked to corruption and favorable treatment.

2008 crisis brought down this financial-real estate model, leading in some cases to unsustainable debt, with failed mega-projects that today continue to represent a very high financial burden.

Given the collapse and the precarious budgetary situation - quite similar among the region of Valencia, Murcia and the Balearic Islands - the only alternative has been to encourage bottom-up processes without institutional support. A smallholding that, however, has allowed Alicante to show more consolidated digital business success stories than Madrid and Barcelona combined. Also providing an interesting paradox in the last four years, the public administrations have tried to support the consolidation of the sector "from above", seeking funds in their empty coffers to promote new digital initiatives with which to complement, two decades later, their emerging companies.

As a result of this effort, the Presidency of the Generalitat Valenciana announced the creation of the Digital District, materializing a concept initially thought to reverse the restrictions of the large investment of the City of Light blocked by the European Commission. The Digital District has started attracting relevant digital companies, such as Accenture's disruptive technologies division for all of Europe and the establishment of Indra, which have joined existing companies such as Everis, Grupo Verne, Energy Sistem, and fifty other foreign companies.[312]

The Alicante Provincial Council has promoted an ambitious digitalization model in its autonomous body SUMA Innova, with very active lines in the digital transformation, a clear commitment to AI, and an annual National Artificial Intelligence Congress that has become a reference. Also, the Provincial Council announced an ambitious digitization plan for municipalities. On the other hand, the Alicante City Council added to the said actions "Alicante

---

312. In the current legislature, the regional government has expanded and materialized its commitment to AI, ahead of the Spanish government. It has quickly achieved European success by landing the said Ellis Center and created in Alicante a Department of Universities, Innovation, Science, and Digital Society. It also has announced through a framework law the assumption of commitments and deadlines to promote industry 4.0, smart cities, the digitization of public administrations, health, education, etc.

Futura", whose objective is to complement the Digital District.[313]

Universities are also bringing priceless value to the ecosystem. Taking Alicante International Airport as a reference, we find a very competitive university system, with seven universities in a radius of 120 km^2 and 2.8 million inhabitants. Many of these universities (Miguel Hernández University, University of Alicante, University of Murcia, the Polytechnic University of Cartagena and the UPV-Alcoy) have generated science parks, technology-based companies, and fascinating synergies.

In the city of Valencia, just over 150 km north of Alicante, there is also a very relevant cluster of startup accelerators, five of which are among the top ten in the Spanish ranking: Innsomnia, Demium-Startups, Plug and Play, Shuttle, and Climate-KicAccelerator. Furthermore, among its universities, the Polytechnic University of Valencia (UPV) is among the most prominent in Europe in terms of the ability to transfer technology, promote entrepreneurship, and develop relationships between the university and the company.

The indicators seem to help Alicante and its surroundings in their new challenge and could become the model to be imitated by the rest of the bottom-up ecosystems in Europe. Alicante is among the six Spanish provinces that have generated the most jobs since 2014,[314] with forecasts for the creation of new STEM jobs for the year 2020 comparable to the Malaga PTA with a thousand jobs per year thanks to the companies located in the District.[315] It is even one of the Spanish provinces where companies are growing the fastest, something that can also be seen in the city of Murcia, both surpassing Barcelona in this indicator.[316]

---

313. alicanteplaza.es/barcala-defiende-el-proyecto-alicante-futura-como-complementario-al-distrito-digital

314. cincodias.elpais.com/cincodias/2020/01/28/economia/15802233 89_171511.html

315. alicanteplaza.es/IndraAccentureEverisyGGTechcontratarnesteaom sde600informticosparasussedesdeAlicante?amp=1

316. elpais.com/economia/2020/01/17/actualidad/1579272449_41368 8.html

6. SOME CONCRETE PROPOSALS: DIGITAL ECOSYSTEMS

Here are some of the strategies and measures that can be extracted from this chapter to favor the development of digital ecosystems and the exploitation of smallholdings:

1. Encourage entrepreneurs and startups, the raw material of digital ecosystems. We refer to the recommendations of the previous chapter. The raw material of digital ecosystems is talent and entrepreneur-disruptors. Without taking care of them, the rest is a toast to the sun.

2. A great ecosystem must develop all its components in a harmonious and integrated manner: entrepreneurial talent, research and training centers, networks of companies and professionals, means of financing, mobility, quality of life, etc. Integrating and promoting all these elements is key.

3. Support hubs and environments where new disruptive technologies such as AI, IoT, and Blockchain have development potential. Europe has a chance if it embraces general utility technologies such as AI, quantum computing, and IoT and generates global reference ecosystems. Promoting a network like Ellis in an ambitious way that serves to boost a real technology transfer is the basis to avoid our dependence on the US and China on this type of technology from becoming absolute.

4. Encourage the university system to become a proactive part of the ecosystem. Promote university-company relations with technology transfer that has an impact on value chains and the real competitiveness of companies. Universities can be a driving force or "retarder" of digitalization. Europe must find its model for universities to become the engine of ecosystems. We should exploit everything that works - for example, an Erasmus of entrepreneurs - and correct the restrictions (lack of employability, anti-business culture, R&D too closely linked to mature technologies, etc.).

5. Promote the location of digital ecosystems in medium cities with high quality of life, thanks to the ability to retain talent without the high costs of diseconomies in large cities (transportation, office prices, average salaries, etc.).

6. Integrate bottom-up and top-down actions. It makes no sense that national and local governments go one way and the market and private initiative go the other. Public administrations must listen and be sensitive to what entrepreneurs and the market indicate. **Learn from the digital smallholding and its startups**, which, with everything against them, became success stories And support their development with ecosystems so that they continue to grow.

7. Europe is moving away from a central Silicon Valley-type model; let's exploit the mosaic of ecosystems and hubs. We must surrender to the evidence. Without a large central hub in the EU, every ecosystem must be taken into account. From large cities such as Dublin, Helsinki, Berlin, Barcelona, Madrid, Lisbon, Amsterdam, Paris, and London, to smaller cases that stand out in their regions, such as Malaga, Alicante, Valencia, and Murcia. Perhaps the model of Europe consists of integrating and connecting to the maximum all these spaces, promoting a real flow between people's ideas, companies, and resources. And for this, we need a true Digital Single Market.

CHAPTER 10: PUBLIC ADMINISTRATIONS IN THE DIGITAL AGE

« A State is governed better by a good man than by a good law. »

ARISTOTLE, *Politics.*

If companies are obliged to innovate continually, why shouldn't the public administration? The opportunity cost associated with an analogical government in the digital age is very high in terms of wealth, employment, and creative and entrepreneurial discouragement. The lack of efficiency and flexibility of public administrations represents an expense of millions of euros for citizens in the form of taxes, which, instead of focusing on education or health, end up supporting an outdated system that deprives our companies of competitiveness in a globalized environment and generates criticism, with the civil servants bearing the break of all anger.

The public administration should be a great ally of companies, especially those of smaller size and startups that are born with almost no funds and dozens of relevant obstacles to overcome, on many occasions putting the savings of entrepreneurs at risk. It should also be considered that SMEs cannot dedicate great efforts or staff to cumbersome procedures such as fighting for the license of technological activity in one place or another, unraveling the GDPR, or spending hours registering invoices. Therefore, when a small business needs a law department to study a tender, or to know how it can use the information generated by users of its apps or website, something is going wrong.

Despite the general misunderstanding due to the misuse of technology in our public administrations, bureaucratic and senseless practices have spread. Innovation has not brought with it the efficiency of the system but has derived from each other the same old tasks. What used to be done by a secretary on paper, is now duplicated with the digital signature and the digitization of documents, but without replacing paper. The result is a parallel and copied administration in two formats.

At the same time, control and monitoring tasks have multiplied, sometimes with tools already in disuse, without incorporating the cloud into the process nor reducing requirements.

If only there were an exercise in self-criticism of both the overall European policy and that of its member countries. However, there is no time to indulge in the debate. Months in digital correspond to years in analogical. For this reason, in this chapter, we want to focus on what, in our opinion, a real digital public administration should be, which technologies could support it, and how an urgent transformation can help society and its companies.

1. OPEN DATA FOR EFFICIENCY WELFARE

At present, the predominance of a bureaucratic culture, the poor functioning of outsourced tools, and a limited knowledge of technological possibilities means that the digitalization of the administration is in most cases a mere computer reproduction of the same old procedures, which even forces citizens to travel to public buildings for some formalities.

Europe and its public administrations should act in two directions. One, digitizing management through process reengineering, [317] and two, making citizen service the central axis under criteria of efficiency and transparency.

The digitization of the Administration requires another vision and treatment, rethinking all our systems and tools, from the information to be stored in a ID card, to the way of issuing invoices with a technology such as Blockchain. For this, a transversal knowledge in the digitization of public processes and services is necessary, in which programming teams, involved citizens, and experts in web design should participate, a process that should begin with a very reliable exercise of transparency and exploitation of open data.

1.1. Transparency and open data policy

The right to data protection, due to its importance for the development of AI, is the most contentious issue in European digital regulations.[318]

---

317. Process reengineering means a radical change for the adaptation of technology in companies and administrations. It is a matter of incorporating technology efficiently, seeking to obtain its maximum potential.Usually entails structural changes at the level of investments and personnel.

See: Hammer, M., y Champy, J. (1993): *Business process reengineering.* Londres, UK. Nicholas Brealey.

318. See Chapter 4 of this book to understand the data privacy debate.

How should an administration deal with a discourse that penalizes the use of data or avoids the debate about its cost opportunity?[319] Should we maintain the fierce European conviction of the right to privacy as something unassailable even in the face of global pandemics? Is China and its centralized planning, with individuals at the service of the State in promoting the digital economy, the model to follow? Should an economistic view of data prevail as in the United States?

Let us start from the premise that Europe, with its strengths and weaknesses, must maintain the status quo that has made it an enviable place of respect for human rights, well-being, and sustainability without renouncing the freedoms of its citizens. We have struck a hard balance that must not be lost in the digital economy, but it is clear that it requires certain adjustments if we do not want to end up in the caboose of progress.

The European Commission, as part of its digitalization initiatives, has made public the need to create a *single space for data*, a cloud in which different countries can upload information that can be useful to key sectors. It certainly looks like good news: 1.6 billion euros are expected to be allocated... although, warns Margrethe Vestager, Vice-President of the Commission, it will be done "in a European way",[320] with the right to privacy at the forefront.

This being so, and despite the goodwill shown, we fear that the desire for regulatory leadership may lead to a half-hearted solution, which, even if it improves the current situation, will leave companies on the sidelines and will not close the gap with respect to the other technological leaders. Because in the case of data exploitation, the best solution for Europe is that the administrations facilitate and encourage the potential use of information through a non-personalized open data policy. An even more ambitious

---

319. We find ourselves in the paradox in which very soon the economic potential of a company or a country will be able to be measured in volumes of data, but at the same time, a European discourse arises that almost criminalizes that a technology company provides a free service at the expense of the collection of information from its users.

320. elpais-com.cdn.ampproject.org/c/s/elpais.com/economia/2020/02/03/actualidad/1580756254_547737.amp.html

online proposal of the Open Government Partnership (OGP) promoted by Barack Obama,[321] which should serve as a starting point for the European Commission.

Why data should be open

Administrations must release both their data and the information generated by users and companies that provide public service (telecommunications, energy, banking, etc.). They should do it in comprehensively anonymized and grouped databases that cannot apply reverse traceability or jeopardize privacy. And after reaching this first objective, invite the rest of the companies to be part of this data lake, incorporating more information.

There are several reasons for orienting public policy towards this degree of transparency:

- **Companies with access to information are more competitive, generating wealth and employment.** At present, only large companies, especially technology, telecommunications, and financial, have easy access to thousands of data, thus exerting a disproportionate force on the rest of the companies. Only by democratizing access to information would it be possible to respond to this imbalance to a certain extent.

- **It would facilitate entrepreneurship and the creation of new companies.** The economic knowledge of the environment would help any citizen look for business opportunities or know where to locate his office.

- **Lower tax burden.** Transparency exercises are accompanied by the detection of inefficiencies and corruption. By increasing public spending on transparency and including companies, tax collection is increased, reducing the burden on the rest of the citizens.

---

321. The initiative sought commitments so that citizens of a country had access to information that would make it possible to fight corruption and strengthen democracies. opengovpartnership.org/

- **A leap in research.** The opening of data would also have a very high impact on university and social research, being able to apply statistical models on a real basis.

- **Better social services.** Open data is the basis for improving care in medical centers and hospitals and the results of treatments. Also, they are used to promote personalized education, finding patterns by student or neighborhood, and enabling the appropriate reinforcements in the most vulnerable areas.

- **Better quality of life.** We cannot ignore how the habitability of cities would improve, with hundreds of uses in the management of tourism, traffic, and the fight against crime. Open databases would also serve to control and preserve our environment, our water resources, or improve energy efficiency.

For all these reasons, it is time to take reasonable risks based on the benefits that society and our countries can obtain. The cost opportunity for Europe as a secondary player in AI and the digital economy is very high.

2. ARTIFICIAL INTELLIGENCE AND THE REVOLUTION IN CITIZEN SERVICE

The quality of citizen service should be a fundamental objective for administrations, yet traditional systems have limitations that prevent individualized attention 24 hours a day, 365 days a year. Digital tools should be the solution to this problem, replacing calls on hold and attention only during office hours with open information that is always available.

However, in most administrations, and also in companies, "digitalization" in communication has been limited to simple web pages, which years ago were interesting as a complement to the analogical forms of contact, but today are insufficient. The information is usually poorly structured, with endless redirections and no interaction possible except for a few forms that take hours or days to be read by an employee.

Twitter and the rest of the social networks provided a partial solution to the problem, often with some ingenuity on the part of the community managers, bringing public service announcements. From the closure of streets for a popular marathon, to the need to donate blood. But its weaknesses are evident: communication professionals are not available 24 hours a day, and making individual and private consultations, in a channel that can be read by millions of people, is not the most suitable.

What is the solution?

The efficiency of administrations depends on the transformation of their citizen service systems with personalized services based on AI, natural language processing (NLP) and chatbots, also known as Intelligent Virtual Assistants. They are revolutionizing public services around the world. Citizens can easily ask questions 24 hours a day, 365 days a year, getting increasingly accurate answers as the systems are trained.

Big tech companies are building AI systems to help address the complexity of conversational language processing, with the goal of having the best answers to increasingly complex questions. Amazon, Google and IBM are already positioning themselves in the sector, aware of its multiple advantages and perspectives. With the timely effort of administrations and companies, soon we will all be able to carry out with our mobile at home, on the street, or in the car, consultations and procedures authenticated by voice recognition and the combination of AI and Blockchain.

Here are some examples that could occur in the future (do not read it aloud if you are near a virtual assistant):

"Alexa, request the renewal of my passport."

"Siri, notify the city council of the pothole in my street."

"Hey Google, send the results of my last test to my GP and make an appointment for next week."

The public uses of this technology are almost infinite: helping students with their university enrollments, requesting the collection of household goods, speeding up assistance to people with reduced mobility, and even coordinating emergency notifications. In fact, during the coronavirus crisis, a chatbot was created in Spain to answer all the doubts and questions about the pandemic that citizens may have in order not to collapse the hospital switchboards.[322]

Imagine the reputation to be gained by a public administration that could attend at all times to its citizens with assistants who can respond from webs, Whatsapp, Telegram, social networks or even with devices such as watches. Imagine now your own satisfaction in getting an answer in seconds whatever time it is about medical care, tax obligations, justice, or any service you might need.

---

322. The Carina chatbot, created by 1millionbot, was recommended by SEGIB and chosen by the United Nations (UNDP) in its tender to provide coverage in Ecuador for the information assistance service created because of the COVID-19 pandemic crisis.
    See: innovadores.larazon.es/es/carina-el-chatbot-espanol-gratuito-que-informa-sobre-el-coronavirus-y-aprende-de-la-conversacion/

The current technological state

The incipient state of this technology allows new startups to emerge in their development, with the markets responding appropriately to the financing of companies, creating employment, and generating wealth.

For example, *Lemonade*, a New York-based insurance comparison and contracting company, raised $480 million in a round of financing, [323] and its current value is more than $2 billion. Lemonade is a potential disruptor of traditional insurance companies, especially home insurance. It promises through virtual assistants the intermediation between insurers and users (notices of repairs, problem-solving, renewal or changes of policies, etc.) without the waiting, thus saving time and costs for policyholders.

Another example can be found in the Spanish *1MillionBot* - a startup of which one of the authors of this book is the founder - that with only 1.5 million euros in funding has entered the market. It provides competitive services of intelligent virtual assistants for e-commerce and manages customer service in different sectors (universities, administrations, online newspapers, retail, health, restaurants, etc.). 1MillioBot, compared to Lemonade, is one more example of the inequality between the US and Europe in digital matters, as well as the difficulty of our startups to scale-up.

Open data and chatbots

If Europe takes the right steps, it has its chance to overtake the United States and Asia in building a smart government. Those governments that begin to integrate AI into their citizen services first will have a clear advantage, but everything will depend on how we treat data. With their analysis, public administrations, in addition to responding to society's problems, will be able to find imbalances, generic needs or problems that affect a large part of cities or that have not been corrected for a long time.

We are aware of the rejection, and almost fear, that many people have because virtual assistants such as Alexa or Google's smart

---

323.   observatorio-ia.com/lemonade-ia-seguros-del-hogar-y-chatbots-ronda-de-480-millones-de

speaker store and use our information for their benefit. But it will be precisely the work with this anonymized information that will be the basis to feed the AI that will improve the welfare of citizens. It is therefore necessary to change our position on the use and exploitation of data, moving from restrictive measures based on the right to privacy to a model in which users have the right to choose:

Option A): I don't want to personalize my services. Delete and do not store my data.

Option B): I do want to obtain personalized service from my provider and I have no problem with it using my data for this purpose.

Citizens must understand that to enjoy increasingly complete and sophisticated public services, which allow personalized and efficient responses, the administrations - as companies do - must not restrict their freedoms, nor doing so will be the beginning of totalitarianism.

We are not advocates of a Big Brother-style administration. In fact, we do not even understand the debate, bearing in mind that all EU countries are active democracies with freedom of expression and citizen demonstration, with political parties in opposition, with independent media of very different ideologies, with prosecutors, police, magistrates and a separation of powers.

If we think that such a system does not guarantee the correct use of data, we should call into question the democratic rule of law itself.

George Orwell said in his *1984* work that ignorance of citizenship translates into the strength of a few.[324] Perhaps the time has come to break that mantra: the era of open data must bring us closer to a new reality from which to perceive the world around us without filters, and then take it to a more sustainable and efficient dimension. Technologically it is possible.

---

324. Part of the slogan of the INGSOC political party: «War is peace; freedom is slavery; the ignorance is strength ».

3. LOCAL ADMINISTRATIONS AND "SMART CITIES"

Europe, in some of its programs, has taken the concept of *smart cities* very seriously. However, although much progress has been made conceptually, in practice, it is a "mixed bag" where according to the authorities they put almost any project that improves the city, such as saving energy or water resources, environmental sustainability, the digital transformation of some services, and the use of AI and sensorization of urban components.

From all this, a certain buzz and confusion have arisen, and almost any municipality can define itself as intelligent by putting a free Wi-Fi network in the *Main street*, installing photovoltaic sensors on street lamps, or publishing a section on "transparency" with little usability and whose sole intention is to host hundreds of PDFs.

Smart cities in Europe have such a broad definition that invites political conformism, if not technological "intrusion" with proposals, sometimes improvised and varied in search of the desired financing. No mayor or local authority should fool themselves or their fellow citizens. Although many are satisfied with the "intelligence" applied to their city out of pure ignorance, and even though these initiatives generate an image of modernity, the smart city concept, if we understand it from a digital perspective, should be more rigorous than it has been up to now that we have accepted it.

The real transformation that European cities require necessarily involves issues already addressed such as government agility, talent attraction, business drive, and human capital training, in addition to the generation and management of data that bring them closer to a state of "intelligence".

These can be summed up in the digitization of urban services and the use of sensorization, monitoring, and IoT; a starting point not only to improve the living space of citizens but also to promote smart tourist destinations or adapt cities to the business needs of the 21st century.

Open data and sensorization of cities would facilitate new applications of maximum interest to know real-time the most polluted areas, the busiest neighborhoods where to locate shops, the waiting time in the emergency room of a hospital, the available parking spaces, or control of political spending.

Reflect for a minute how Google Maps has changed our lives (avoiding traffic jams, route recommendations, comments, etc.). Now think about the hundreds of tools that could help us in our day to day if there were more companies with access to a similar volume of data and that translate the information into something tangible and of general utility.

Without them, citizens are blind, and we become ignorant, unable to know what is truly happening in our environment. We even end up taking for granted the fake news that approaches us without control due to the impossibility of checking them.

4. THE REAL ELECTRONIC ADMINISTRATION IN THE ERA OF BLOCKCHAIN

The best thing about well-understood technology is its strength. Politicians, economists, lawyers, and sociologists could cover shelves with manuals, treatises, and speeches on how a state can and should defend its economic, normative, or and democratic sovereignty and the efficiency, effectiveness, and intellectual re-armament that it entails. For the more practical engineers, one term is enough: "distributed ledger"[325] - the basis that defines Blockchain. Its attributes, authentication, traceability and security, define all the needs and structures necessary to guarantee auton-omy, transparency and public freedoms in the digital era.

Blockchain is a completely revolutionary technology, and if well used by the administration, has enormous potential, with ad-vantages such as those discussed below [326]:

1. Provide maximum security to citizen data, with absolute inviolability of transactions, financial records, and electoral ones.

2. The use of smart contracts with which to digitally man-age and securely process property records or titles, payments, legal documents, health certificates, etc

---

325. A distributed ledger is a consensus of replicated, shared, and syn-chronized digital data geographically laid out across multiple sites, countries, or institutions. There is no central administrator or centralized data storage. en.wikipedia.org/wiki/Distributed_ledger

326. We have followed here the work of Vilarroig Moya, R. and Pastor Sempere, C. (2018). Blockchain: technological, business, and legal aspects. Navarra, Spain: Thomson Reuters Aranzadi.

3. Advance in the fight against fraud, with a completely unbreakable record of transactions between individuals and companies for the collection of taxes or other administrative acts.

4. Decentralize processes and offer citizens transparent and safe management that allows, for example, to know the contribution of each company or person to the value chain of a product.

5. Ability to streamline thousands of procedures and help overcome the concept of 'bureaucracy' with the consequent savings in paper and administrative costs.

6. Improve all bidding processes and public tenders, with the ability to resolve disputes and save time in processing, thanks to its impregnable record system.

7. Solve communication problems between public administrations in different regions or countries, with data availability and accessibility for anyone authorized to consult it.

8. Data is made available to the groups entitled to access (treasury, doctors, judges, police, etc.) efficiently and without the possibility of alterations.

It would be wise for the EU to back a single regulatory framework aimed at leading the use of Blockchain in the public administration, supported by developers (large and small companies) from the different regions of the old continent, and thus anticipate overtake China and the United States. Estonia could become the engine of a much more dynamic new European administration. In a small country in which any management is done in a matter of seconds from their mobile phones.[327]

---

327. qz.com/1535549/living-on-the-Blockchain-is-a-game-changer-for-estonian-citizens/

The EU has already announced the creation of an Observatory on Blockchain.[328] Yet we have already heard these siren songs after many times - promising technologies that end up after years of delay, as a partial commitment by the authorities; regulations that harm their technological development in the face of disagreements between jurists, politicians, and interest groups; or in potential restrictions that instead of facilitating, discourage this type of initiative.

Europe needs to act immediately. The chances for it to lead the way towards a Blockchain-based digital Administration are shrinking with each passing day. China has already started to take the first steps, both in cryptocurrencies and in incorporating technology into the Administration.[329] The US doesn't look like it will sit idly by either, with crowdfunding initiatives targeting security, health and the tax system underway for years.[330]

What are you waiting for, Europe?

---

328. euBlockchainforum.eu/
329. cnbc.com/2019/12/16/china-looks-to-become-Blockchain-world-leader-with-xi-jinping-backing.html
330. datafoundation.org/bringing-blockchain-into-government

5. CONCLUSIONS FROM THE CASES OF SPAIN AND ESTONIA

5.1. Spain and the delay in the application of the digital administration

In Spain, in 2006, a very commendable and early attempt was made to promote electronic administration to reduce bureaucratic procedures, with Jordi Sevilla being the Minister in charge. For the government, it was urgent to "suppress 10 million annual registration forms, eliminate photocopies of the national ID, create a single telematic registry, and incorporate 800 standard forms of the General State Administration to the internet".[331]

For this purpose, the Ministry of Public Administrations created an Electronic Administration Advisory Council[332] with experts in the field. One of the authors of the book had the privilege of collaborating and being a partner in the experience. The initiative took the form of a law (Law on Electronic Administration) with competencies and deadlines -although extensions had to be granted due to non-compliance- and an attempt to make all the process mandatory. Local or regional administrations could not refuse to offer electronic services, thus avoiding any political bias or disobedience.

With a 14-year perspective, we must affirm that, despite its shortcomings, the statement that "working in the right direction, even making mistakes, is correct" applies: eight years later, in 2014, the Spanish President Mariano Rajoy (leader of the opposition during the promotion of the digitization project) estimated at 20,000 million the savings of the public sector brought about by

---

331. elpais.com/diario/2006/03/03/economia/1141340404_850215.html

332. europapress.es/nacional/noticia-consejo-asesor-administracion-electronica-apoya-ley-acceso-electronico-ciudadanos-20061130174827.html

the electronic administration promoted by his political rivals.[333] He also highlighted milestones such as that "99% of the processing dependent on the General State Administration can now be carried out electronically and not at the window". Or that in 2013, "95% of business procedures and 65% of citizens' procedures were carried out through the internet".

Although the achievements cannot hide the failures such as the electronic national ID or delays in tackling such a complex task, from a current perspective, this Law on Electronic Administration was a success. Certainly, in 2019 a moratorium was created until October 2020 so that the different Spanish public administrations could complete the digitization of processes started more than a decade earlier, such as electronic signature or registration or notifications via mobile phones.[334]

What we have learned

The case of Spain serves well to make some observations and recommendations:

1. The Law on Electronic Administration has not streamlined management and administrative procedures, which in many cases remain complicated and uncomfortable for users.

Many officials allege that this Law has led Spain to the purchase of "the most important scanners in the world", with a veiled criticism of the creation of a "double administration: that of paper and electronics", the latter being subject to the first.

---

333. rtve.es/noticias/20150219/rajoy-asegura-administracion-electronica-supondra-ahorro-20000-millones-ano/1101401.shtml

334. A principios de 2020 ninguna Administración autonómica, provincial o municipal ofrecía al completo todos los servicios digitales impuestos en 2015 por la Ley (normas 39 y 40/2015), según un informe que elaboró la consultora Ernst & Young

Ver: innovadores.larazon.es/es/el-reto-imposible-de-lograr-una-administracion-publica-electronica-en-2020/

In summary, a thorough reengineering of administrative processes has not been carried out, which could have brought simplification, agility, rationalization of resources, transparency, and control - a misunderstood digitization raised with fear and dire results.

2. Technology has evolved enormously since 2006, and yet in Spain, there are still delays that will make them obsolete when the adaptation process ends.

The introduction of AI and Blockchain may represent a revolution for public administrations; however, without the disruption of the previous technological wave embedded in their general system, what hope do we harbor that Spanish administrations will know how to adapt to the challenge posed by this new paradigm?
New technologies would eliminate bottlenecks, streamline and make transparent aid procedures or concessions, and prevent political corruption. At this rate, we will never see such advantages in our system.

3. To adopt great changes, you need the right profiles. On many occasions, this is at odds with the bodies of civil servants of an administration.

There are highly trained professionals but who, for a mere generational issue, are unaware of the digital medium. Let's take as an example the Valencian government, which has made a concrete and determined commitment to the digital future, but which in its application finds that of its 122,564 employees, more than 60% of the workforce is over 50 years old and only 58% are less than 30 years.[335]

There are only two solutions to this problem: the first is the entry of new public workers, which would double spending on salaries or pensions and end up paying all citizens of a country.

---

335. lasprovincias.es/politica/funcionarios-publicos-peligro-extincion-20190722111946-nt.html

The second is the continuous learning of the professional already hired, not through incentives, but as something mandatory within the job description. That could lead to a reduction in salary or dismissals due to lack of competitiveness or public service interest of professionals.

Despite all this, Spain has bodies and institutions that, in an almost isolated way, try to instill distributed ledger technologies that could well develop ambitious plans for local, regional, and national governments. Alastria[336] has been able to bring together a large number of institutions, companies, and organizations in a large network-integrating platform that encourages the development and application of Blockchain. In universities, initiatives such as BAES[337] promote multidisciplinary research in the fields of technology, economics, and law. And some Spanish institutions have encouraged the Institute of Electrical and Electronic Engineering [338] to present a standardization proposal to promote this technology from Europe at a Congress on Blockchain.

Spain and the rest of the EU have a growing digital life, with outstanding cases of smallholdings, as we have already explained. However, for technology companies and entrepreneurial talent to multiply, the commitment of governments and the European Commission to go through electronic administration must be a priority.

5.2. Estonia as an example of the new digital administrations

In 1991, when Estonia left the orbit of the Soviet Union, the different political parties set out to encourage the creation of companies and the growth of its economy.

Since then and until today, with the digitalization of its administration, Estonia has become the country with the most startups

---

336. alastria.io/

337. baes.iei.ua.es/

338. Institute of Electrical and Electronics Engineers is a global association of engineers with about 425,000 members, dedicated to standardization and development in technical areas.

per capita in Europe. It is also the country with the highest average internet connection speed in the world, and the first to allow voting from a computer or mobile terminal, guaranteeing access to the network of all its educational centers, digitally registering its inhabitants, and reflecting 100% transparently the public spending of its administrations, the agreements between ministries, and the assets of its public officials.

Estonians can do almost any bureaucratic management quickly, online, and without wasting paper: like requesting a change of residence or registration, renewing the doctor's prescriptions, processing bills, paying taxes, or voting. Baby registrations are made automatically in hospitals, sending an email to parents welcoming the newborn to the Estonian nation. And, of course, we do not forget the possibility of creating an online company easily, quickly, and from abroad.

We can say that Estonia, due to its size (it barely has one million inhabitants), can be managed better than other EU countries. But if it were a single question of population, all the councils or sub-national divisions of Europe today should be an example of e-administration, at least as far as their possibilities go. Therefore, let's banish that idea and think more about the conviction of a country that since the end of the 20th century has opted for innovation as the central focus of its policies.

To accomplish this, it was not necessary to invest large amounts of money but to trace the possibilities that technology allowed to be pioneers in the encryption of digital identities, the acceptance of the digital signature, and a protected system that lets administrations share information.

In addition to speed, the digital system of the Estonian administration has saved its citizens millions of euros, if we compare it with what it would have cost to hire tens of thousands of public officials in the areas now digitized (registries, records of invoices, employment offices, property registration, etc.) and the opportunity cost derived from the loss of time from analog services.

All these advantages (cost savings, efficiency in procedures, transparency, and business drive) should be enough for the rest of the European countries to draw up urgent digital transformation strategies for their administrations. Unfortunately, there is generally a short-term view of political strategies, mostly limited to the duration of a legislature. The lack of continuity of proposals and agreements between parties is a significant restriction for many projects, especially for those that involve profound transformations.

One of the achievements of Estonia has been to extend for more than two uninterrupted decades the attainment of the same goal for the benefit of all.

"State pacts for the digital economy" would be the corollary derived for Europe and its member countries.

6. SOME CONCRETE PROPOSALS: EFFICIENCY IN THE ADMINISTRATIONS

To turn the powerful European administrations into more creative and efficient entities and even to become engines of the digital revolution, we suggest the following lines of action:

1. Make the digitization and efficiency of the European public sector one of its hallmarks, based on technologies such as AI, IoT, and Blockchain - a leap of giants that helps make the old continent an example of a new administration, a Europe of digital citizens of the 21st century, which should have an impact on Europeans who are better aware and educated in digital matters, lowering costs for companies, increasing transparency and control of public resources, lessening uncertainty, and augmenting legal guarantees.

2. Emphasize that digitizing the administration is not "scanning the paper and uploading it to the cloud". It is about taking advantage of the full potential of software to rethink and clean processes (reengineering) that add value to decision-making or in the provision of public services, simplifying them and making them more transparent, and creating a more productive and efficient administration without compromising the guarantee of control.

3. Promote continuous learning among staff. In the face of automation processes, assign public professionals to more creative and social tasks linked to healthcare, education, and environmental sustainability, eliminating repetitive and worthless tasks.

4. Change the concept of public administration and employees with respect to citizens, moving from a current situation in which we are "administered-to citizens" to a future one where we radically speak of "public services to citizens."

5. Back an open data policy so that companies and researchers have access to information that allows significant social advances and innovations.

6. Educate citizens in the use of digital public services to speed up the transition to more efficient systems.

7. Test all new digitized processes, ensuring that citizens understand how they work in a completely intuitive and easy way.

3ʳᵈ **PART:** UNSATISFIED GODS AND A NEW ECONOMIC THEORY

CHAPTER 11: EUROPE AT THE CROSSROADS: BRINGING DISSATISFIED AND IRRESPONSIBLE GODS TO HEEL

« The ability of technology to improve human life critically depends on parallel moral progress in man. Without the latter, the power of technology will simply be used for evil purposes, and humanity will be worse off than before. »
FRANCIS FUKUYAMA. *The End of History and the Last Man.*

« Is there anything more dangerous than dissatisfied and irresponsible gods who don't know what they want? »
YUVAL NOAH HARARI. *Sapiens. From animals to gods.*

In just a few decades, Europe has gone from the most exultant optimism of Fukuyama in "The End of History and the Last Man"[339] for embracing democracies and free-market economies over totalitarianisms, to the political uncertainty and unrest that creates a disturbing haze. The recent Brexit, the financial crisis of 2008 that almost caused the breakdown of the Euro, the existence of tax havens, political radicalization, or the COVID-19 crisis and the confrontations over the financing of the most affected economies are just some examples of this situation.

Furthermore, our common project has not succeeded in closing the welfare gap between the economies of the North and the South, and the disparity of criteria between countries has prevented the integration between European regions similar to that of the US or China.

---

339. Fukuyama, F. (1992). *The end of history and the last man.* Simon and Schuster.

All this occurs in a global context of a lot of instability, which requires rapid progress. But the EU does not react to the competitive grip of the US and Asia. The private sector appears as a passive agent in investment plans, the development of entrepreneurship ecosystems is not a priority, and European regulatory leadership threatens the development of the digital economy.

In early 2020 the European Commission announced that it was moving towards a *green and digital* strategy. However, today its interests are specifically focused on its anti-digital crusades. The aim is more to preserve privacy and bring the technological giants to heel than to respond to challenges such as climate change, immortality or the utopia of singularity. The book "The end of the world as we know it" shares this perception, although its author Marta García Aller knows how to fill us with optimism, revealing how "digital threats" are opening up new opportunities.

For our part, we are not political analysts, and we know that there are areas where our input will be much less consistent than that of well-versed experts on geopolitics. Yet we are clear that a proposal like the one we are making, which aims for the EU to regain its fullness and global leadership, could fall on deaf ears if it remains at a political and economic crossroads where the very union of the member countries is called into question.

Therefore, we believe it is necessary to make a small analysis of the context in which we have drawn our proposals from the previous chapters, thus weaving the arguments with geopolitical reality. Our goal so far has been to come up with a series of drivers that will push digital development in the EU; however, the reader will observe that many of these proposals would also mitigate transcendental problems for Europe.

1. A CONTEXT OF POLITICAL AND ECONOMIC UNCERTAINTY

1.1. Brexit and other destructive processes: is there a relevant future commitment in Europe?

Brexit has been seen from continental Europe with a certain arrogance. It is almost like the British fickleness that capriciously leads to economic suicide, according to some analysts, and the "deconstruction" of their kingdom, with the threat of referendums in Scotland and Northern Ireland.

To close this conformist picture, many have also wanted to observe in this process the reflection of a society of subjects of Her Majesty Queen Elizabeth of England, supposedly xenophobic and with an irrational hatred towards Europe. There have been many videos we received in recent years about verbal or physical attacks on foreigners by a series of "criminals" (they cannot be called otherwise) in buses or public places.

Yet before qualifying the United Kingdom as a racist nation, it is worth to considering that the main British cities were pioneers in growth with migrants from many parts of the world and that its army lost the lives of its best men to help Europe in the two bloodiest wars of the 20th century. Anyone strolling the streets of London notices how mixed race it is, and students and professors from every imaginable country fill its universities.

In the economic sphere, the predicted catastrophe has not occurred either despite the fluctuations inherent to the uncertainty of the process. Moreover, once the break-up agreement has been ratified, sterling maintains its 2018 values.[340] Meanwhile, the EU has been engaged in a deep debate about the hole in the budgets created by the British exit, which threatens the future of agricultural aid.

The UK will now be able to unilaterally seal new alliances with

---

340. We wrote this in 2020.

the United States, Japan, Israel, China, etc. It will have a free hand to deregulate or regulate its digital economy more efficiently. It can consolidate its geographic leadership in AI and reinforce it with agreements with the tech giants and any other country, something that it could not do in the current EU. UK will surely lose the negotiating capacity and the advantages in terms of investment and scientific and economic collaboration with the continent; however, it has before it the possibility to correct the weak commitment of the Union in the future sectors.

This whole process should make our European leaders self-critical. There have always been mutual reservations and reluctance between the UK and the rest of Europe, something staged when the Pound was maintained against the Euro. However, the truth is that little has been done from Brussels to excite British citizens, and, to tell the truth, those of the rest of Europe. Remember that turnout in elections to the European Parliament has only exceeded 50% once in the last five elections. Something that denotes who are fed up ignorance or lack of information, or citizens with their political class. Possibly the combination of high salaries and empty seats has much to do with this disenchantment.[341] Nor does the existence of "tax havens" on European borders or relaxed bilateral relations help. One does not have to go to Puerto Rico or Singapore. Multinationals can move their profits to Ireland, Luxembourg, or the Netherlands to evade large sums of money from the national treasury. And some recognized athletes and YouTubers end up residing in nearby Switzerland or Andorra to pay less income taxes.

The building of a united Europe in the last 50 years has been an exciting process. Our politicians, driven by an open society and in search of opportunities, made History with a capital letter, overcoming restrictions that had not been possible in 2,000 years of wars and conflicts. While there were great goals, solidarity and cohesion have led to this impossible union of countries in peace. We

---

341. Juncker, president of the European Commission, criticized absenteeism in the European Parliament. "Parliament is ridiculous," he went on to say. See news: vozpopuli.com/internacional/inasistencias-eurodiputados-Juncker-Parlamento-Europeo_0_1041496599.html

have witnessed the fall of the Berlin Wall, the constitution of democracies throughout the continent, the construction of a single currency, the establishment of mutual university bases, and the free mobility of citizens.

Yet today, Europe seems to blur between disintegrating processes and the consolidation of populisms and nationalisms.[342] It has the traditional parties as accomplices, unable on the one hand to park their differences to make a common front, and willing, on the other hand, to cover up the shame and corruption in their formations. Faced with popular boredom, society ends up voting for anyone who promises them a real change.[343]

What is the EU response to these situations? How does it protect unemployed citizens when their leaders are robbing them of their future? How is it acting before the disintegrating processes that are contrary to the idea of Europe in freedom, without borders, global and digital? How is it possible that situations like *LuxLeaks* are not acted upon even until the press does not report it anymore?[344]

The lack of political entity and the fragmentation between countries means that there is no response, or at least not with the strength that the current convulsion requires. Many citizens will wonder: why do we want a supranational political body if it stands idly by in the face of the real problems of the people?

With Brexit, the EU losses its best-positioned partner in the digital economy, London being the European capital of startups in AI and fintech. It also loses a historic cultural door that linked

---

342. An economist like Luis Garicano has pointed out in his book *El contrataque liberal* (2019, Peninsula) that "The world seems to be going back to the 1930s" in the face of the rise of political positions such as those of Donald Trump (United States), Matteo Salvini (Italy), Viktor Orbán (Hungary), Tayyip Erdogan (Turkey), or Nigel Farage (United Kingdom).

343. We have the closest example in Spain: with youth unemployment that reached 50%, the media woke us up every morning with the waste of billions of euros destined for investments based on quick buck, with bites of the public coffers, corruption schemes, and off-shore companies of political representatives.

344. lavozdegalicia.es/noticia/mercados/2019/04/07/paraisos-fiscales-ue-enemigo-vive-casa/0003_201904SM7P2992.html

it with the United States, Australia, South Africa, and the rest of the Commonwealth countries. And of course, it is distancing from the synergies with one of the best existing university systems, with flagship institutions such as the London School of Economics, Oxford, and Cambridge and their respective science parks, capable of competing with the large North American institutions in some relevant and prestigious areas.

All this leads us to think that an EU without a common commitment to the future, or exciting projects and objectives for its citizens, is frankly weak and prey to a disruptive and exhausting discourse. If it does not react in time, the geopolitical situation will foreseeably get worse.

1.2. The depletion of the European traditional economy

The economic crisis of 2008 was a profound burden on European economies, shattering the anchored foundations of a weak and exhausted traditional model. The mature industries suffered more than the rest of the effects of the dowturn, generating higher unemployment rates and rapidly losing importance in the creation of wealth in countries. In Spain alone, industrial manufacturing production in 2017 was at levels below those existing before 1994.

The timely decisions of the European Central Bank - albeit somewhat late - did not prevent the suffering of the weakest regions, which translated into an unprecedented drain of young talent, a reduction in wages, and record figures in child poverty levels, with thousands of families with all its members unemployed. The economies of southern Europe had to carry out tough adjustments in their public accounts that still persist in order to avoid over-indebtedness, and whose cuts have meant a certain defenselessness of medical professionals in the face of the coronavirus pandemic.

But the impact of the economic crisis goes far beyond the indicators of production, employment or public and private debt. The mistrust of the markets, especially of the economies of the south, including France, shook the foundations of the EU that we know today.

In this convulsive stage of transition from crisis to recovery, while the old continent was licking its wounds and planning how to recover its levels of well-being, on the other side of the Atlantic a new entrepreneurial replacement was rising from the "ashes" with the best of Silicon Valley. The depletion of the traditional model had a counter in a new industry that emerged on the US East Coast that displaced the economic leadership of banks, oil, automobile, and electrical industries to the current technological giants.

With a crisis in between, we have gone from a decade in which the euro disputed the hegemony of the dollar, to another in which Europe did not keep up with the technological pace set by the US and China. Let us remember that even from a starting position infinitely less favorable than that of many European countries and without a consolidated market as a foothold, China has shown that technological leadership is possible if the drive is right. The EU has become a complacent observer under the syndrome of population aging, chronic debt, and technological dependence. The speeches of its political leaders, Merkel, Macron, Sánchez, and all their predecessors in the last decade are very far from the discourses of the Clinton and Obama administrations or of Trudeau. In Europe, we continue to incorporate digital policies at forced marches and almost by obligation, not in a disruptive way.

Without a benchmark industry or digital ecosystems to highlight, beyond islands like Spotify or Nokia in its time, the EU has opted for digital protectionism and the grandiloquent discourse of the current major laws. Senior officials in Brussels and national governments themselves have reacted as "lifesavers" for sectors subject to technological disruption. Let us stress once again: while in the last fifteen years, the US has been the place of creation of companies such as Amazon, Google, Apple, Facebook, Microsoft, and hundreds of new digital startups called to change the world, in Europe, we have specialized in designing laws and taxes to fight them, and not in creating ecosystems to compete.

The economic crisis has revealed the reality of two Europes. There is an exhausted Europe, with a chronic slowdown due to the lack of global competitiveness of its traditional sectors, and another that is struggling to stand out and be seen in a legal and economic framework that has not understood digitization and disruption. The challenge for the EU as a whole is to understand that the collapse of the old economy based on finance and brick must give way to a comprehensive - not patched or dispersed – economy of the 21st century.

2. TECHNOLOGY DEPENDENCY

2.1. Brussels: it's digital services!

A young man from anywhere in Europe wakes up and looks at his calendar on his mobile, synchronized with his *Gmail* account. "Well, there is nothing important for today." He writes to his friends, "are you meeting for lunch on the beach?" using *Whatsapp*; checks Instagram and *Tinder* accounts ("another match? I'm in luck") and puts some songs on *Spotify* while having breakfast and waiting for the response of his contacts. "What a great day...". Impatient, he only wants to get in the car, set the location on *Waze*, and keep an eye out for traffic jams.

One of his friends receives the message: "I'm sorry ... I have to present a proposal on Wednesday". For a couple of hours, she has already been working on a final document in *Google Docs* with her partners, each one from home. Her startup keeps giving her good news: the campaign in *Adwords* and *Facebook Ads* have been two hits, so much so that they have a waiting list of clients. "The online marketing course I took at *Coursera* is the most profitable thing I've done in my life" she thinks, as she builds metrics and reviews KPIs with *Google Analytics*. Time to take a look at *Asana*: "Come on, there's nothing left. If I hurry, I can wear today my new swimsuit".

Surely the reader, as a professional or user, recognizes on herself in some of these daily tasks or in others such as using professional networks like *Upwork* or *LinkedIn* to work with people from all over the world, find work documents in *Google Scholar*, answer questions in developer communities, or turn to *TensorFlow* to build and train neural networks. Thus, you can imagine how Google, Facebook, Apple or Microsoft have contributed to the competitiveness of European companies, or even to improve your lives.

But beware! Open your eyes wide! These tools are not free!

You are paying with your data, young dupes! Read the cookie message well every time you access a website! Here's the truth that evil tech companies hide from us! Read!

This is what they seem to tell us again and again from the high European spheres. Because the harsh reality is that while a digital culture was being built in companies, society and our technology sector demanded a real transformation of the productive fabric, European and national authorities bet on an oversized ethics of data privacy to prevent exactly... what? That the mail service should be free of charge? That we can access an infinite number of songs and movies for the price of a vinyl record or a pack of popcorn in a movie theater? That we can contact our loved ones on a daily basis without spending a fortune on calls or putting their lives at risk in the middle of the coronavirus pandemic?

A report for Spain by the ADEI Observatory shows how companies value free tools such as email or search engines at tens of thousands of euros.[345] Without these services, there is no doubt that millions of companies across Europe would suffer grave deterioration in their operation and productivity. Moreover, the technological dependence of Europe on the US and China is also seen in key sectors such as security, healthcare, and education.

Will the EU be able to neglect its defense and sovereignty, or refuse to incorporate tools for the prevention and cure of cancer? Europe will continue to set limits on the use of data, even in times of global pandemics, but its dependence will establish *de facto* and have to resort to the tools created in the East and West so as not to lose a competitive warfare or suffer a popular uprising.

Without technological giants or benchmark digital ecosystems, Europe will need to create alliances with the large North American or Asian companies to develop its own technology and overcome its current delay. The disagreements and disputes between Huawei

---

345. In the report "The value of the Internet" from the ADEI Observatory (2019) and through representative fieldwork of the universe of Spanish internet users, value is placed on the free services that we use daily. For example, the Spanish user derives well-being from the internet priced around 10,000 euros per year, while e-mail (€ 5,000), search engines (€ 4,000), and messaging applications (€ 3,000) are the best-valued digital services.
See: observatorioadei.es/publicaciones/valor_internet_final_nov19.pdf

and the US government over the implementation of 5G networks in Europe is a good example of our weak position between the two axes.[346] For all this, the sometimes arrogant attitude from the European political and regulatory spheres, capable of giving lessons on AI ethics and morals, is surprising. Like those who have lost the notion of reality granted by experience after studying so much theory.

Now reconsider. What has had the most impact on your daily lives and well-being? The advances that are taking place in California and increasingly more frequently in China, or the lofty European ethics of data protection, which has even led to the imposition of sanctions on those who suffer hacker attacks or use facial recognition to improve student productivity?

Our advice is that before setting global digital rules, Europe must *be* a digital economy.

2.2. The side effects of lag in AI and the cost of being analog

We must demand that the administrations defend users and that our governments be able to penalize companies that use data fraudulently or against the interests of their customers. This does not justify a preventive policy that treats individuals as criminals and companies as presumed culprits. In the old continent, a proactive position has been adopted from a legal perspective, justifying the law against the result of its actions.[347] This excessive protection for users contrasts with the position of the United States, where in recent decades the regulation of technological progress has been very cautious, taking into account the benefits and

---

346.   abc.es/economia/abci-estados-unidos-presiona-paises-europeos-para-excluya-totalmente-huawei-despliegue-202002201931_noticia.html

347. See: Majone, G. (1994). The rise of the regulatory state in Europe. *West European Politics, 17*(3), 77-101.

Löfstedt, R. E., & Vogel, D. (2001). The changing character of regulation: A comparison of Europe and the United States. *Risk Analysis, 21*(3), 399-416.

Wiener, J. B., & Rogers, M. D. (2002). Comparing precaution in the United States and Europe. *Journal of risk research, 5*(4), 317-349.

costs of its actions on industry and economic growth,[348] something that has not prevented the American courts from acting outright against large digital companies when it has been necessary.

A good example is the case of the US administration against Facebook, which was sanctioned with more than 4 billion dollars[349] for the cases of experimentation on the emotions of users[350] and the famous transfer of information to Cambridge Analytica. In Europe, Mark Zuckerberg's company only had to face a fine of 11 million euros.

Thousands of criminal acts occur daily in the digital economy: hackers who ask for a ransom with bitcoins, fake retail websites, the sale of weapons or drugs on the Deep web, and the duplication of credit cards. Fake news flood social networks and condition citizens to vote in one way or another. Even photos and videos are stolen from the cloud and shared without consent by millions of people. But in the face of the new cyberattacks, we can only rely, first, on prevention through education, and then on technology, the most effective response to solve security problems.

Because AI is making it possible to end spam in emails. Biometrics makes any financial transaction more secure. Drones and facial recognition can enable a new era of protection and surveillance. Blockchain can end political corruption in one stroke. To do all this, it is necessary to experiment with the potential of new technologies and to persecute those who misuse them, not to establish excessive limits to their use.

The digital delay also endangers the European capacity to cure diseases, prevent and act in the face of pandemics, create jobs, ensure road safety, or fight against climate change as we campaign for in the EU. However, great bureaucratic Europe seems more concerned with disciplining those dissatisfied and *irresponsible gods* of Silicon Valley than with looking to the future. "Do we already

---

348. Movius, L. B., & Krup, N. (2009). US and EU privacy policy: comparison of regulatory approaches. *International Journal of Communication, 3*, 19.
349. bbc.com/news/world-us-canada-48972327
350. Facebook Tinkers with Users' Emotions in News Feed Experiment, Stirring Outcry; The New York Times, 29 de Junio de 2014.

have regulation? Let's sleep peacefully! The tech companies are already on their toes."

We will talk about this below

3. "FROM ANIMALS TO GODS": HUMANISTIC AND JURIDICAL EUROPE IN THE FACE OF AI FIRE

Yuval Noah Harari concludes his work "Sapiens: from animals to gods", the world best-seller that has created awareness and culture of human activity throughout history, leaving us with a disturbing question: "Is there anything more dangerous than dissatisfied and irresponsible gods who do not know what they want?".[351]

The great humanistic and juridical Europe had taken up the gauntlet years ago, determined to answer these rhetorical questions. "Those dissatisfied and irresponsible gods must be disciplined, especially now that science has focused on issues that deserve profound moral and ethical debate such as defeating death, bionics, singularity, Frankenstein's prophecy,[352] advanced molecular nanotechnology…" Even in the United States, fierce allies emerge to this need to limit the human drive to achieve new goals, such as the admired Elon Musk.[353] The founder of Tesla vehemently warned that "AI is the greatest existential threat facing humanity".[354]

However, the difference between the United States and Europe is that in the North American country, the responses to these types of statements do not take long thanks to sound technological consciousness and, above all, the existence of references in new

---

351. Yuval Noah Harari (2013): *Sapiens: de animales a dioses.* Debate. pp 456.

We thank Nacho Amirola for sending us this book some time ago. We dedicate this small reflection to him.

352. Ibídem page 451.

353. To know well the history and the surprising journey of Elon Musk, we recommend reading Ashlee Vance (2016): Elon Musk: "The businessman who anticipates the future". Editorial Península.

354. cnbc.com/2018/03/13/elon-musk-at-sxsw-a-i-is-more-dangerous-than-nuclear-weapons.html

disruptive technologies and forums in which to speak out. Elon Musk was kindly answered by Andrew Ng, co-founder of Coursera, director of the AI Lab at Stanford University, former head of AI at Google, and one of the world's greatest AI talent. The response is worth reproducing in full:

"I think he said something like that we are summoning the devil … In my opinion, that of worrying about AI as a superintelligent thing, smarter than any of us, that will end humanity is similar to worrying about over-population of the planet Mars.

Maybe a day will come in hundreds of years in which we have colonized Mars and, perhaps, we have overpopulated it. And you could tell me, Andrew, what do you think of those poor children of Mars, dying from pollution? How come you don't care about them? My answer would be that we haven't even landed on another planet yet.

That is why I find it so difficult to develop a productive concern on that subject."[355]

Thinkers, jurists and technological development

Europe - and a large part of the West - is heavily under the *"Harari"* syndrome. Apart from enjoying the historical, scientific, political and philosophical perspective of the best-seller, it seems that we have taken to heart the crusade for the preservation of the species in the face of the threat of ourselves, the "dissatisfied and irresponsible gods".

In the near future, science will confront us with such complex issues as technological singularity or the possibility of defeating death and will require great decisions for humanity as a whole. We will have to avoid discrimination between rich and poor and learn how to organize a completely new planet with rules that perhaps now we are unable to imagine.

If only another wave of great thinkers would emerge in Europe equivalent to Marx, Nietzsche, and Freud, the "philosophers of

---

355. retina.elpais.com/retina/2019/09/30/innovacion/1569842076_18
1883.html

suspicion"[356] as Paul Ricoeur described them, with their unusual critical capacity in economic, social, and human aspects, they would give us broad perspectives. However, even then, with their possible diagnoses and theoretical proposals, we should not lose the real perspective of our environment and our time.

We have to ponder well how to adapt the philosophical conclusions or even the economic theory, which stands so well on paper. Let us remember how a misconception of the solution to the ills of capitalism led Eastern Europe to decades of backwardness, and how Ukraine, Belarus or Russia still today suffer the consequences of a bureaucratic oligarchy that generated a tragedy, that of Chernobyl, which could devastated half of Europe.

The EU, now more than ever, must proudly display its defense and banner of rights, principles, and freedoms. In very recent times we have learned its value from the hand of devastating totalitarianisms. However, we cannot hide our fear of the future with a Herculean defense of rights that did not exist twenty years ago and for which there is a double yardstick depending on whether we are in the analog or digital world.

We should not fear competition but incompetence. We must flee from a bureaucratized Europe anchored in technophobic immobility, weighing progress and development against grandiloquent speeches, seemingly sheltered by the law, that prevent the need to reinvent ourselves.

Does this mean opposing any technological regulation? Turning a deaf ear to what our fellow lawyers, philosophers, or technologists say? Quite the opposite. We want to make clear our absolute commitment to ethical values and to the need to design efficient regulations that minimize the risks of our era. How can we not agree to prohibit new technologies from being used to manipulate our decisions? How can we not penalize those who steal user data or use it for spamming?

However, we want and must claim the importance of not getting stuck only in the speeches and diagnoses of thinkers or in the foundamentals of law. Europe needs action. It has a technological

---

356. es.wikipedia.org/wiki/Maestros_de_la_sospecha

gap to close and an uncertain economic future. Because the exercise of freedoms is much more restrictive for nations that are economically dependent. And Europe increases day by day this dependence on China and the USA.

Remember the fire metaphor with which we began this book, following Harari. One could imagine a small tribe of sapiens trying to manipulate a fire, perceiving its danger: *fire hurts, fire kills. Let's put out the fire, let's forbid the fire.* We can even visualize a sort of sorcerer evoking "demons and evils", claiming to be the only one with the gift to dominate them, and directing a whole community under the mantra of the danger of flames.

But we can also imagine those other hominid communities that bravely and responsibly assumed the risks of fire. Despite the burns, they quickly learned to exploit its benefits, to dominate it, to minimize its damage. Around their bonfires, they established the origin of great landmarks: conversation, agriculture, mythology, money, or culture, until we reached the science that made us unstoppable.

The EU anti-digital regulations and many of the debates around artificial intelligence, its ethics, and data protection closely resemble the fire-averse tribe, with wise wizards instructing to stay away from the fire. To them, it is necessary to respond: "of course, the AI presents potential risks! That is why we must embrace them, evaluate them, and be highly effective in controlling them. But never extinguish the flame of technology."

4. CHINA AND EUROPE: LESSONS FROM THE CORONAVIRUS AND AI

China, which at the beginning of the 20th century remained under the feudal Qing dynasty, and which until Mao's death (1976) maintained a Soviet-style planned economy with collective farms, has shown the world its technological power in the midst of the coronavirus crisis. COVID-19 has cleared up the doubts of who is the great dominator of the digital economy. AI, big data, and even drones have fought and controlled the pandemic in record time -weeks- with measures that in the West seemed very drastic but were extremely useful.

Part of the success in fighting the virus must be attributed to the tracking hundreds of millions of smartphones, obtaining the information necessary to contain the outbreak. Specifically, the algorithms designed estimated whether an individual had been exposed to the virus from the location of known infected cases. Those who had shared space with the carriers of the virus also became potentially infected. In this way, medical resources and tests could be optimized, targeting high-risk individuals identified by the AI system. Even electronic records of drug purchases were used to detect uncontrolled cases.

The use of digital technologies in China has been overwhelming and served as a role model for South Korea, Singapore and Japan, with the impact of the virus infinitely less than what we suffered in Europe. Big data analysis, made up of information from customs and health insurance, has enabled Taiwan to detect both patients with early symptoms as well as visitors from countries with confirmed cases. Those potentially infected had to be quarantined and tracked through their mobile phones to ensure that they complied with the recommendations. South Korea also followed a model based on technology, and a large number of tests were carried out very efficiently. Information became a key factor: the South Korean Ministry of Health created an online registry in which each person with symptoms entered their data and waited for an appointment for a medical examination, preventing hospitals from collapsing. To these actions, of course, other measures were added such as quarantine, in addition to the excellent work of its health professionals, as has happened in the rest of the world. However, it is fair to say that digital technology has saved thousands of lives in Asia.

According to the *Stanford Health Policy*[357] the chances of a massive contagion in Taiwan were very high. Some predictive models also alerted Japan, Indonesia, South Korea, and the whole of Asia in general to a health catastrophe.[358] However, at the time of writing, Taiwan barely added 5 deaths due to coronavirus, Singapore 20, and South Korea just over 250, compared to the tens of thousands of cases that were sadly counted in Europe.

Europe and the coronavirus

In Europe, coinciding with the first outbreak of coronavirus in China, we received with carelessness and almost gracefully the photos of Wuhan, with families dressed as "Martians" with hoods, masks and gloves. Memes were even made, lowering the tension of what already threatened to be a global problem.

Before long, the Western Stock Exchanges collapsed. Governments around the world began to decree exceptional measures such as the suppression of classes in schools and universities. This was followed by instructions to leave only pharmacies and food centers open. Italy was the first in the old continent to be confined: restrictions throughout its territory, even accompanied by riots in its prisons[359] and campaign battles in supermarkets.

The Spanish government was the next to place its citizens under mandatory quarantine. It was March 14, 2020, only three days before the WHO had certified that we were facing a pandemic.

---

357. healthpolicy.fsi.stanford.edu/news/how-taiwan-used-big-data-transparency-central-command-protect-its-people-coronavirus

358. McKibbin, Warwick J. and Fernando, Roshen, The Global Macroeconomic Impacts of COVID-19: Seven Scenarios (March 2, 2020). CAMA Working Paper No. 19/2020. ssrn.com/abstract=3547729.

359. lavanguardia.com/internacional/20200309/474066507094/coronavirus-revuelta-carceles-italianas.html

Every few hours, the positives and deaths were multiplying around the world. Even those countries who had opted not to take action had to change their policy: the United Kingdom canceled all its classes, and Trump closed borders while offering billions to get an urgent vaccine against COVID-19.[360]

In this global chaos, the figures left no room for doubt: Asia had overcome the virus with fewer infections and deaths than Europe and the United States. In two months in Beijing, 435 cases and 8 deaths had been counted. In the first week in Madrid, there were 1,300 known cases and 35 deaths, despite the efforts made by a health system classified by some to be the "best in the world."

Then the question arose: why aren't the same tools that had served China, Taiwan, and South Korea used to control the pandemic? We already talked about this in Chapter 4 of this book. However, it is something of such magnitude that it is necessary to reiterate it. Europe potentially has the same technology, with our GPS smartphones and telecommunications providers capable of facilitating an accurate record of each user's itinerary.[361] However, privacy laws prevent governments from collecting and employing individualized data.[362] The Asian alternative was invalid.

The Spanish Data Protection Agency warned: "the purposes for which the data can be processed are only those related to the control of the epidemic, including providing information on the use of self-assessment applications carried out by public administrations or obtaining statistics with aggregated geolocation data to generate maps that inform about areas of greater or lesser risk".[363] In other words, there is no question of locating potentially infected persons or identify them. The right to data privacy remains inviolable.

---

360. businessinsider.com/coronavirus-germany-covid-19-vaccine-not-for-sale-donald-trump-2020-3?IR=T

361. ncbi.nlm.nih.gov/pmc/articles/PMC4528087/

362. asiatimes.com/2020/03/china-suppressed-covid-19-with-ai-and-big-data/

363. aepd.es/es/prensa-y-comunicacion/notas-de-prensa/aepd-apps-webs-autoevaluacion-coronavirus-privacidad

In this situation, the European Commission has had to do a very complicated job. National teleoperators do not provide information about citizens, but rather add their data and anonymize them. With these data Nuria Oliver points out that it will be possible to save lives, since it will make it possible to estimate the number of people located in each area, the crowds, and "hot spots for the spread of the disease."[364] However, this solution is a far cry moved away from the ones provided by China, Taiwan, and South Korea.

This debate is of profound significance. There are fears of a dangerous privacy gap. However, in this situation, even specialists like Ricard Martínez have called for an ethic in the use of data for the common good. There is a need for "global public health decisions based on a model centered on the ethics of life and the guarantee of fundamental rights".[365] The key is proportionality. Let's only use the data we need to save lives, because there is no greater fundamental right than this.

As we have already explained, if we had conducted a spontaneous survey on the street before the pandemic on whether or not citizens would be willing to give their data temporarily to their government to reduce contagions, protect thousands of lives, help health professionals and reduce the dates of confinement, even knowing that the technology is not perfect, we are convinced of a majority positive response. Privacy takes a back seat when people see their jobs, their well-being, and the health of their loved ones at risk.

The cost of inefficiency and digital backwardness has already translated into hundreds of thousands of human lives and a dramatic economic and social impact that should at least serve to help Europe overcome its contradictions. COVID-19 has forever changed the way we understand globalization and digital technology. Short-term decisions and models that renounce the future are no longer valid.

---

364. elpais.com/elpais/2020/03/12/opinion/1584016142_423943.html
365. Ricard Martínez (2020): "An ethic of privacy, an ethic of life in the times of COVID-19". eldiario.es/cv/opinion/Ricard_Martinez-opinion-datos-privacidad-COVID-19_6_1005859406.html

CHAPTER 12: PROPOSING NEW THEORETICAL APPROACHES TO THE DIGITAL ECONOMY

By: L. Moreno-Izquierdo, A. Pedreño Muñoz y L. Tormo García[366]

« The illusion that we understand the past encourages over-confidence in our ability to predict the future. »

DANIEL KAHNEMAN. *Think fast, think slow.*

Paul Romer, 2018 Nobel Laureate in Economics, has come to consider that economic science has become a discipline too dependent on mathematics. Macroeconomic models that, on many occasions, have proven useless and dangerous for the management of the real economy, reinforce, as in the case of the Great Recession of 2008, a purely ideological position that ignored and denied its causes.[367]

Romer has even charged against neoclassical economists, calling them "post-realists and a product of neoliberalism", demanding a realistic approach of theory towards economic agents. Abstract economic orthodoxy, with idealized movements and hypotheses, must give way to the study of the behavior of firms and individuals and the determinants of any choice.

He does not expect that we economists renounce our models, but he does require that we should build them from the reality that surrounds us. We need to get out of the watertight compartments and the "homo economicus" to hybridize in a multidisciplinary

---

366. Luis Tormo García is Professor of Fundamentals of Economic Analysis at the Universitat de València.

367. Romer, P. (2016). The trouble with macroeconomics. *The American Economist*, 20, 1-20.

way with problems that go beyond economic decisions and corseted laws. We need a more global, critical, and nonconformist vision.

The Royal Swedish Academy of Sciences has known how to weigh the value of all the fields to which the economy was in debt, awarding its Nobel Prizes to areas related to law, psychology, climate change, and social policies. Perhaps it is because, as many colleagues have told us, economists tend be "jumping the gun", more focused on the research opportunities that datasets offer us than on making novel advances beyond econometric models. Giving more importance to time series than to foresight. A static view of our science that makes models barely withstand the passing of the years, economic crises, and geopolitical and technological disruptions.

In a few decades, when the next generations of Europeans analyze our performance, it may be difficult for them to understand what happened in the first half of the 21st century. Despite all the information we have, we did not know how to anticipate the real estate bubble or the financial crisis. Neither do we foresee the decline of Europe in the perfect storm and technology gap described in previous chapters. The absence of tools for prediction and avoiding the effects of the greatest known technological disruption seem to be the reasons for the lack of response to our economies.

For this reason, we want to share some proposals, working hypotheses, and concerns about the changes that the digital revolution implies, and how economics should respond to the challenges of the new reality. Hopefully, they will motivate students, faculties, and professors to debate and critique the limits of traditional models in the digital economy and lead to research that can shed light on current problems that are extraordinarily relevant for the European economy.

1. WHY IS IT DIFFICULT TO EXPLAIN THE DIGITAL REVOLUTION FROM TRADICIONAL ECONOMICS?

1.1. A black swan in our economics faculties

More than a decade ago, the authors of this book began to question whether the theoretical models reflected the profound changes brought about by the new economy. Together with Professor Ana Ramón, from the Department of Applied Economic Analysis of the University of Alicante, we made some approximations in papers that then spoke of an *cutting-edge economy*[368], giving rise to the doctoral thesis *"Pricing strategies of low-cost airlines: an approach to the extended rivalry model"*[369].

This thesis analyzed how the use of large databases was giving Ryanair and Easyjet a competitive advantage over traditional companies. At that time, there was hardly any talk about the dependency of companies on the new technological paradigm, and the emergence of low-cost airlines was seen as a change in the business model, and as a revolution.

But the digital economy is a *black swan:*[370] its emergence generates atypical situations, at a pace beyond all expectations and with an extreme and transversal impact. Traditional companies that did not know how to adapt to the speed of change suffered the consequences. And so did economic theory, because although technology is present in almost all growth models, it has never

---

368 . Pedreño Muñoz, A.; Ramón Rodríguez, A. & Moreno Izquierdo, L. (2011): The road to new construction sustainability, innovation and cutting Edge. Mètode Science Studies Journal: Annual Review, 194-199.

369. Open access at: rua.ua.es/dspace/handle/10045/36090. Thesis prepared by Luis Moreno and co-directed by Andrés Pedreño and Ana Ramón, qualification of cum laude and extraordinary doctorate award.

370. Taleb, N.N. *The black swan: The impact of the highly improbable*. Random house, 2007.

been so important or involved such continuous and complex disruptive changes.

Economics faculties try to make sense of these new developments within classical theoretical principles. But can traditional pricing models and their comparative statics explain the strategies of Amazon or Ryanair based on AI? Do theories of internationalization reflect how the expansion of Google, Spotify or Netflix has occurred? Does labor market theory address a hypothetical situation of mass automation? Is a new monetary theory necessary to explain the creation and value of money with the emergence of cryptocurrencies? And most importantly, does foresight have the place it deserves in a digital economy facing unknown scenarios for which predictions based on past data are not valid?

Of course, answering these questions should not be taken lightly, nor should they be thought of as isolated cases of general theory. Economists cannot be satisfied with easy answers but must explore the effects and find the optimal solutions to improve the welfare of the citizens of our time. That is our role in the world. Even if this takes us away from our understanding of economic science itself and into uncharted territory.

In recent years bitcoin has been able to challenge the age-old concept of "money". Digital startups have reached every corner of the planet at zero cost and without physical infrastructure. The collaborative economy has blurred the boundaries and diluted the differences between supply and demand. AI is able to optimize prices without a theoretical framework to adhere to, without us being able to know what processes of relationship between variables are taking place within the algorithms. And everything will change again with quantum computing and nanotechnology.

These are transformations of such magnitude that they require teachers and researchers all over the world to reflect and ask their students questions about the adaptation of our economic science to the new technological and social framework. It is possible that we will err on the side of boldness with these first approaches, but you will share with us that what lies ahead of us is an exciting theoretical and empirical challenge.

2. ECONOMIC GROWTH AND DISRUPTION

2.1. Disruption in the Schumpeterian technological component and technological leaps

Schumpeter's pioneering work intuitively defined innovation as a dynamizing instrument of productivity and wealth, differentiating it from the traditional factors of production (land, labour and capital). The "traditional factors" (FP) were considered by Schumpeter as finite or outdated, since they are conditioned by natural resources, the number of inhabitants or the tools available[371].

On the other hand, factors that are not assumed to have limits to growth because they depend on intangible elements were considered. Specifically, Schumpeter defines "socio-cultural aspects" (ASC) such as entrepreneurship, education or public policies, and the "component" or "technological development" (A) which incorporates the accumulation of knowledge. In this way, the expression of the potential income of a country h in a period t is:

$$\text{GDP}_t^h = f_t^h(\text{FP}_t^h, \text{ASC}_t^h, A_t^h).$$

The relationship between technological improvement (A) and the increase in a country's output (GDP) has been extensively addressed by economic theory from different perspectives. To cite the most relevant, Nobel laureate Robert Solow explained the changes in the A component exogenously in each economic cycle, while fellow Nobel laureates Paul Romer and Robert Lucas have treated technology as an endogenous element, which depends on human capital, educational policies or investment in R&D in each country[372].

---

371. Under certain conditions, traditional factors of production may cease to be finite. For example, a technological improvement could make minerals that are currently unusable very useful, or the capital stock could increase its value significantly with the right investments.

372. See: Romer, P. M. (1990). Endogenous technological change. *Journal*

Despite the positive relationship between *A* and *GDP*, achieving significant technological leaps that allow for continued convergence or a change of economic leadership is not simple. It is not enough to increase public spending or to ask our companies to make a greater investment effort. The differential impact of the A component on economic growth will ultimately depend on the technological specialization of each country.

Three types of regions

Throughout the previous chapters we distinguished the disruption of innovation, emphasizing key aspects such as STEM hybridization, talent or digital ecosystems as opposed to the traditional indicators referring to education, technological work or R&D investment. In doing so, we showed that not all improvements in human capital have the same effect on wealth, or that the performance of public spending on innovation depends more on quality than quantity. For example, the US and Germany have similar R&D investment rates, public spending on education or scientific publication ratios. However, the productivity associated with cutting-edge technologies is much higher in the US economy. Similar relationships can be found between Ireland and Spain, or Estonia and Italy.

From these examples we understand that the returns derived from an economy's innovation effort will depend directly on its specialization, generated from the rational combination of its productive factors. By way of simplification and as theoretical support, in the following sections we will identify three types of regions according to their productive and technological specialisation:

- **the less innovative regions** focus on traditional factors of production, and promote sectors such as tourism, construction or manufacturing industries;

- **the innovative regions** find a balance between traditional and knowledge-related factors. They promote the automotive,

---

of political Economy, 98(5-2), 71-102; Lucas, R. E. (1990). Why doesn't capital flow from rich to poor countries? *The American Economic Review*, 80(2), 92-96.

chemical or mature technology sectors;

- **disruptive regions** are committed to factors related to the technological avant-garde, promoting the most advanced sectors in each new paradigm, and re-enforcing traditional sectors.

2.2. Incorporating disruption into economic theory

In the growth models of economic theory, due to their lack of definition or by mere omission, the effect of disruption is included as part of the technological component A or of the error (e) in the calculation of a country's production, such that:

$$GDP^h = \beta FP^h + \beta SC^h + \beta A^h + e^h.$$

However, not taking into account different types of "innovation" in an era in which technology is becoming increasingly important as a differentiating factor can lead to a lack of precision in our applied models, as well as hindering decision-making by companies and administrations. The cases of Israel, Estonia, Canada and Ireland are good examples of why the traditional A component distorts the relationship between technological progress and economic development. The four aforementioned countries, recognised as a benchmark in their commitment to digital transformation, had a starting position that was not at all outstanding in technological sectors, with less investment capacity than the countries around them and even with a traditional dependence on primary industries.

Taking into account the technological specialisation referred to above forces us to disaggregate our production function to include a **coefficient of disruption** (δ), thus distinguishing between traditional innovation ($\delta^{Tr}A^{Tr}$) and the commitment to the technological vanguard ($\delta^D A^D$), such that:

$$GDP_t^h = GDP_t^{h,Tr} + GDP_t^{h,D} \begin{cases} GDP_t^{h,Tr} = f_t^{h,Tr}(FP_t^{h,Tr}, ASC_t^{h,Tr}, \delta^{Tr}A_t^{h,Tr}) \\ GDP_t^{h,D} = f_t^{h,D}(FP_t^{h,D}, ASC_t^{h,D}, \delta^D A_t^{h,D}) \end{cases}$$

As an economy becomes more disruptive, the value of GDP^D driven by the combinatio $\delta^D A^D$ increases relative to GDP^T.

Intuitively, the δ coefficient will rise in value through cutting-edge actions such as those already described in this book: the integration of Blockchain in administrations, computational education at all levels of training or the empowerment of digital startups in an ecosystem, among others. These not only distinguish between more or less disruptive sectors, but also between companies or administrations.

The disruption multiplier and economic growth

From the model described we can establish a series of relationships between "traditional" (r), "innovative" (v) and "disruptive" (s) economies in which we can differentiate the economic convergence of the economy as a whole, from the contribution of the leading-edge sectors, such that:

$$\left.\begin{array}{c} \dfrac{GDP_t^{s,D}}{GDP_t^{s}} > \dfrac{GDP_t^{v,D}}{GDP_t^{v}} > \dfrac{GDP_t^{r,D}}{GDP_t^{r}} \\[2ex] \dfrac{GDP_t^{r,Tr}}{GDP_t^{r}} > \dfrac{GDP_t^{v,Tr}}{GDP_t^{v}} > \dfrac{GDP_t^{s,Tr}}{GDP_t^{s}} \end{array}\right\}$$

It is thus easy to explain why over long periods the less innovative regions can grow more than the disruptive ones, coinciding with the global depletion and catching-up of technology, and driven by the incorporation of these into traditional GDP. However, it will be the difference in the contribution of disruptive GDP that will explain the processes of divergence in the face of the arrival of new technological paradigms.

This is the situation described between Europe and the US in previous pages, with an evident convergence in production for three uninterrupted decades, until the moment of consolidation of ICTs in the 1990s. Since then, productivity in the US economy has been boosted more than in Europe, with the gap widening as we move into the age of artificial intelligence.

Measuring disruption

Defining our δ coefficient or multiplier for incorporation into economic theory and its applied study is not without complexity. Disruption can be understood as a set of actions and factors that bring an economy, its sectors and its companies to the technological forefront, but in practice these actions are difficult to measure, and can even be confused with socio-cultural aspects (ASC).[373] It is therefore interesting to understand in this first stage of definition the disruption coefficient as a differential in the use of technology over time, assuming that the factors of production are static over a technological paradigm, such that:

$$GDP_t^{i,D} = \overline{FP}_t^{i,D} + ASC_t^{i,D} + \delta^D A_t^{i,D}$$

including $ASC_t^{D,i}$ social effects that may or may not have a direct relationship with a country's disruptive impulse ($ASC_t^{D,i} = \delta^{D,i} + e_t^{D,i}$), such that:

$$\delta^{i,D} = \frac{GDP_t^{i,D}}{(1+A_t^{i,D})} - e_t^{i,D}.$$

differentiating $A_t^{D,i}$, or the determinant of the productive potential of disruptive sectors and firms, from the disruptive technological level ($\delta^D A_t^{D,i}$) which also includes external economies and which determine their overall potential impact on the economy.

The disruption differential will allow us to study the relationship between countries to obtain the returns of the innovative effort in terms of disruption for each moment of a technological paradigm (**figure 12.1**), thus identifying leaders from followers. In addition, the results can be used to study international best practices, observing which actions are enabling some economies to be more disruptive than others, and serving as inspiration for the rest of the planet.[374]

---

373. This book has presented examples such as digital regulations adapted to the exploitation of data, policies dedicated to attracting talent or the scalability of start-ups or university flexibility.

374. In the article by Peretó-Rovira, A., Moreno-Izquierdo, L. and Pedreño Muñoz, A. (2020): "Un índice para medir la apuesta de los países por la inteligencia artificial" Ekonomiaz, 98 (2), 26-53, a first compilation of disruption indicators is carried out.

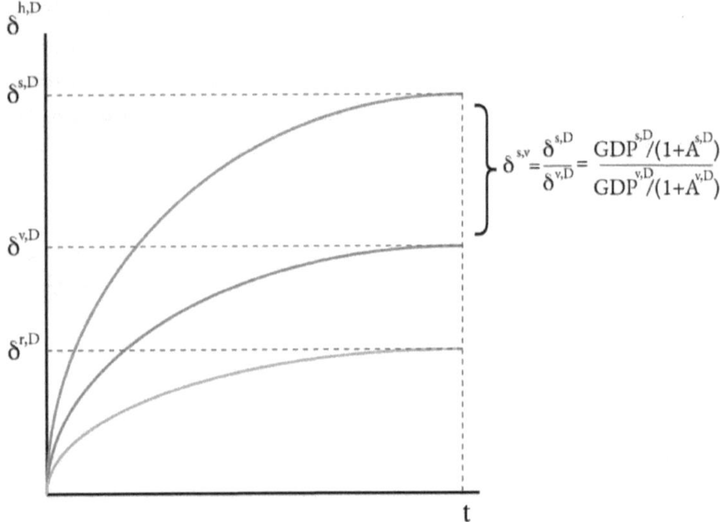

Source: own elaboration

3. CHANGES IN TECHNOLOGY LEADERSHIP

3.1. The waves of disruption in the AI era

The economic impact of AI, which is expected to contribute more than 16 trillion dollars over the next decade,[375] will mean a new global geopolitical order. A situation that historically repeats itself with each technological leap, and in which the most disruptive regions become economic leaders.

As we have already explained, the adaptation of countries to each of the stages of the Kondratiev waves (exploration, acceleration and maturity) has determined their productive and competitive position since the first Industrial Revolution, and this same process will occur again in the revolution that has just begun.

United States, Europe and China

To understand how the disruption coefficient explains the change in technological leadership, we will use the experience of China (C), the USA (U) and Europe (E) in the last three technological leaps: the computer age (A_1), the internet economy (A_2) and artificial intelligence (A_3), measured by their productive capacity or impact on global wealth.

From the indicators presented in this book, we understand that the US has been the clear technological leader in the last two technological leaps $(t_0 - t_1,$ and $t_1 - t_2)$, while it is competing with China for the leadership of the current technological wave $(t_2 - t_3)$. For its part, Europe has remained a step behind the US in technological matters, [376] while with respect to China the gap began to open

---

375. pwc.com/gx/en/news-room/press-releases/2017/ai-to-drive-gdp-gains-of-15_7-trillion-with-productivity-personalisation-improvements.html

376. Although the policies of countries such as Sweden or even Germany have led to a higher number of patents per capita or higher R&D investments as a percentage of GDP than those of the US, it is the North American country that concentrates most of the technological ecosystems, the most innovative universities and the creation of the leading digital start-ups.

up with the explosion of internet 2.0 in favour of the Asian giant. Formally, we could describe the relationships at the end of each technological leap (t = 1, t = 2, t = 3) as follows:

$$\delta^D A_t^{U,D} > \delta^D A_t^{D,E} \; \forall \, t,$$

$$\delta^D A_t^{U,D} > \delta^D A_t^{C,D} \text{ if } t \leq 2; \; \delta^D A_t^{U,D} = \delta^D A_t^{U,C} \text{ if } t > 2,$$

$$\delta^D A_t^{E,D} > \delta^D A_t^{C,D} \text{ if } t > 1; \; A_t^{E,D} < \delta^D A_t^{C,D} \text{ if } t > 1$$

The hypothetical variation of countries along each paradigm is depicted in Figure 12.2.

Figure 12.2: Disruption and change in technological leadership

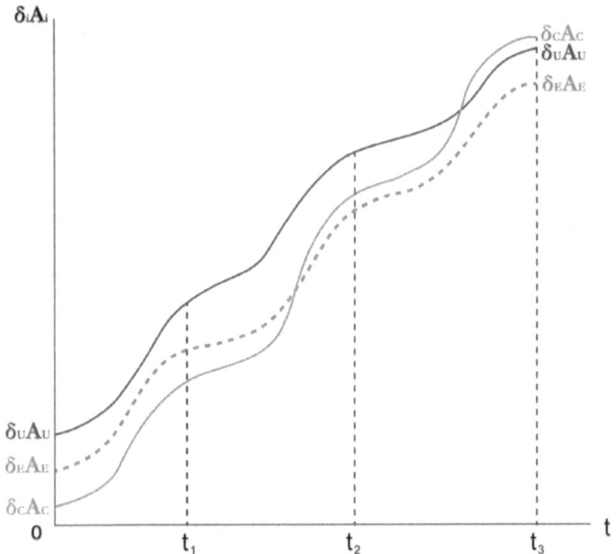

Source: own elaboration

This theoretical exercise reflects Europe's technological reality and its loss of economic influence, as previously exposed: while in the US and China a new generation of leading technology companies such as Google or Tencent was growing, Europe did not develop a relevant technological sector, meaning a loss of 7 percentage points in the world's GDP.

This loss of relative weight is not due to a problem of access to technology ($A_t^{D,E}$), and even less so in a globalized world where all innovation is shared at a very fast pace, but of its exploitation and the capacity to generate external economies, something determined by the disruption multiplier (δ^D). Europe has maintained high technological investment, and its universities have training programmes in digital areas, yet it is far from matching the disruptive capacity of its main competitors.

The previous graph also serves to explain the case of China, the most paradigmatic in the digital era. The Asian giant's transformation process begins in the first technological leap (t_0 to t_1) through the attraction of companies and the purchase of innovation, but in the last two stages it takes off thanks to its own technology sector with strategies such as the MIC 2025 plan for leadership in the fourth Industrial Revolution.

3.2. R&D in the race for technological leadership

According to our classification, Europe would be an innovative region, while China and the US are disruptive. Although we are aware of the differences within their borders, as we have already explained, this distinction will allow us to better understand the logic of the R&D system and how it brings countries closer to or further away from technological leadership in this theory of disruption.

To do so, we will establish periods of scientific maturation in each technological paradigm, which run between t and t+n. In this period, regions accumulate disruptive innovation, or $(R\&D)^D$, until they undertake potentially disruptive investments. Once the investment in innovation (In^D) has been made, efforts are required to consolidate it in products or services in the market or as a public good, which we will call disruptive products (Q^D). These efforts have to do with the rest of the productive factors, since taking advantage of disruptive innovation requires investments in physical capital in the cutting-edge sectors (K^D), but also the interest of society and companies in adopting these advances (ASC) and of course the rest of the more advanced technological components (A^D) that must adapt to the continuous improvements.

At the same time, disruptive products generate external effects, encouraging other sectors to initiate or adapt their production processes to the improvements created, and motivating competition in the rest of the environment. We cannot ignore the fact that these advances also generate diseconomies, especially in traditional sectors, which can be substituted by these new products. However, the historical evolution of the economy has shown us that creative destruction motivates improvements in the regions that develop.

Formally this relationship would be summarised as follows:

$$[(R\&D)_t^{h,D}+...+(R\&D)_{t+n-1}^{h,D}] \Rightarrow In_{t+n}^{h,D} \Rightarrow \begin{Bmatrix} \Delta K_{t+n}^{h,D} \\ \Delta ASC_{t+n}^{h,D} \\ \Delta A_{t+n}^{h,D} \end{Bmatrix} \Rightarrow Q_{t+n}^{h,D} \Rightarrow \begin{bmatrix} \Delta GDP_{t+n+j}^{h,D} > 0 \\ \Downarrow \\ \Delta GDP_{t+n+j}^{h} > 0 \end{bmatrix}$$

Global overview

From this relationship, we can clearly identify technology leaders as those in which technology sectors are able to transform and improve their economies, or in other words, carry out a complete process of disruption that goes far beyond mere investment in R&D, which is only the first step.

Once an economy achieves leadership, it also manages to increase its influence over its technological followers, who become dependent on its advances in order not to lose competitive advantage. This relationship is set out in the table in **figure 12.3**, which determines the production and consumption of *disruptive* and *innovative technology* in disruptive, innovative and traditional countries.

According to this model, the corollary of innovation policies that are incomplete or do not lead to disruption is subordination and loss of relative weight in the global economy, something that Europe is already experiencing. China and the US are not only vying for leadership in the age of AI, but also to increase their influence over the rest of the world through the expansion of their companies and the diffusion of their technology. If Europe does not curb or minimize this situation through policies such as those described in this book to embrace disruptive processes, it will continue to irremediably lose economic relevance and ascendancy over third regions, with no *Brussels Effect* or normative leadership to compensate for the loss of welfare.

Figure 12.3. Classification of countries according to their contribution to technological progress

Technology production			Technology consumption		
			Disruptive region (s)	Innovative region (v)	Traditional region (r)
Disruptive region (s)	Innovative technology	Yes	$TI_{s,s}$	$TI_{s,v}$	$TI_{s,r}$
	Disruptive technology	Yes	$TD_{s,s}$	$TD_{s,v}$	$TD_{s,r}$
Innovative region (v)	Innovative technology	Yes	$TI_{v,s}$	$TI_{v,v}$	$TI_{v,r}$
	Disruptive technology	No	-	-	-
Traditional region (r)	Innovative technology	No	-	-	-
	Disruptive technology	No	-	-	-

4. SUPPLY AND DEMAND IN THE FACE OF DISRUPTION

4.1. Generational change: a question of survival

In addition to the macroeconomic movements explained in the previous section, the disruption multiplier δ can also be seen in the interaction between users and consumers. Think of how technology enables on the one hand the creation of new goods and services and increases production capacity, and on the other hand how consumers learn to use these new creations and change their consumption preferences.

In the first chapters of this book we already introduced the concept of "creative destruction" introduced by Schumpeter, which would explain how continuous innovation leads to an unstoppable substitution of products and firms as demand becomes aware of the advantages of its improvements. But R&D strategies are not cheap, and there is a high risk that the results will not be as desired or will not satisfy demand. So the key question is: how much and in what to invest?

Disruption in the firms' production function

To explain the effect of disruption on the relationship between supply and demand, we will start with three types of firms offering different varieties of the same product in a specific market: a variety "x", a variety "y" and a variety "z". These varieties are differentiated from each other by the degree and type of innovation implemented in each of them, so that version "x" would be the least advanced, "y" would be a relevant innovative improvement, and "z" would be a disruptive transformation.

Each of the companies will have a production function such that:

$$q_{it} = f(I_{it}, FP_{it})$$

where q_{it} is the maximum production capacity of each firm determined by the elements that make up its production function, I_{it} is the innovative component of each firm[377] and FP_{it} is the combination of the traditional factors of production described above.

This function is subject to many variations, as the extensive literature shows. One of the most interesting would be the division of factors of production into non-digital and digital, as carried out by Jalava and Pohjola (2002), Stiroh (2002) or Timmer and van Ark (2005), among others. [378] However, in our case we will focus on the differences in the innovative component, distinguishing between linear process improvements (I_{iTt}) and those that incorporate elements of technological leadership (I_{iDt}). In addition, we added our disruption differential, which we used to measure the degree of efficiency of the investment made. In this way:

$$I_{it} = f(\partial I_{iTt}, \partial I_{iDt})$$

$$q(q_{iTt}, q_{iDt}) = \partial I_{iT} F(L_{iTt}, K_{iTt}) + \partial I_{iD} F(L_{iDt}, K_{iDt}),$$

given for the example provided that firms type "x" and "y" determine their output solely on the basis of their innovativeness, while firm "z" does incorporate disruption, so that:

$$\partial I_{xT} F(L_{xTt}, K_{xTt}) > 0; \; \partial I_{yT} F(L_{yTt}, K_{yTt}) > 0; \; \partial I_{zT} F(L_{zTt}, K_{zTt}) > 0$$

$$\partial I_{xD} F(L_{xDt}, K_{xDt}) = \partial I_{yD} F(L_{yDt}, K_{yDt}) = 0; \; \partial I_{zT} F(L_{zTt}, K_{zTt}) > 0.$$

Determining the type and degree of innovation

In our three-firm model, the cost associated with process and product improvement (cI_{it}) will be the sum of innovative (cI_{iTt}) and

---

377. In the economic literature, the value of I is usually represented by the letter A, since it represents the technological component of the firm. This change is made so as not to confuse the reader, given that the macroeconomic value of A studied in the previous section would be similar for all companies in the same environment: ($A_t^x \approx A_t^y \approx A_t^z$).

378. See: Jalava, J. and Pohjola, M (2002): Economic growth in the New Economy: evidence from advanced economies. *Information Economics and Policy*,14(2), 189-210; Stiroh, K.J. (2002): Are ICT spillovers driving the New Economy? *Income and Wealth*, 48(1), 33-57; Timmer, M.P. and Van Ark, B. (2005): Does information and communication technology drive EU-US productivity growth differentials? *Oxford Economic Papers*, 57(4), 693-716.

disruptive (cI_{iDt}) investments, with different alternatives, among which we highlight:

Alternative 1
$cI_{zTt} > cI_{yTt} > cI_{xTt} > 0$ $cI_{zDt} > 0; cI_{yDt} = cI_{xDt} = 0$
$cI_{zt} > cI_{yt} > cI_{xt}$

Alternative 2
$cI_{yTt} > cI_{zTt} > cI_{xTt} > 0$ $cI_{zDt} > 0; cI_{yDt} = cI_{DTt} = 0$
$cI_{zt} > cI_{yt} > cI_{xt}$

Alternative 3
$cI_{yTt} > cI_{zTt} > cI_{xTt} > 0$ $cI_{zDt} > 0; cI_{yTt} = cI_{xTt} = 0$
$cI_{yt} > cI_{zt} > cI_{xt}$

Alternative 4
$cI_{yTt} > cI_{xTt} > cI_{zTt} > 0$ $cI_{zDt} > 0; cI_{yTt} = cI_{xTt} = 0$
$cI_{yt} > cI_{zt} > cI_{xt}$

In the first two scenarios, company "z" is the company that invests the most resources in total in improvements, although in the second case company "y" invests more in innovation (remember that the investment of "y" in disruption is equal to zero). In the third and fourth cases, firm "y" would be the clear leader in innovation investment. In these two alternatives, company "z" turns to disruption, even absolutely in the fourth scenario.[379] he latter situation would occur, for example, in companies that spend years developing new products before launching them on the market.

Rationally, companies will choose the investment alternative that brings the greatest expected benefits, something that is not simple as it depends on multiple factors: financing possibilities, knowledge of the market, the speed of technological advances, expectations of demand acceptance of new products, and of course risk aversion, given that there is a possibility that investment in innovation will generate more cost than the benefit provided.

This can be seen in **figure 12.4**, which reflects alternative 1 above ($cI_{zt} > cI_{yt} > cI_{xt}$), with demand gradually accepting technological change. The ordinate axis of the first graph represents the

---

379. Scenarios where $cI_{yt} > cI_{xt} > cI_{zt}$ have not been incorporated as their effects are easily deducible from the fourth scenario.

value of the production of a good or service according to the investment in new developments made by the three types of firms. Greater innovation leads to greater market value, on the understanding that this innovation translates into improvements in the product. In the second graph, the y-axis reflects the consumption of aggregate demand given a level of technology applied to the product. Rationally, buyers will opt for more advanced products as long as they meet their budget constraints. The x-axis presents the time evolution.

Figure 12.4. Production strategy and demand decisions

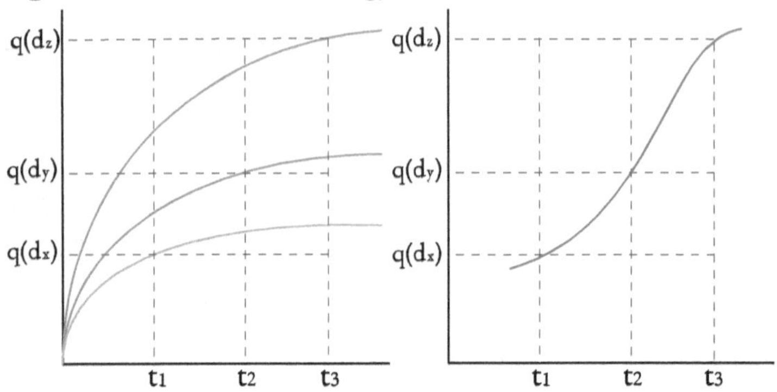

Strategically, and with demand described as in figure 12.4, in the period $t_0 - t_1$ it will not be profitable for companies to invest too much in innovation: most consumers still demand traditional products, and only early adopters will want to spend their savings on upgradeable prototypes. In the $t_1 - t_2$ period, technology has already permeated society, with widespread interest in innovative products. Companies will need to be ready in period t2 to meet the booming demand for improved products, or to accelerate their innovation. In the period $t_2 - t_3$, firms must become disruptive in order to take full advantage of the benefits offered by new technologies and thus respond to demand.

Conservative, innovative and disruptive companies: an explanation of the European problem

The transition proposed in the previous section is optimal from a theoretical perspective, but ineffective in reality: the big tech

416

companies are so because they have detected and invested before anyone else in discoveries that normally require years of development until they begin to yield positive returns. It would be a mistake for a company that wants to be a leader in innovation to wait for a consolidated demand to make the relevant investments.

However, we must understand that, just as demand has budgetary constraints to buy one product or another, firms decide the type of investment they make in innovation or disruption ($cI_{iTt} \geq 0$; $cI_{iDt} \geq 0$) based on the availability of funds. Such funds can derive both from the net profits generated by a firm's core business (g_{it}) and the savings and assets accumulated to date (si t-1), and from external financing (m_t). In this way we could define the economic situation (r_{it}) of a company as:

$$r_{it} = g_{it} + s_{it} - (cI_{it} - m_{it}),$$

being aware that if $r_{it} < 0$ we would be talking about bankruptcy. And this bankruptcy could be due to a loss of customers (demand prefers a more advanced version of the product), or because the investment made has not led to greater demand (customers choose a less advanced version of the product).

With this formula we can explain one of the most transcendental European problems of those analyzed in this book: the lack of disruptive companies in comparison with China and the US. Because even if a company director is aware of the great expectations of wealth that investment in disruptive technologies (such as artificial intelligence, Blockchain, or quantum computing) could bring, the room for manoeuvre available to him/her will determine his possibility of leading a conservative, innovative or disruptive company.

Think of the big tech companies and how they needed billion-dollar capital injections to get started, and how the stock markets have continued to fund their growth. Disruption requires effort and years of development: the algorithms that amaze the world by winning games of Go[380] or that detect skin cancer[381] are the product of continuous effort and sunk costs.

---

380. Watch the documentary "AlphaGo" on Netflix.
381. Jaleel, J. A., Salim, S., & Aswin, R. B. (2013, March). Computer aided

Companies without easy debt or access to venture capital will fall into the camp of the conservative, or at best the innovators, even if they know the future benefits of new technologies. And the real problem lies in the fact that as the technological paradigm advances, it becomes increasingly complex to achieve higher degrees of disruption, as it requires, in addition to investment, drastic changes in business models, in the training of human capital and even in the legislative or political-economic environment.

It is clear that not all projects achieve their innovation objectives, that many run out of funding halfway through the process, and that bankruptcies of young projects are a constant occurrence. However, taking refuge in mature sectors and companies is never the solution. If Europe continues to be anchored in its industrial heritage and its anti-digital regulation, it will condemn its economies to a constant loss of technological competitiveness.

This, as we have already explained at length, will result in the closure of companies and the loss of jobs and welfare for its entire population.

<hr>

detection of skin cancer. In 2013 International Conference on Circuits, Power and Computing Technologies (ICCPCT) (pp. 1137-1142).

5. PRICE FORMATION IN THE DIGITAL WORLD

In economic theory, "perfect information" is considered a necessary issue to reach an equilibrium that maximizes social welfare. However, this assumption has always been seen as unrealistic. Neither companies can enter the brains of consumers, nor can buyers sit on the board of directors of companies.

The digital economy and e-commerce have brought both demand and supply closer than ever before to a near state of perfect information. The former can compare in seconds the characteristics of all products on the market and choose between different sales channels. The latter have more information about their potential customers (sales history, web visits, A-B tests, etc.) and their competitors. In addition, physical and investment barriers to entry have been eliminated, and buyers and sellers are multiplying.

This being the case, we should think that the equilibrium between supply and demand for any good or service should be very close to that defined by economic theory as "perfect competition". A static point in the long run that relates quantity consumed and price paid, and which assumes that the profits of companies fall to zero. [382] But, evidently, this does not happen. First, because price-cutting agents with high market power (also intermediaries) continue to exist. And secondly because, even assuming almost impossible perfect competition, the digital economy is revealing new behaviors of economic agents. Let focus on them.

5.1. AI in pricing: Psychology and economics

Microeconomics, throughout the last century, has offered a multitude of models of how our economic reality works, with predictions very different from the ideal competitive model.

---

382. They are not negative since all costs are covered, including the opportunity to do another activity.

However, and given that in this chapter we simply want to make a brief outline of the differences between traditional and digital economics, we will take the license to go to the most basic concept to explain the functioning of markets: Adam Smith's "invisible hand".[383]

Prices are the fundamental element of this theory, as they are the mechanism we all accept for making consumption decisions based on assumptions of rationality and budget constraints. But human beings are very complex and reducing consumption decisions to budget and quality is incomplete. Emotions, brand values, intuition, passion and many other elements that escape the rational logic of homos economicus are also essential to understanding the choices of economic agents (buyers, sellers, investors, employers, even the government), as Robert J. Shiller and George Arkeloff[384] have reflected in their book *Animal Spirits*.[385] And this puts a strain on the classic principle of market equilibrium, especially in the information age.

Low-cost airlines asked themselves the following question a few decades ago: Why accept a single price for all consumers, if each of them values the "flying experience" differently? A user could pay twice as much as the person sitting next to him just for having booked 48 hours later, requesting priority boarding, or self-assigning the seat 14F.

Compared to classic pricing models, with fares that barely change with occasional discounts, new airlines such as Ryanair or EasyJet worked with real-time information and complex algorithms to automatically modify their rates. This does not mean that each of us will see a different price (which is forbidden in the EU), but so many extras and shopping possibilities are included that price discrimination is highly segmented.

A good way to summarize this strategy would be:

---

383. Smith, A. (1759) (ed. 2010): *The theory of moral sentiments*. Penguin.

384. Nobel laureates in Economics in 2013 and 2001 respectively.

385. Akerlof, George A., and Robert J. Shiller. Animal spirits: *How human psychology drives the economy, and why it matters for global capitalism*. Princeton University press, 2010.

$$\text{Digital company} \Rightarrow \left\{ \begin{array}{c} \text{Big Data (real time)} \\ + \\ \text{AI algorithms} \end{array} \right\} \Rightarrow \left\{ \begin{array}{c} \text{Price} \\ \text{discrimination} \\ \text{policy} \end{array} \right\} \Rightarrow \begin{array}{c} \text{Profit} \\ \text{maximisation} \end{array}$$

In this context a "digital company" is defined as a company that introduces digitalization systems into its business structure. In fact, we are seeing more and more examples of dynamic pricing, even in supermarkets, which take advantage of information about their customers' consumer habits to know exactly when to play with the prices of fresh products.

This strategy increases the market power of supply over demand. It is true that digital consumers, i.e. those who use digital tools in the selection and consumption process, have more access to information and especially to the experiences of other users to maximize their utility:

$$\text{Digital consumer} \Rightarrow \left\{ \begin{array}{c} \text{Big Data} \\ \text{(third party} \\ \text{information)} \end{array} \right\} \Rightarrow \left\{ \begin{array}{c} \text{Online} \\ \text{reputation} \end{array} \right\} \Rightarrow \begin{array}{c} \text{Utility} \\ \text{maximisation} \end{array}$$

But we cannot deny that dynamic pricing causes psychological pressure on consumers, who lose decision-making capacity. Faced with this situation, platforms such as Kayak or some Google tools are emerging that try to predict market movements in the short and medium term, generating a new relationship between digital economic agents:

$$\text{Digital consumer} \Rightarrow \left\{ \begin{array}{c} \text{Big Data} \\ + \\ \text{Predictive} \\ \text{algorithms} \end{array} \right\} \Rightarrow \left\{ \begin{array}{c} \text{Online} \\ \text{reputation} \\ + \\ \text{Predictions} \end{array} \right\} \Rightarrow \begin{array}{c} \text{Utility} \\ \text{maximisation} \end{array}$$

The power of data and discrimination

Perfect discrimination, or near-perfect discrimination as discussed in this chapter, has been addressed theoretically by microeconomic fundamentals usually under monopoly conditions. This is the case in traditional agricultural or manufacturing markets, even in air transport, with a specific number of flights per destination. However, the digital economy is enabling such discrimination in almost any sector, with companies using algorithms and large volumes of data to optimize performance and attract new users.

This raises interesting theoretical questions because, if a company is able to differentiate each user, or each user is able to be noticed as unique by expressing his or her differential interests, what is the point of talking about market equilibrium? Equilibrium, in short, is nothing more than a common point for all supply and demand, and the digital economy is proposing an absolute individualization of one or the other based on the intangibles that surround the product or the seller. Intangibles such as the usability of a website, the online reputation based on information from other users, the delivery time of the product, or even the possibility of paying with Paypal, among countless other factors.

Each user's valuation of these intangibles will ultimately form a unique utility curve for each product, which the supply tries to capture in order to exploit with price segmentation. With this we could move from a single equilibrium to a sum of aggregate equilibria with a multitude of implications for economic theory, but also for the real economy. Because companies that employ technology to provide an almost exclusive service to each customer will end up displacing from the market those that use traditional pricing mechanisms.

We have already mentioned the case of Ryanair, and how, despite the obstacles, it became the most profitable airline in Europe, based on a new business model and dynamic pricing. [386] This formula is repeated today in the big platforms, analyzing user behavior to adjust their fares or prices, modifying them according to the volume of visits, the number of clicks, the day of the week, or any external shock that alters the data, even if nobody has noticed. But to establish these strategies, companies need data. Lots of data. Masses and masses of data.

Regulatory challenges in the face of digital discrimination

---

386. This is known as the "low cost paradox". See: Moreno-Izquierdo, L. (2013): "Pricing strategies of low-cost airlines: an extended rivalry model approach" (doctoral thesis): rua.ua.es/dspace/handle/10045/36090

Big data and artificial intelligence will continue to make the competitive differences between large and small businesses if governments do not act, leading to digital monopolies wiping out every other business. Small businesses find themselves in the position of selling on aggregators such as eBay, Amazon or Booking, but they do not know how many users search for the destination, or how many click through and do not go on to buy. They feed the platforms' offerings, but receive little information other than sales, playing at a disadvantage to companies that develop their own product lines based on this data.

Digital regulations should not give disproportionate weight to privacy, as happens in Europe, because it is a brake on the exploitation of data, preventing companies from making the necessary competitive leap. However, they should be based on a comprehensive open data policy, for example by establishing KPIs to which any business owner selling on digital platforms should have access. The case of Google Analytics is a magnificent example that should be highlighted and serve as a model to follow.

The second point to address is transparency in business strategies. Algorithms can automatically assign rates that maximize sales, but with neural network or random forest models, for example, not even the companies themselves know what relationships are occurring. Administrations should set limits to ensure that users are not negatively discriminated against for reasons such as gender, geographic location or ethnicity, for example, and work with companies that fail to reach minimum rates. This does not mean hindering the exploitation of data but setting limits so that the digital economy can expand in a safe and equal environment.

Economic theory must open up to these new challenges facing economists. It will not be easy to explain, analyze, determine and predict the consequences and effects of pricing systems that tend towards clustering, if not individualization, in all sectors. Our mission will be to measure their effect on business performance, social welfare or the wealth of countries, but also to denounce inefficiencies and ensure that all citizens and entrepreneurs enjoy the same opportunities.

6. THE SHARING ECONOMY AND OVER SUPPLY

One of the most outstanding effects of the digital economy has been the formation of a *collaborative* branch, referring to the direct exchange of goods and services between users through digital platforms, leaving the private sector and administrations on the sidelines. Although the concept itself has been blurred and has given way to a *platform economy*, [387] its emergence has raised a truly interesting new perspective in which each individual is both producer and consumer at the same time.

Theoretically, this would mean an ecosystem with a number of producers who are permanently tending towards oversupply, which forces us to ask ourselves again about market equilibrium, sensing that its emergence should lead to lower prices and an improvement in product quality. Or at least that is the case in classical theory.[388]

However, if we maintain the idea of the previous section of access to almost perfect information on the part of demand, and therefore of the absolute segmentation of production, the excess supply is no longer such, and therefore prices should not experience any variation.

Let's take the example of Airbnb to explain this phenomenon: Airbnb's price recommendation system facilitates a first approach between supply and demand, but customers see each product as a unique element based on the rating of other users, the existence of photographs, the response time of owners, the location, or even

---

387. On platforms such as Airbnb or Uber, it is increasingly common to find companies offering their services that do not purchase products from third parties. By merging both activities, it is difficult to distinguish the interaction between users of traditional online sales, leaving the term collaborative economy in question.

388. The reader can turn to the famous manual "Principles of Economics" by N. Gregory Mankiw if he is unaware of this type of theoretical approach.

variables that are not controlled, but can have an effect on the final decision, such as the color of the walls or the image projected by the owner.

This absolute discrimination of supply will mean that, if a new company or property enters the market, the information available will mean that users may or may not see it as competitive or a substitute for an existing one. In fact, in many cities, more than 60% of the properties offered on Airbnb have never been rented, not even for a day, but their presence does not bring down the price of the rest of the apartments or the hotel offer.

Does this mean that the price in the sharing economy does not depend on the quantity produced or on competition? Not exactly: the emergence of Airbnb has caused significant adjustments in the hotel and holiday rental sector; just as low-cost airlines have altered the strategy of traditional airlines. However, it is necessary to understand that access to near-perfect information by buyers makes goods or services in the digital economy difficult to substitute perfectly, and therefore we should treat the market not as an aggregate of offerings, but as a mesh of differentiated product groups.

7. AUTOMATION, EMPLOYMENT AND PRODUCTIVITY

7.1. A classical approach to automation and employment

Another area that economists will need to review closely is the impact of the digital transformation on employment, and more specifically the challenges that automation presents. The idea of an extraordinarily automated economic system may sound like a science fiction scenario, but it is not so much the case that many professionals will lose their employment if there is no upgrading of job skills and business management.

As explained earlier in this book, technology is a factor that has traditionally affected both labor supply $S(w)$ and demand $D(w)$, generating changes in both the volume of workers employed (q) and wages received (w). Techno-logical paradigm shifts, as well as the occurrence of external shocks or economic crises, lead to changes in the equilibrium point of the labor market, given by $q*$ and $w*$ when $D(w) = S(w)$.[389]

However, the emergence of new disruptive technologies is causing a change in the job market that has never been seen before: while until now innovation has mostly replaced dangerous, repetitive or rudimentary tasks, it is now also targeting cognitive jobs, ranging from identifying cancerous tumors, tracing stock market investment patterns or driving a vehicle autonomously, to making scientific discoveries. This could mean a possible automation of millions of jobs, which could lead to a collapse in wages, as some entrepreneurs such as Elon Musk and Mark Zuckerberg, who openly advocate a universal income, have already warned.

Much earlier, in 1984, Nils J. Nilsson, one of the most relevant researchers in the field of AI,[390] already predicted that people will

---

389. Again, see "Principles of Economics" by N. Gregory Mankiw.

390. See: Nilsson, N. J. (1984). Artificial intelligence, employment, and income. *AI magazine*, 5(2), 5-14.

be dispensable from any future production of goods and services. This statement should have awakened economists decades ago to the prospective study of employment in the new technological paradigm.

Subsistence wages and the cost of automation

To understand the effect of mass automation on the labor market, we will start from the elements described above ($S(w)$, $D(w)$, q^*, w^*), and add two more: the cost of substituting the activities for which the job is offered by automation processes (Ca) , and the minimum wage below which no worker will fill the vacancy (w_s). This wage w_s indicates a subsistence level and does not necessarily coincide with the minimum wage. [391]

From the relationship of these variables we can understand the functioning of automation on labor market:

Scenario 1: $Ca > w^* > w_s$

In this situation there is no real possibility of automating employment, since the marginal cost of doing so is more expensive than the wage received by workers.

This situation can occur for two reasons: either because workers are highly specialized and technology does not yet cover that area, which is related to high wages and good bargaining power of employees, or because there is excess demand for employment and wages are very low, so that $Ca > w^* \geq w_s$.

Nilsson is an Emeritus Professor of Computer Science at Stanford University and a former chair of the same department, founding member and former president of the American Association for Artificial Intelligence, and a great disseminator as a writer and editor in several scientific journals.

391. The subsistence wage is a real drama for thousands of people, with payrolls that do not allow them to emancipate themselves or barely make ends meet. This question gives rise to so many reflections that would require another book, although the recommendations made in the previous chapters should also respond to this problem.

Scenario 2: $Ca < w^*$; $Ca \geq w_s$

In this second scenario there is a realistic possibility of automating employment, unless workers decide to decrease their wages to a point w' such that $w' < Ca < w^*$, and $w' \geq w_s$.

The total number of workers who will remain in the firm with this wage reduction depends on the elasticity of supply itself: if there are other job options, they will look for another firm in which to work; in an environment of high unemployment, they are very likely to accept the worst conditions to secure a wage above the subsistence level.

This theoretical scenario is highly socially sensitive, as pressure from trade unions or public intervention to increase the value of w_s to w_s' could lead to an acceleration in job destruction if $w_s' > Ca > w_s$.

Scenario 3.1: $Ca < w_s$, no government intervention.

When the marginal cost of automation, Ca, is lower than the minimum wage a professional is willing to pay (w_s), firms have no competitive incentive to keep employees. It is very likely that firms will end up laying off workers in order not to lose competitiveness in the market.

Only preventive regulations or too high dismissal costs could stop this action, although such actions put the company itself at risk, especially if it operates in the global market.

Scenario 3.2: $Ca < w_s$, with state intervention.

Another way to stop the mass dismissal of employees when $Ca < w_s$ is through government intervention, which will use public money to compensate for the difference between the marginal cost of automation and at least the subsistence wage.

These actions guarantee the employment of thousands of people, but they entail an opportunity cost of not reinvesting that amount in other areas such as health or education, in addition to the increase in public debt or the increase in taxes that fall on the rest of the citizens. They also hinder technological progress, as companies lose incentives to improve innovation in their production processes. All these effects are known as social loss.

These three scenarios, four counting the duplicity of scenario 3, and although they are mere simplifications of the effects that automation could have on the labor market, they reflect well the situation of wage reduction and job destruction that our economic sectors are facing, as well as public indebtedness to alleviate the resulting social problems. Only a constant improvement of workers' skills and an increase in business competitiveness will be able to maintain the situation in which $Ca > w^*$.

Therefore, the best labor policy that can be envisaged is the productive transformation towards the sectors of the future with a twofold objective: firstly, to boost new jobs in cutting-edge technological industries such as AI or quantum computing. Secondly, to create non-existent jobs that hybridize and renew mature industries in which the regions are specialized.

7.2. Emotional employment and the new diseconomy

The Fourth Industrial Revolution, that of artificial intelligence, could drive enough actions globally to autonomously generate all the goods and services we humans need without having to carry out productive activities. But even in this scenario, including a universal income, people would not stop working.

Historically, every past technological leap has raised productivity, destroying and creating activities. The surpluses generated from productive improvement are distributed in society with professions that cover new needs, and that can be as unlikely as crisp inspectors, flag wavers, candy tasters, duck walkers, or dice shooters. Perhaps the 21st century will see the generation of a new type of job, the "emotional job".

The philosopher and scientist I. Kant argued that all co-knowledge requires the concurrence of two radically heterogeneous faculties of the mind: sensing and understanding.[392] We

---

392. Kant, I. (2009). *Crítica de la razón pura.* Ediciones Colihue SRL.

assume that new generations of robots and algorithms will gradually gain the ability to receive representations (receptivity) or be affected by and interact autonomously with their environment. But we humans will be left with our monopoly to manage emotions, feelings and passions, built in an environment of freedom. This translates into an infinite number of tasks linked to creative education, health care, leisure or personal relationships that will remain the responsibility of human beings. Such inexhaustible fields as emotional care for the sick and disabled, the fight against poverty and social cohesion, the preservation of the environment, putting an end to gender violence, the development of literary creativity, or directly making other human beings or animals happy.

New disruptive technologies will force the human species to identify what we know how to do with greater skill and enjoyment. Playful and emotional jobs will be the new way of compartmentalizing the economy.

Automation, surplus, prices, and sustainable production

Faced with the challenges that lie ahead, the economic analysis needs new players interested in foresight. The digital economy can make the invisible hand of the market less necessary, paradoxically the work of Piero Sraffa[393] more readable, and even bring the end of the capitalist economy as predicted by Schumpeter in his 1942 work "Capitalism, Socialism, and Democracy". However, unlike Karl Marx's negative vision, for the father of innovation, it would be a positive ending, with the technological leaps separating human beings from the need to produce.[394]

It is not easy to answer how a future fully automated economy would work, or how we could provide a universal basic income to

---

393. Sraffa, P. (1960). Produzione di merci a mezzo di merci: premesse a una critica della teoria economica. G. Einaudi.

394. For Schumpeter, automation and the coverage of all needs could lead to disinterest in entrepreneurship and continuous improvement, the foundations on which capitalism is built. Consequently, market economies would disappear to make way for socialism.

Schumpeter and Marx arrive at the same point from two opposite positions: by reaching an optimal situation based on increased productivity and the inefficiency of the system, respectively.

all the inhabitants of the planet, although we will try to imagine a first approximation based on the disruption that the traditional economy is undergoing. This future scenario with automated routine jobs can only be understood with a centralized AI capable of anticipating the needs of the "market" and translating them into direct orders to production chains. Supply and demand for all types of goods and services would be covered, eliminating business uncertainty based on algorithms, and ensuring efficient and clustered distribution of products.

We are not envisioning an *Orwellian* world, as in 1984, or a rationing system, but rather large surpluses and freedoms according to the income of each person, with a production defined by the predictions of the algorithms. Automation linked to AI could allow a country like China to reconcile a "gamified" mixed economy with an environmental, social, creative, and innovative economy, where social entrepreneurship would continue to be fundamental, a fusion between the fundamentals of the centralized economy and the market economy in which an intelligent platform like *Alibaba* as a central authority executed an idyllic *sraffian* system.

These new societies will require basic incomes guaranteed under agreed political and social criteria. Once all needs are met, they will need rules and token-based incentives to cover social or creative jobs, or to reward scientific advances or environmental responsibility. This may all sound like a distant future. Neither employment nor the market economy will disappear for the time being, and it is difficult than AI will reach the cognitive levels of *Bender*[395] or *Hal 9000*.[396] However, when we talk about the possibility of a new economy, even if remote, it is necessary to turn to John Kenneth Galbraith[397] as soon as possible.

The influential economist popularized the term "affluent society" in the 1950s - the existence of poverty as the failure of developed economies, generators of surplus wealth and employment but driven more by accumulation than by the "distribution

---

395. Futurama by Matt Groening and David X. Cohen.

396. 2001: A Space Odyssey (novel and film) by Arthur C. Clarke y Stanley Kubrick.

397. Galbraith, J.K. (1958) (ed. 1998): *The affluent society*. Houghton Mifflin Harcourt.

of rewards." Faced with this social reality, we believe that there is a way for capitalist opulence to give way to a system with the capacity to produce and redistribute what people need. A possibility that turns social value into a structuring element, which we should explore.

Perhaps society has been in bondage to the constraints of the market for too long. Maybe AI can answer many of the advanced hypotheses of Galbraith and Schumpeter.

8. OTHER THEORETICAL QUESTIONS

8.1. Productivity and bureaucracy

One of the issues referred to in this book is the importance of having an agile administration for business scalability and the creation of a framework consistent with the development of the digital economy. To explain why, we are going to resort to a basic and traditional formula for measuring productivity: wealth or production generated (x) divided by hours of work (t):

$$Pr = \frac{x}{t}$$

However, as we all know, not all working hours are equally important to productivity. Therefore, we can differentiate between the time spent on actions that generate wealth (t_r) such as devising new products, analyzing the market, or looking for clients, and the time spent on procedures already mentioned (t_b) - paying taxes, submitting invoices, or requesting grants. Entrepreneurs, businessmen, and any administration that wants to be effective should be concerned that it takes up as much time as possible in generating wealth (t_r). The longer their bureaucratic time (t_b), the less total time (t) they will spend growing their project:

$$Pr = \frac{x}{t_r}; \ t_r = (t - t_b)$$

Unfortunately, there are no official statistics today that allow us to carry out this calculation, beyond the Doing Business indicator of the World Bank that we presented previously. Yet with or without indicators, the administrations should realize that the time that workers dedicate to solving tedious obstacles and fulfilling bureaucratic requirements is nothing but the wealth that a whole country loses, and therefore jobs, tax collection, and general welfare of the population. This model can also be used in companies or jobs that make "inefficiency" their day to day: hours that are lost due to the transfer to the office, meetings that drag on without a specific goal, excessive pauses, and so on.

After a reflection of this style, probably many readers will end up questioning the unproductiveness of working hours established by hours and not by objectives or the effectiveness of teleworking. Nevertheless, that is not the point of this book.[398] We only want to highlight that countries such as Ireland, Norway, Denmark, and especially Estonia are making their governments become great allies of their companies, seeking greater flexibility and agility of the processes for the benefit of the private sector, which translates into the location of great technology and the creation of startups, wealth for its citizens, and employment.

Perhaps they can inspire the rest of the European regions.

8.2. The new finance: disintermediation and cryptocurrencies

The financial theory will also have to be revised in the not too distant future with the consolidation of cryptocurrencies and the global consensus around new forms of payment without the intermediation of banks or governments. Most economists to date have analyzed the emergence of bitcoin from a legal and tax perspective. However, it is necessary to ask whether cryptocurrencies for global use are not the best possible adaptation for the efficient functioning of the economy of our time: without exchange policy decisions that affect consumers and companies, suppressing the effects of variations in the quotation and facilitating the detection of fraud thanks to the registration of activities.

Blockchain, the technological pillar that supports bitcoin, has many other derivatives beyond the currencies themselves; so much so that they could redefine the economy from a more advanced and efficient base, consistent with the digital society and the massive international movement of people, goods, and money[399] - even to answer basic questions of public sector theory such as the

---

398. For this, the reader has other works such as "The 4-Hour Workweek" by Tim Ferriss (RBA Books) and especially "The Clockwork System" by Mike Michalowicz (Conecta).

399. See the Foreword 'Blockchain: a new economic model?' written by A. Pedreño in Pastor Sempere, M.C. & Vilarroig Moya, R. (2018). Blockchain: Technological, business, and legal aspects. Thomson Reuters.

stowaway problem. [400] The possibilities of Blockchain (100% secure and certified transactions with information that cannot be altered, accurate information on each movement, and detection of intermediaries who do not add value, among others) have led renowned economists to propose its anonymous author[401] as a Nobel Prize winner.

8.3. The scalability of digital companies

Many digital businesses show us a break from the traditional economy. The classic internationalization theories, such as those of Uppsala[402] or Vernon,[403] or the theories of industrial location of the behavioral and structuralist schools do not quite adjust to the new disruptive startups destined to "change the world".

Many colleagues have highlighted in recent years the structural characteristics of the so-called "born-global" - companies that are born thanks to the internet with a global dimension, or the big bang disruptors - companies that, despite their limited size, can generate profound changes in an entire sector.

Expansion and growth processes no longer occur sequentially, and location loses the strength to explain the activity carried out by companies.

The digital economy has democratized and internationalized access to talent, with free and open global training from the best universities and professionals (Coursera, Udacity, Udemy), and the possibility of hiring remote workers from all over the planet (Upwork, Linkedin). It has also opened access to funding (Kickstarter,

---

400. es.wikipedia.org/wiki/Problema_del_poliz%C3%B3n

401. Satoshi Nakamoto is the identity assigned to its author. Nakamoto's true identity remains unknown and has been the subject of much speculation. It is undiscovered whether the name "Satoshi Nakamoto" is real or a pseudonym, or if the name represents a person or group of people. Hopefully, if he or they receive the Nobel, at least we get to eliminate doubts.

402. Johanson, J., & Vahlne, J. E. (1977). The internationalization process of the firm—a model of knowledge development and increasing foreign market commitments. *Journal of international business studies*, 8(1), 23-32.

403. Vernon, R. (1992). International investment and international trade in the product cycle. En: *International economic policies and their theoretical foundations*, 415-435. Academic Press.

Indiegogo). However, even so, we find large differences between countries that should be concerned and employ our science.

The economic theory should work to discover the factors that drive the creation and scalability of successful digital startups since they represent the best basis for the future growth of a country.

9. THE VARIABLE *"T"* AND THE PROSPECTIVE IN THE ECONOMY

As we hope you have realized, in almost all the hypotheses put forward in this chapter, "time" has taken on a fundamental relevance. In the new technological paradigm, changes occur faster and more profoundly than ever, and models must also adapt to this new reality.

Our idea of disruption as the engine of economic development is inspired by the assumptions of Schumpeter, Romer,[404] and Brynjolfsson,[405] among others. However, the exponentiality and acceleration of the transformations force us to seriously review the implication of the variable time (t) in the short and long term. In the first place, when processes occur in such an accelerated way, decisions cannot be understood as isolated events at t or $t + 1$, but rather a multitude of interactions and decisions of vital importance arising between the two periods. Perhaps nothing that we can give as valid today will have a reason to be in a year, a month, or even a day.

The word "pivot", very widespread in the entrepreneurial world, gives a good account of the need to understand the economy from a flexible and lively perspective. Business plans for three or five years end up in a drawer or in the bin and are replaced by a *lean canvas* or similar tools in which the source of income, costs, competition, problems, solutions, and opportunities are visualized and corrected every day. Guiding ourselves by long-term plans will surely make us incur mistakes and confusion due to the difference between what is projected and the real world.

Information and data should guide decisions in very short terms, even in seconds, happening that if in the analog economy

---

404. Romer, P. M. (1986). Increasing returns and long-run growth. *Journal of political economy*, *94*(5), 1002-1037.

405. Brynjolfsson, E., & Kahin, B. (Eds.). (2002). *Understanding the digital economy: data, tools, and research*. MIT press.

we could divide time into t, $t + 1$, $t + 2$ ... in the digital economy we should subdivide those periods almost infinitely because one day in the analog economy means years in the digital economy. In addition, the variable t is also taking another turn in the long term in the digital economy, with prospects gaining ground in the economic study. No doubt to many colleagues it will seem like a leap into the void. Our science has generally relied on the facts of the past to interpret the present and make predictions. However, governments, companies, and citizens are extremely concerned about the uncertainty and complexity of changes that are completely new and for which there is no previous data.

Do we from the academy know how to respond to this challenge?

While only isolated works such as the said article by Osborne and Frey on job market automation gain some fame from universities, consultancies such as Gartner, Accenture, PwC, Everis, and Deloitte are the ones that monopolize the media attention, thanks to their analyses in very long-term horizons.

However, most of the academic publications in scientific journals on economics are forgotten in a very short time and have little notoriety. Mathematics has become strong in economics, and the most prestigious magazines hardly publish articles that are not supported by rigorous models that leave little room for imagination. Another reason is the disconnection between universities and the business world, making a harsh self-criticism of our institutions. In Europe, it is not promoted but penalized when teachers have professional experiences that they can transfer to the academy.

An economy of foresight

Working with short-term data on the prospect is the key to efficiency. A company that makes decisions based on reports made a month ago may be losing competitiveness compared to those that do so with real-time information. A university that creates new training programs based on the job demand last year may be putting an entire generation of students who in four years could find their knowledge out of date for unemployment. An investor who allocates money on the basis of historical series may be throwing savings away.

A good example of this policy is Google. Currently, it maintains one of its greatest sources of income in the online advertising business, with continuous updates and a team dedicated entirely to it. However, for years it has known how to look at the revolution of smartphones, the cloud, Deep Learning, and quantum computing. Risking its present assets, it embarked on a disruptive bet that will surely allow it to remain the global technology leader in the era of AI. Yet it did not do it statically or follow a long-term plan but corrected its projections and perspectives every day, making mistakes countless times along the way but with enough flexibility and money to correct the course and continue sailing.

All these clues should make us economists see that we have to build a prospective economy, which provides us with tools and criteria to minimize uncertainty and the problems that change potentially entails, but be quick enough to make corrections based on information from the real world, reflecting how an economy that can read and adapt agilely to future events brings its environment closer to a competitive improvement and well-being. Understand that anticipating is much more effective than being a follower.

We want to end the book with a statement by Andrew Ng that poses a real challenge to economists: "AI will be like new electricity",[406] which, remember, will leave unrecognizable any sector that the reader has in mind, from agriculture to medicine and from tourism to education. Economic agents are aware that they face changes that are no longer linear but exponential. They are not an innovation anymore but a disruption. Perhaps the time has come to adapt our economics manuals as well. The work ahead is as exciting as it is complicated: understanding how each industry must reinvent itself to take full advantage of the new possibilities of the fourth industrial revolution, even planning a future in which economic relations will not be at all like they are today.

However, to do this, we must first reinvent ourselves: hybridize with other branches of knowledge, learn new research techniques, give prominence to algorithms, and, especially, provide the agility that our science requires in this new era of artificial intelligence.

---

406. gsb.stanford.edu/insights/andrew-ng-why-ai-new-electricity

SYNERGIES AND ENTREPRENEURIAL CULTURE

Farewell and Closing

ABOUT THE AUTHORS, BY ANA B. RAMÓN

The authors Andrés Pedreño and Luis Moreno express in this work their concerns and fears about a fragmented Europe losing in technological warfare and weakened by the advance of the 21st century. A vision that, although a priori seems very critical with some administrations and legislators who have not understood the magnitude of the digital transformation in the making, is at the same time and above all optimistic before the emergence of notable technological projects that are consolidated in places like Alicante with almost everything against them.

Since I was a student of Andrés Pedreño at the University of Alicante and began to understand and be fascinated about economics, I knew that I wanted to grow professionally by his side because nobody like him was capable of motivating me and awakening my concern. Fifteen years later, what was my surprise when I saw that one of my economics students, Luis Moreno, showed the same admiration and enthusiasm when he spoke of his professor Andrés Pedreño whom he had just met.

The three of us began to work together, and I had the honor of co-directing Luis's doctoral thesis with Andrés (2010-2013) - a completely transgressive PhD work in which already then we began to talk about smart pricing systems, digital innovation, and knowledge as competitiveness differentials. Since then, Luis and Andrés have not stopped collaborating on papers and participating in congresses in which they have expressed their concern about the lack of perspective of Spain and Europe in the digital economy.

Andrés is the compass, the rudder, and the boss; he never misses the mark, and he is a born leader. That he is a visionary ahead of his time is perhaps what I have heard most about him. His greatest merit consists of being able to extract the best of each one of the members on board his team because rowing his boat is always a collective project, almost a familial one. Luis has understood Andrés' obsession and concern for innovation and digital disruption like no one else, bringing each project down to earth and giving it a unique personality. Sharing the look to the future, but without losing the rigorousness of the analysis or his millennial vision.

Generational complementarity undoubtedly reaffirms Andrés and Luis in their commitment to improving the economic and social well-being of our environment through innovation. This book is the penultimate fruit of this fruitful feedback.

Although it may seem otherwise given the age difference of more than thirty years, Andrés is the disruptive soul of the team, capable of reinventing himself at every stage of his life, even after his 60s. He has been an entrepreneur in spirit since his university days, being the driving force behind innovative projects such as the Miguel de Cervantes virtual library or Universia in the 90s. Outside the university, he promoted successful startups with an enviable spirit and presided over the association for the promotion of the knowledge society, AlicanTEC. Andrés taught throughout his teaching career that the mission of economists cannot remain in the explanation of the events that occurred but rather to help improve the well-being of our society either by creating employment from a company or with research and forecasts that allow making decisions.

Since I have known Luis, I have always seen him as a dreamer with great projection who has learned from the best of teachers that thinking big requires honesty and humility. Today he is already a brilliant professor with a bright future ahead of him who has proven his worth with dozens of published international articles, in stays at prestigious universities, and in his participation in international congresses all over the world. Luis provokes in his students the same feeling of improvement and motivation that Andrés instilled in him. He is a staunch advocate of education that hybridizes the best of face-to-face and online, and a promoter of innovative and pioneering projects from the public university, such as UniMOOC, with hundreds of thousands of students enrolled.

In short, they are two generous, committed, perfectionist, and demanding people who above all enjoy their work, accept any challenge as long as they believe in it, and who end up turning it into reality by sharing proposals and energizing ideas, no matter how crazy they seem at first. In this book, they have managed to find again that balance between rigor and usefulness that characterizes them, first through a brilliant analysis of the reason for the digital divide and then the proposal of solutions.

You may or may not agree with them, but no one will deny the seriousness of the arguments and the courage in the proposals.

On a personal level, if there is something clear to me, it is that nothing is too serious for them to not enjoy a good time together, always in a relaxed and informal fashion, without ever losing their sense of humor, optimism, and proactive perspective. Even when things go wrong and projects collide with harsh reality, positive philosophy emerges to give the best possible response. One day, Andrés revealed his secret to Luis and me. It does not consist in having more or less vision but in being passionate and obsessed with absolutely any project. Make it your own until you stop thinking about anything else. Every page of this book reflects that spirit - a work resulting from years of study and a special closeness to the startup world that is very difficult to find.

You can be sure that all the chapters in this book have been discussed and worked on together. It is not a work resulting from a division of sections but the sum of efforts between two colleagues and friends who for years have tried to generate debate and create awareness that European society, our society, is at stake in the era of greater disruption more than the human being has ever seen. The era of artificial intelligence.

Ana B. Ramón Rodríguez
Full Professor of Applied Economics
University of Alicante

OUR ENVIRONMENT: FROM THE GAULISH VILLAGE TO PINK FLOYD

« All Gaul is occupied by the Romans. All? No! A village popu-
lated by irreducible Gauls still and always resists the invader. »
R. GOSCINNY and A. UDERZO. *Astérix.*

« Hey! Teachers! Leave them kids alone!
All in all, it's just another brick in the wall.
All in all, you're just another brick in the wall. »
PINK FLOYD. Another brick in the wall.

In this book we have tried to show how a social climate has been generated in Europe over the last few years that is far removed from its economic reality. Where it seems advisable to avoid "uncomfortable truths" and to go beyond "political correctness", even if our future is at stake. There are hardly any critical voices in the media against European policies, nor are the outdated ideas and regulations that limit our development being questioned. Privacy is a dogma that is neither debated nor discussed. Neither are entrepreneurs given space in the news, with few exceptions, nor are their interests protected in debates as they are for other groups.

Intellectual and productive dissidence has no visibility, and this has impoverished the debate and almost clipped the wings of the digital economy.

Aware of this situation, the authors have spent many years trying to promote a change in the mentality of each new generation of students who have taken our subjects. Even before web 2.0 was born, we were already trying to explain the keys to the success of the first internet companies, which today are technological giants. In those years, we could not imagine how the digital economy was going to unfold.[407] Google did not even have a defined business model, but, in the eighties and early nineties, a change of mentality already had begun in the US that served as inspiration: consultants demanded from companies and administrations "thinking outside the box," and later the so-called reengineering process would appear.

The digital revolution was unstoppable, calling for "scaling the wall or redefining the problem," as Apple CEO Tim Cook claimed. However, from the very beginning it was clear that Europe did not understand the changes it was facing. The complexity, acceleration and intensity of the new technological era required exploration, research and investment, not defensiveness. Instead, Europe used its banners of "security" and "ethics" to raise principles that hide impotence and protectionism, against which we rebel in this book. Europe's intellectual heritage and its humanist and even philosophical legacy must be absolutely preserved, but this should not be a restriction or an excuse to hide inefficiency.

We have tried to set a good example of this idea that we convey in lectures, and we have been able to embark on very disruptive projects with which to imbibe the entrepreneurial spirit. We have continually left the comfort zone, without fear of political incorrectness in the face of the inefficiency of the system. Of course, we have sometimes failed, with all its consequences, but it is an insignificant price to pay compared to the satisfaction of being "outside the box".

Despite an ecosystem completely dominated by the analogue economy of tourism and real estate, and an administration oriented towards megaprojects and speculation, one of the authors participated first hand in the construction of the campus of the University of Alicante, [408] in the creation of the first Vice-Rectorate

---

407. Our students fifteen years ago were skeptical about our predictions on the scope of the digital economy. Today they stop us when they see us and thank us for having introduced them to these issues.

408. Pedreño, A (1998): Universidad de Alicante, utopías y realidades (University of alicante, utopías and realities). cervantesvirtual.com/descargaPdf/universidad-utopias-y-realidades-universidad-de-alicante-19941997--0/

for New Technologies in a European university, [409] or in a Med-park Science Park completely ahead of its time, but which was cornered by a policy.

This same ecosystem, which was not very conducive to the digital economy, was still in place when, years later, the authors participated in the development of the UniMOOC project. Motivated by previous experiences, we were filled with the spirit of non-conformism and resistance with which Goscinny and Uderzo drew Asterix's village, and we named our meeting place the Gaulish village.

UniMOOC was a unique project: it became the first free open education platform in the world oriented towards entrepreneurship and innovation, served as a think tank for some fifteen institutions and large companies interested in the education of the future, opened up the knowledge of over two hundred teachers to more than half a million students around the world, and allowed us to connect with brilliant initiatives such as The Hackers Club, which is still promoted today by Eduardo Manchón and Andrés Torrubia. The scalability problems described in this book meant that the project did not reach the expected heights, but it served as an inspiration for other platforms such as "Google Actívate", which today train millions of people around the world.

UniMOOC also allowed us to get to know and even participate in new "Gaulish villages", such as Torre Juana or Alican-TEC, which in turn spread to Murcia, La Rioja, Valencia, Cantabria, the Balearic Islands .... They are all part of this "European digital mini-foundation" described in chapter 9, which claims scalability and future, and which is not resigned to the decline of Europe.

The true adventure begins here

History is full of lessons, but they will be of no use to us if we are the prisoners of Plato's cave myth.[410] The only way to understand the whole context is to break the chains of the established

---

409. This vice rector's office promoted dozens of innovative projects, including the Miguel de Cervantes Virtual Library (Stanford University Award for the best digital library).

410. es.wikipedia.org/wiki/Alegor%C3%ADa_de_la_caverna

and reinvent ourselves to accommodate a new era that is just beginning. For this reason, as well as raising a necessary debate, this book seeks to invite young people not to accept unemployment, low wages or the cuts that threaten their future. To be creative, to get out of your comfort zone and to lose your fear of incorrectness.

As poetic as the metaphor may be, the "villages" of digital resistance must be torn down from within and contaminate the rest of the economy with disruption. Our young people must be battering rams of rebellion to tear down every brick of "no education" in the wall immortalized by Pink Floyd.[411] We face challenges that require us to take risks, to learn new skills, to break out of our comfort zone, to scale the wall, or to break it down directly, to analyze and solve problems from different and much broader perspectives. If young people do not urgently lead this change, we are bound to be affected by the more negative side of AI and automation. Or worse, we will be unable to cope with new crises like the coronavirus, in a world very different from that of the 19th and 20th centuries.

In our time we have no alternative. Each fall must serve as an impetus to get up and take on new and increasingly complex challenges, such as the preservation of the environment, the fight against cancer or the global redistribution of wealth.

And to do so, we must face the future with as open a mind as possible.

Luis Moreno and Andrés Pedreño.

---

411. youtu.be/YR5ApYxkU-U

451

ACKNOWLEDGMENTS

Our most sincere thanks to all those who in one way or another have contributed and helped make this book a reality:

-   Vinton Cerf and José Carlos Díez, for their generosity writing the prefaces to this book.

-   Laura Cárdenas, friend and editor of the Spanish version, for her comments, the long hours spent correcting us, all her writing tips, and her generosity and willingness to help us when we need her.

-   Pedro Pernías Peco and Ana Ramón, for being part of the first team of "irreducible Gauls" of the village and always being ready to join any new adventure, being a fundamental part of many of the projects, and having taught us many things that are written here.

-   To the Alicante entrepreneurship ecosystem, especially to Andrés Torrubia for reading this work and proposing a podcast where we can delve into and discuss many aspects of the book. He is joined by Eduardo Manchón and Javier García, synonyms of disruption and entrepreneurial drive. To the entire Board of AlicanTec and to Manuel Bonilla, who is always ready to support good ideas and causes.

-   Manuel Desantes Real, for so many things, but especially for being an ally, for his infinite wisdom and putting sanity to crazy ideas on more than one occasion.

-   Manuel Marco, Juan C. Trujillo, and the entire Lucentia EBT team, for their support and willingness.

-   Ismael Parrilla and Pedro Moreno, for being inexhaustible sources of bibliographic resources, recommendations, and citations.

- Heriberto Araujo, for his editorial advice and sharing his experience as a writer. We recommend his works: "La silenciosa conquista china" (The silent Chinese conquest) (2011) and "El imperio invisible" (The invisible empire) (2013) to better understand China's economic expansion model.

- Lasse Rouhiainen, an AI expert and a friend who has shared knowledge and advice as a writer. We recommend his book "Artificial Intelligence: 101 Things You Should Know Today About Our Future" (2018).

- To the entire Department of Applied Economic Analysis of the University of Alicante and the Faculty of Economics, especially to its director Martín Sevilla Jiménez, our dean Raúl Ruiz, and all our vice deans, for always giving us the freedom to address the economy of innovation and globalization from a critical and prospective angle, always with positive and constructive evaluations.

- To the environment born of the Alicante Conference on Spanish Economy, especially to Juan Velarde, José Luis García Delgado, Gloria Pardo, Álvaro Anchuelo, and the director of the Institute of International Economics, José Manuel Casado. For more than three decades, the Conference has served as a unique forum for debate in which to learn and share knowledge and which has enriched us intellectually year after year.

- To our colleagues Carmen Beviá, Carmen Martínez, Antonio Escudero, Aurelio López-Tarruella Martínez, Ricard Martínez, Carmen Ródenas, Hipólito Simón Pérez, and Ángel Sánchez among many others for their recommendations and reviews and giving us assurance when we doubted whether this book was a good idea. We are still doubting but there is no going back.

- To the think-tanks and groups that at TJ OST have helped us through many debates, activities, and events such as Friday Tech Fever in which numerous experts have participated; especially to the group that supports us and has provided coverage for many activities: Marilú Hernández, Trini Mora, Julia Castillo, Assumpta Ricard, along with the teams of people linked to 1MillionBot[412] and IT&IS.[413] We recommend observatories on digital technologies and entrepreneurship by these teams to all readers.

- To the entire team that worked at UniMOOC for almost a decade: Adrián, Alberto, Alicia, Anna, Arancha, Asun, Carlos, David, Elena, Eva, Felipe, Fran, Héctor, Judit, Joan, Marta, Martín, Miriam, Miguel, Nerea, Paco, Rebeca, Rubén, Sandra, Vicente, Ximo, and especially the "Fight Club": Adam, Álex, Andreu, Jesús, María, and Naomi.

- To our families, friends, and colleagues who have supported and assisted us during almost a year of intense writing, especially Rebecca Rippin, María Salud García, and María Luisa Izquierdo. Also, a great recognition to Andrés's children: Loli, Andrés, Joaquín, and David, who were companions on many Sundays in discussions about the content of the chapters of this book. We love you all.

- To Spotify and especially Los Planetas, Xoel López, Love of Lesbian, The National, Editors, Death Cab for Cutie, Jack Bisonte, Sam Fender, and Viva Suecia, among many others, for filling hours and hours of work with music. Here are our favorites: https://sptfy.com/hBaR.

- We must not forget our roots, Villarrobledo and Balsapintada, in La Mancha and Campo de Cartagena (Murcia) respectively. For giving us such a humble and nonconformist character, having taught us with the example of so many that the future is only built with effort and determination.

---

412. Celia Sánchez, Raquel Pomares, Ramón Pedreño, Carolina López, Andrés Pedreño Lloret, Constanza Casquet, Jorge López, Joaquín Pedreño, Gonzalo Faus, Amanda Cabezas, Takwa Rejeb, Javier Ruiz, Berta Marco, Antonio Gimeno y Víctor Vidal.

413. Assumpta Ricart Gimenez, Julia Castillo Garcia, Ana Marilu Hernández Olivares, Andrés Pedreño Lloret, Marian Anyeline Gomez Murillo, Irenice Ferreira Dos Santos, Said El Ouardi, Fouzia El Ouardi y Laura Server Valera.

Acknowledgments for this edition:

Thanks to the people who have sent us proposals for improvement and debate as well as some corrections that improved the second and third editions of this work, particularly Manuel Atienza, Carlos Barciela, David Cano, Isabel Echeverria Mir, Salvador Enguix, Casimiro García Abadillo, Juan José Landazuri, Tíscar Lara, Aida Lillo, Lucas Martínez Clar, Pedro Mier, Beatriz Moreno Serrano, Juan Ruíz Manero, Alexandre Peretó, Álvaro Rodelgo, José Juan Ruiz, Jordi Sevilla, Manuel Tarín, and Mario Villar.

JUNE – 2021